Meditative Pathways

by Alex McCann Johnson

Meditative Pathways

Alex McCann Johnson

Published by Guided by Spirit Publishing

Guided by Spirit Publishing
203 Main St.
Williston, ND, 58801, USA
www.guidedbyspiritpublishing.com
info@guidedbyspiritpublishing.com

Guided by Spirit Publishing
203 Main St.
Williston, ND, 58801, USA

The information in this book is provided for informational purposes only. The author and publisher make no representations as to the accuracy or completeness of any information in this book and are not liable for any errors or omissions or for the results obtained from the use of such information.

ISBN: 979-8-9913133-5-3

Printed in the United States of America

Cover Design by Eugine Johnson

Dedication

To all those seeking stillness, connection, and meaning.

*This book is for you. May this be a year of practice,
a sacred rhythm of prayer and meditation
woven into the tapestry of your everyday life.*

*To my friends and family, who have walked with me through every
season, thank you for your love and presence.*

*To my mom, who always had a prayer on her lips, your faith lives
on in me.*

*And to my husband, my grounding force and constant support,
you are the calm in my storm and the rock beneath my feet.*

Let this journey begin.

Table of Contents

INTRODUCTION TO
Meditative Pathways

Welcome to *Meditative Pathways*, a year-long journey designed to guide you on a path of spiritual growth and transformation. This book is not bound by a specific start date or order. It is here to be your companion, offering a daily lesson and prayer to support you in your spiritual journey, whenever you choose to begin.

Each day, you will find a lesson that invites you to explore, reflect, and deepen your connection with your inner self and the divine. The accompanying prayer serves as a tool to ground your practice, helping you align with the wisdom of the universe and open your heart to the growth you seek. Whether you're looking for peace, clarity, healing, or insight, the combination of daily lessons and prayers will help you move toward a life of greater presence, love, and spiritual alignment.

No matter what you believe or where you are on your spiritual path, this book is for you. It transcends specific religious or spiritual frameworks. Whether your divine is a name, a force, the universe, or simply the energy of life itself, this book is an invitation to deepen your relationship with that higher power and to nurture your growth as a spiritual being.

You don't have to follow a specific order, nor do you need to start on a particular date. You simply need to approach each day with an open heart, a willingness to grow, and a desire to connect with your higher self. Each meditation serves as a gentle nudge to deepen your spiritual practice, cultivate peace within, and align with the path that is uniquely yours.

May this book serve as a reminder that the journey of spiritual growth is ever-unfolding, and that every day offers new opportunities to expand, to heal, and to become more in tune with your true essence.

Are you ready to walk this path? Let us begin, one step at a time.

How I Found Meditation

My name is Alex McCann Johnson, and I've been honored to share messages of guidance with people for over a decade. Along the way, I've come to understand the incredible power of meditation, a practice that has shaped my personal growth and spiritual development in ways I never could have imagined.

I first encountered meditation as a college student studying psychology. At the time, I was shocked by how little meditation was emphasized, especially given its proven benefits for mental health and well-being. It seemed strange to me that such a powerful tool was not being integrated more into therapeutic practices. But that initial introduction sparked something within me—a curiosity to learn more.

When I began studying hypnotherapy, I was introduced to a form of meditation through focused, guided visualization. This experience opened up a whole new dimension of awareness for me. I started to understand the subtle yet profound ways meditation could deepen our connection to ourselves and the universe. I realized that meditation wasn't just about quieting the mind; it was about creating space for transformation, healing, and insight.

As I continued my journey through energy work, intuitive development, shamanism, yoga, and even theology, I began to see meditation's universal presence across cultures and spiritual traditions. We've always meditated in some form or another, whether through prayer, focused breathing, or ritual practices. Yet, even with its long history and widespread use, there is still a stigma surrounding meditation. Many people don't fully understand it or know how to practice it. This lack of understanding often leads to resistance or reluctance to embrace the practice.

A few years ago, I taught a class on meditation for teachers. To my surprise, many of them expressed concern about practicing meditation in their classrooms, fearing that parents might disapprove or misunderstand the practice. They were worried about the stigma surrounding it, not realizing that meditation, especially short, focused sessions of breathing or mindfulness, can have profound benefits for students' focus and emotional regulation. Studies have shown that just two or three minutes of meditation at the start of a class can center and calm students, allowing them to be more present and engaged in their work. If you're interested in exploring this further, there are countless studies available that outline the many benefits of meditation, and there are entire books dedicated to this topic.

As I've continued my own growth—an ongoing process that will never truly end—I became increasingly intrigued by the idea of creating a year-long meditation plan, one that would guide people spiritually and mindfully, helping them to deepen their practice and connect with their higher selves. This book is the result of that vision, and I'm so excited to finally present it to you.

In *Meditative Pathways*, you'll find daily lessons and meditative prayers designed to support your spiritual journey and personal growth. Each day is an opportunity to reflect, center yourself, and deepen your understanding of yourself and the world around you. I've crafted this book with the hope that it can be a daily resource for you, offering inspiration, peace, and connection to the divine.

This book can also be shared with others. Perhaps you're leading a yoga class or a group meditation. Before you settle into Shavasana or any quiet moment, you could open this book to a random page and read the lesson and prayer aloud to your students. You never know what may come up—there's always something that resonates with the group, a message that speaks to them exactly where they are in that moment. It's a beautiful way to connect and share the wisdom within these pages.

I invite you to embark on this journey with me, and to allow these meditative lessons and prayers to guide you through your own cycles of growth, understanding, and transformation. May this year-long practice deepen your connection to yourself and to the divine, and may it bring you peace and wisdom as you walk your path.

How to Meditate

Meditating with this book is simple, yet profound. Each day, you are invited to read a lesson that offers wisdom and insight. This lesson is designed to guide your thoughts and reflections, helping you deepen your connection to your spiritual path. After reading the lesson, you will find a meditative prayer, crafted to center your mind and open your heart to the divine presence in your life.

To begin, take a moment to settle into a comfortable space where you can sit undisturbed. Close your eyes gently, allowing your body to relax and your mind to slow. Take a few deep breaths, inhaling deeply through your nose and exhaling slowly through your mouth. With each breath, feel yourself becoming more grounded and present in the moment.

Next, read the lesson for the day. Allow the words to wash over you, absorbing the essence of the teaching. Let your mind engage with the message, but also let it flow freely without judgment or expectation. Simply be present with the words, allowing them to resonate with your inner being. If a particular phrase stands out to you, take note of it—this may be an area of focus or insight for your practice.

After reading the lesson, move into the meditative prayer. Read it slowly, taking in each word with intention. As you read, allow the prayer to become your own. You may wish to repeat it aloud or silently, letting the words deepen your connection to your inner wisdom and the divine. Feel the energy of the prayer as it fills your heart and mind. Allow it to guide you into a state of stillness and openness.

Once you have read both the lesson and the prayer, sit in stillness for a few moments. Close your eyes and simply *be*. Reflect on the lesson and prayer, and let them settle within you. Let your thoughts float by like clouds, gently returning to the peace and clarity that comes from within. If your mind begins to wander, gently guide it back to the prayer or the feeling of peace in your heart.

This practice doesn't require long periods of time or rigid rules. The key is to take the time to be present, to allow the lesson and prayer to enter your being, and to sit with them long enough for their message to settle deeply into your soul. There is no rush; there is no perfect way to meditate. Simply allow yourself to be open, to absorb, and to trust that in this quiet time, you are connecting with something greater than yourself.

As you continue this daily practice, you may notice shifts in your awareness, in how you relate to your spiritual path, or in your ability to move through life with peace and clarity. The more you engage with the lessons and prayers, the more you will deepen your connection to your true self and the divine. Meditating with this book is not about achieving anything, but rather about allowing yourself to be present with the divine energy that flows through you, guiding you to greater wisdom, healing, and growth.

Let each day be an opportunity to simply sit with the lesson, feel the prayer, and allow the peace and purpose of your journey to unfold in its own time.

DAY 1:

The Gift of a New Day

Lesson for the Day

Each morning, as the sun rises, you are given a gift—a fresh start, a blank canvas, a new opportunity to live with purpose and intention. No matter what happened yesterday, today is a new beginning, filled with endless possibilities. The breath you take in this moment is a reminder that life is moving forward, and you have the power to shape this day with your thoughts, words, and actions.

A new day invites you to release past regrets and embrace the present moment fully. What if you approached today as if it were a sacred offering? A chance to bring light where there was once darkness, to speak kindness where there was once silence, and to love where there was once fear. Each sunrise whispers a divine invitation to step forward with renewed faith, hope, and gratitude.

Honor this day by being fully present. See the beauty in small moments—the warmth of the morning sun, the laughter of a loved one, the peace in your breath. Let go of worries that do not belong to today. Trust that whatever you need will be revealed in perfect timing. This day is a gift—accept it with an open heart and a spirit ready to receive.

Meditative Prayer

Divine Light,
Thank You for the gift of this new day.
May I rise with a heart full of gratitude,
Embracing the fresh start You have given me.

Help me release the weight of yesterday,
And step forward with lightness and joy.
Fill my mind with peace,
My words with kindness,
And my actions with love.

May I see the beauty in each moment,
And trust in the unfolding of my path.
I welcome the lessons, the blessings,
And the opportunities this day holds.

With each breath, I am renewed.
With each step, I walk in faith.
With each moment, I honor the sacredness of today.

DAY 2:

Embracing the Stillness

Lesson for the Day

In a world that moves so quickly, stillness can feel uncomfortable, even unnatural. We are taught to always be doing, achieving, and progressing, yet there is deep wisdom in the act of pausing. Stillness is not empty. It is full of presence. It is in the quiet moments that we can truly hear—our own heart, the whispers of the Divine, and the gentle guidance of our soul.

Embracing stillness is an act of trust. It is trusting that we do not need to have all the answers right now. It is allowing space for clarity to unfold, rather than forcing it. When we slow down, when we breathe deeply, when we allow ourselves to just be, we create room for peace to settle within us. We realize that we are not defined by our productivity but by our presence.

Today, invite stillness into your life. Find a moment to sit in quiet, even if just for a few minutes. Listen to your breath, feel the rhythm of your heartbeat, and notice how stillness gently brings you back to yourself. You do not need to fill every space with noise or movement. In the stillness, you are already whole.

Meditative Prayer

Sacred Stillness,
I welcome Your presence into my heart.
In the quiet, I find peace.
In the stillness, I hear Your voice.

Help me release the need to always do,
And allow myself the gift of simply being.
Let me rest in the fullness of this moment,
Trusting that all is unfolding as it should.

When my mind races, bring me back to my breath.
When the world feels loud, be my refuge of peace.
When I feel lost, guide me home to stillness.

May I embrace the quiet as sacred.
May I listen deeply to the wisdom it holds.
May I find peace in simply being here, now.

DAY 3:

A Heart Open to Change

Lesson for the Day

Change is one of life's certainties, yet it is often met with resistance. We hold onto what feels familiar, even when it no longer serves us, fearing the unknown. But when we open our hearts to change, we step into the flow of life rather than resisting it. Change is not here to break us. It is here to shape us, to expand our understanding, and to invite new opportunities for growth.

A heart open to change is a heart that trusts. It trusts that endings lead to beginnings, that uncertainty holds possibility, and that transformation is part of our soul's journey. When we release the need to control how things unfold, we allow the Divine to guide us toward what is truly meant for us. Every change, whether small or life-altering, carries a lesson—a gift waiting to be received.

Today, welcome change as a companion rather than a threat. Breathe into the unknown with faith. When you feel fear, ask yourself, "What if this change is leading me somewhere beautiful?" Your spirit was made to evolve, and with an open heart, you will always find your way.

Meditative Prayer

Divine Guide,
Help me open my heart to change.
Let me release my grip on what no longer serves me,
And trust in the beauty of the unknown.

When fear arises, remind me that I am held.
When I resist, soften my heart with faith.
Help me see change not as an ending,
But as a doorway to new beginnings.

May I welcome growth with open arms.
May I trust in the unfolding of my journey.
May I walk forward in courage, knowing You are with me.

Change is not my enemy. It is my teacher.
I surrender to the flow of life.
I embrace the new with an open heart.

DAY 4:
Trusting the Path Unfolding

Lesson for the Day

There are moments in life when the road ahead feels unclear. We long for certainty, for a clear sign that we are moving in the right direction. Yet, the path is not always meant to be fully revealed. Sometimes, we are asked to walk in faith, trusting that each step will lead us exactly where we need to be.

Trusting the unfolding path requires patience and surrender. It means accepting that delays, detours, and even moments of stillness are part of the journey. It means believing that the Divine sees the full picture, even when we can only glimpse a small part. When we release the need to control every outcome, we make space for miracles, unexpected blessings, and lessons we never could have planned.

Today, take a deep breath and trust. Trust that you are exactly where you need to be. Trust that the doors meant for you will open at the right time. Trust that even in uncertainty, you are being guided. Let go of the need to rush or force the process. Walk forward with faith, knowing that the path ahead is unfolding perfectly.

Meditative Prayer

Divine Creator,
I surrender my need to know every step.
I trust that the path before me is unfolding
With wisdom, purpose, and grace.

When I feel uncertain,
Fill my heart with faith.
When I am impatient,
Remind me that Your timing is perfect.

Help me release the need to control,
And instead walk in the flow of Your divine plan.
Let me find peace in the journey,
Even when I do not see the destination.

I trust that I am guided.
I trust that I am supported.
I trust that every step I take is leading me
Exactly where I am meant to be.

DAY 5:

The Power of Intention

Lesson for the Day

Every thought, word, and action carries energy. When we move through life without intention, we allow external circumstances to shape our path. But when we set clear intentions, we become conscious creators of our reality. Intention is the invisible force that directs our energy toward what we seek, aligning our actions with our highest purpose.

Living with intention does not mean controlling every outcome—it means choosing how we show up. It means starting each day with clarity, focusing on what truly matters, and aligning ourselves with the energy we wish to bring into the world. When we set intentions with faith and purpose, the universe responds, opening doors and guiding us toward the life we are meant to live.

Today, pause and ask yourself, *What energy do I want to bring into this day?* Set an intention that aligns with your heart's desires— whether it is peace, love, courage, or clarity. Hold that intention close and walk through the day with purpose. When you act with awareness, even the smallest steps carry great power.

Meditative Prayer

Divine Light,
I set my intentions with love and faith.
May my thoughts be clear,
My words be kind,
And my actions be aligned with my highest good.

Help me move with purpose today.
Let my heart lead me toward what is true.
May my energy be focused,
And my spirit be open to divine guidance.

I release all distractions and doubts.
I trust that my intentions,
When set with love,
Will create ripples of goodness in the world.

With each step, I walk in purpose.
With each breath, I create my reality.
With faith, I align myself with the highest good.

Day 6:

Finding Peace in the Present

Lesson for the Day

So often, our minds drift between the past and the future—rehashing old memories or worrying about what's to come. But true peace is only found in one place: the present moment. The more we center ourselves in the here and now, the more we discover that peace is not something we must chase. It is something we allow.

Being present means letting go of distractions, surrendering the need to control, and trusting that this moment is enough. It means finding joy in the simple things—the warmth of the sun on your skin, the rhythm of your breath, the beauty of a quiet pause. When we stop resisting the present, we begin to see life as it truly is, as sacred unfolding, moment by moment.

Today, give yourself permission to slow down. Notice the small details around you. Breathe deeply and feel the gift of this moment. Release any regrets about the past and any anxieties about the future. Peace is here, now. All you have to do is step into it.

Meditative Prayer

Divine Presence,
Help me find peace in this moment.
Quiet my restless thoughts,
And bring my heart into the here and now.

When I am lost in the past,
Remind me that today is where life is unfolding.
When I worry about the future,
Let me trust in Your perfect timing.

May I embrace the beauty of this moment,
Finding joy in the simple and the small.
May I breathe deeply and rest in Your presence,
Knowing that all is well.

Peace is not something I must chase,
It is something I allow.
And so, I surrender to this moment,
Where peace, love, and grace already exist.

DAY 7:

Letting Go of Yesterday

Lesson for the Day

Yesterday is a story already written, a chapter that has passed. Whether it was filled with joy or struggle, it no longer defines you. Holding onto the past—whether through regret, guilt, or longing—only weighs down the present. True freedom comes when we release what was and embrace what is.

Letting go does not mean forgetting. It means making peace with what has been, learning from it, and choosing not to carry its weight into today. Every sunrise offers a fresh start, an opportunity to step forward with lightness and clarity. The past may have shaped you, but it does not have to confine you.

Today, take a deep breath and let go. Release any burdens that no longer serve you. Trust that what is meant to stay will remain, and what is meant to leave will make space for something new. Move forward with grace, knowing that today is yours to embrace fully.

Meditative Prayer

Divine Source,
Help me release the weight of yesterday.
What has passed is no longer mine to carry.
I surrender my regrets,
I forgive myself and others,
And I open my heart to this new day.

May I learn from what was,
But not be bound by it.
May I walk forward in freedom,
Trusting that I am always being guided.

I welcome the freshness of today,
The lightness of an unburdened heart.
I trust that what is meant for me will come,
And what is not will gently fade away.

With each breath, I let go.
With each step, I move forward.
With grace, I embrace this moment.

DAY 8:

The Strength in Surrender

Lesson for the Day

We are often taught that strength means holding on, pushing through, and staying in control. But true strength is also found in surrender. Surrender is not about giving up—it is about trusting that we don't have to carry everything alone. It is the deep knowing that we are supported, guided, and held, even when we cannot see the way forward.

There is freedom in releasing the need to force outcomes. When we surrender, we allow divine wisdom to unfold in our lives. We let go of resistance and open ourselves to possibilities greater than we imagined. Surrender does not mean weakness. It is an act of faith, a choice to trust in the unseen.

Today, practice surrender. Release the burdens you have been gripping tightly. Breathe deeply and allow yourself to rest in divine flow. Know that you are not alone, and that whatever is meant for you will come in perfect timing. Strength is not always about holding on—it is also about knowing when to let go.

Meditative Prayer

Divine Wisdom,
I release my need to control.
I surrender my worries, my fears,
And the weight I was never meant to carry.

Teach me to trust in Your perfect plan.
When I do not see the way,
Help me walk forward in faith.
When I feel lost,
Remind me that I am always held.

I embrace the strength in surrender.
I let go with grace,
Knowing that what is meant for me
Will never pass me by.

I trust. I release. I surrender.
And in doing so, I find peace.

DAY 9:

Clarity in the Quiet

Lesson for the Day

In the stillness, there is wisdom. When we quiet the noise of the world—its demands, distractions, and expectations—we create space to hear what truly matters. Clarity does not come from overthinking or forcing answers, it comes when we allow ourselves to be present and listen.

In the quiet, our spirit speaks. The Divine whispers guidance, and our own inner wisdom rises to the surface. When we pause, breathe, and let go of mental clutter, the path ahead becomes clearer. Answers that once felt distant reveal themselves in gentle, unexpected ways.

Today, embrace a moment of quiet. Step away from the rush, turn inward, and simply be. Let your breath steady you, let your heart soften, and trust that clarity will come. The answers you seek are not lost—they are waiting for you in the stillness.

Meditative Prayer

Sacred Stillness,
In the quiet, I find clarity.
When my mind is restless,
Calm my thoughts and bring me peace.

Help me release distractions,
So that I may hear the wisdom within.
Let me trust that the answers I seek
Will come in perfect timing.

May I embrace the pause,
Finding peace in the space between.
May I rest in the knowing
That I do not need to rush or force.

In Your stillness, I am guided.
In Your quiet, I am renewed.
In this moment, I am at peace.

DAY 10:

Awakening to Possibility

Lesson for the Day

Each day is an invitation to see the world with fresh eyes. Possibility surrounds us, waiting to be noticed, but too often, we limit ourselves with doubt, fear, or past experiences. Awakening to possibility requires a shift in perspective—a willingness to believe that life can unfold in ways greater than we have imagined.

When we open our hearts to possibility, we step into the flow of divine creation. We recognize that new opportunities, insights, and blessings can arrive in unexpected ways. Instead of clinging to what is familiar, we embrace what could be. The universe is vast, and within it, endless potential exists for growth, healing, and joy.

Today, choose to see beyond limitation. Instead of asking, *What if it doesn't work?* ask, *What if it does?* Instead of fearing change, welcome it as a doorway to something beautiful. Life is filled with divine possibilities—you need only open your heart to receive them.

Meditative Prayer

Infinite Creator,
Awaken my heart to possibility.
Let me see beyond my doubts,
And embrace the limitless potential within me.

Help me release the fears that hold me back.
Replace my hesitation with faith,
And my uncertainty with trust.

May I walk with an open heart,
Ready to receive the blessings
That are already making their way to me.

Today, I choose expansion over limitation.
I welcome divine opportunities.
I believe in the beauty of what is yet to come.

ALEX MᶜCANN JOHNSON

DAY 11:

The Breath of Renewal

Lesson for the Day

Each breath is a reminder that renewal is always within reach. Just as the seasons change and the earth is refreshed, so too can we release the old and welcome the new. The breath is sacred—it grounds us in the present, clears stagnant energy, and fills us with life-giving force.

Renewal does not require grand gestures. It begins with something as simple as an intentional breath. With each inhale, we invite fresh energy, hope, and clarity. With each exhale, we let go of stress, doubt, and the weight of the past. Renewal is not about becoming someone new—it is about returning to the truth of who we are.

Today, pause and take a deep breath. Feel the air fill your lungs, awakening your spirit. Let it remind you that you are alive, capable, and worthy of new beginnings. No matter what has come before, you can always start again.

Meditative Prayer

Sacred Breath of Life,
With each inhale, I welcome renewal.
With each exhale, I release the past.
I breathe in clarity,
I breathe out fear.

Fill me with fresh energy,
Restoring my mind, body, and spirit.
Help me embrace this moment,
Knowing that I am always being renewed.

May I trust in life's cycles of growth.
May I welcome transformation with grace.
May I walk forward, refreshed and open,
Ready for the blessings ahead.

With this breath, I begin anew.
With this breath, I am whole.

DAY 12:

Moving Beyond Fear

Lesson for the Day

Fear is a powerful force—it can keep us safe, but it can also keep us small. When fear takes hold, it whispers doubt, plants hesitation, and builds walls where there should be open doors. But fear is not meant to be our guide. It is simply a signal, reminding us of where we need to grow.

Moving beyond fear does not mean eliminating it altogether. It means acknowledging it, but choosing faith instead. It means stepping forward even when the path is uncertain. The Divine does not call us to live in the shadows of fear, but to walk boldly in the light of trust and possibility.

Today, take one step beyond fear. Whether it is a small act of courage or a shift in mindset, move forward with faith. Trust that you are supported. Trust that strength rises within you the moment you decide to step beyond what holds you back.

Meditative Prayer

Divine Protector,
When fear rises, fill me with courage.
When doubt whispers, speak truth to my heart.
Let me walk forward in faith,
Knowing that I am never alone.

Help me release the fears
That keep me from my highest path.
Replace them with strength,
With trust, with unwavering confidence.

I choose to see beyond fear.
I choose to embrace the unknown.
I choose to walk in light,
Knowing that I am always guided.

Fear does not define me.
Faith leads me forward.

DAY 13:

The Light Within

Lesson for the Day

There is a light within you that has always been there—steady, radiant, and divine. This inner light is not dependent on external circumstances, nor can it be diminished by the darkness around you. It is the essence of your soul, the spark of the Divine that lives within.

At times, life may make you feel dimmed, burdened, or disconnected from your own brilliance. But just as the sun continues to shine behind the clouds, your light is never truly gone. When you turn inward and reconnect with your spirit, you remember the truth: you are luminous, created in love, and meant to shine.

Today, honor the light within you. Let go of self-doubt and allow yourself to be seen, to express, to love. Trust that your inner light is strong enough to guide you, no matter how uncertain the path may seem. You are radiant. You are divine. You are enough.

Meditative Prayer

Divine Light,
You shine within me,
A flame that can never be extinguished.
Help me to see myself as You see me,
Whole, radiant, and full of love.

When I feel lost,
Let Your light guide me home.
When I feel unworthy,
Remind me of my divine essence.

May I shine brightly in this world,
Spreading love, hope, and kindness.
May I embrace my light,
Without fear or hesitation.

I am created from light.
I am surrounded by light.
I am the light.

DAY 14:

Courage to Begin Again

Lesson for the Day

Life is a series of beginnings. No matter how many times we stumble, fall, or lose our way, we are always given the chance to start anew. Beginning again requires courage—the courage to release the past, to step into the unknown, and to trust that something beautiful awaits on the other side of change.

It is easy to believe that past failures define us, but they do not. Every ending is simply a transition into a new possibility. The Divine does not count our missteps. Instead, we are met with grace, encouragement, and an open invitation to try again. Strength is not found in never falling—it is found in rising each time we do.

Today, give yourself permission to begin again. Whatever has weighed you down, whatever has held you back, release it. Breathe in fresh hope and take the first step forward. You are not starting over—you are starting from wisdom, from growth, from renewed faith.

Meditative Prayer

Divine Source,
Grant me the courage to begin again.
When I feel weary, renew my strength.
When I doubt myself, remind me of my resilience.
When I fear the unknown, fill me with trust.

Help me release the past,
Knowing that each day is a fresh start.
Let me walk forward in faith,
Believing that new beginnings hold new blessings.

I am not defined by what has been,
But by the courage I have to rise again.
With every step, I am guided.
With every breath, I am renewed.

Today, I choose to begin again.
And with You by my side, I am unafraid.

Day 15:

Honoring Your Journey

Lesson for the Day

Your journey is uniquely yours—filled with experiences, lessons, challenges, and triumphs that have shaped you into who you are today. Too often, we compare our path to others, questioning if we are where we are "supposed" to be. But the truth is, every step you have taken, even the difficult ones, has carried purpose.

Honoring your journey means embracing your growth, acknowledging how far you have come, and trusting that every season of your life has meaning. There is no right timeline, no perfect path—only the unfolding of your soul's evolution. Each moment, each lesson, and each experience is sacred.

Today, take a moment to reflect on your journey with gratitude. Release self-judgment and trust that you are exactly where you need to be. Honor the road you have walked, the strength you have shown, and the wisdom you have gained. Your journey is not just about where you are going—it is about who you are becoming along the way.

Meditative Prayer

Divine Guide,
I honor the journey that has shaped me.
Every step, every challenge, every lesson
Has brought me to this sacred moment.

Help me release comparison and self-doubt.
Let me embrace my own path with gratitude and trust.
May I see the beauty in my growth,
And the wisdom in my experiences.

I trust that I am where I need to be.
I honor my struggles, my victories, my evolution.
With each step forward, I walk with faith,
Knowing I am always guided and supported.

I am growing. I am learning. I am becoming.
And for this, I give thanks.

DAY 16:

Releasing the Old, Welcoming the New

Lesson for the Day

Life is a continuous cycle of endings and beginnings, and each transition offers us a choice—to hold on or to let go. Releasing the old does not mean forgetting or rejecting what once was; it means making peace with the past and creating space for new blessings to enter.

Clinging to what no longer serves us—old patterns, past hurts, or limiting beliefs—only keeps us stuck. True growth requires trust. Trust that what has left was meant to go, and trust that what is coming will be exactly what we need. When we welcome the new with an open heart, we allow life to unfold in ways beyond our imagination.

Today, take a deep breath and release. Release old burdens, old fears, and anything weighing you down. In that release, make room for fresh opportunities, renewed hope, and divine possibilities. You are not meant to stay the same—you are meant to evolve. Welcome the new with faith, knowing it is leading you to your highest good.

Meditative Prayer

Divine Creator,
Help me release what no longer serves me.
I let go of the past with gratitude,
And open my heart to the blessings ahead.

Where there was doubt, let there be faith.
Where there was heaviness, let there be lightness.
Where there was fear, let there be trust.

I make space for the new,
New wisdom, new love, new possibilities.
I welcome change as a sacred part of my journey,
Knowing that all things unfold for my highest good.

With each breath, I release.
With each moment, I welcome.
With each step, I trust in the divine flow of life.

DAY 17:

Strength in Vulnerability

Lesson for the Day

True strength is not found in perfection or invincibility—it is found in the courage to be real, to be open, and to be vulnerable. In a world that often equates strength with self-reliance and emotional armor, it takes deep inner power to show up as your authentic self. Vulnerability is not weakness. It is the gateway to connection, healing, and transformation.

When we allow ourselves to be seen, we create space for love to flow freely. When we release the need to have all the answers, we make room for divine wisdom to guide us. Strength is not about never falling—it is about having the courage to rise, to share our truth, and to embrace our humanity with grace.

Today, let go of the fear of being vulnerable. Allow yourself to express your heart, to ask for support, to acknowledge your emotions without judgment. There is strength in openness, and there is power in embracing yourself exactly as you are.

Meditative Prayer

Divine Love,
Help me find strength in my openness.
Let me release the fear of being seen,
And trust that my authenticity is a gift.

When I feel the urge to hide,
Remind me that I am worthy just as I am.
When I fear rejection,
Let me know that true love embraces all of me.

May I walk with courage,
Not as someone who never struggles,
But as someone who knows that vulnerability
Is the foundation of strength.

I am safe in my truth.
I am strong in my openness.
I am whole in my willingness to be seen.

DAY 18:

The Whisper of Your Soul

Lesson for the Day

Deep within you, beneath the noise of the world and the chatter of your mind, there is a quiet voice—a whisper that has always been there. This is the voice of your soul, guiding you with love, wisdom, and truth. It does not shout or demand attention, but it speaks in the moments of stillness, in the gentle nudges of intuition, and in the deep knowing that cannot be explained.

Listening to your soul requires trust. It asks you to pause, to breathe, and to tune in beyond distractions. The world may pull you in many directions, but your soul will always bring you back home to yourself. When you feel lost, confused, or uncertain, return to this whisper. It will not lead you astray.

Today, take a moment to listen. Set aside the noise, close your eyes, and breathe deeply. What is your soul whispering to you? What truth is waiting to be heard? You are already connected to the wisdom you seek—it has always been within you.

Meditative Prayer

Sacred Spirit,
Help me quiet the noise around me,
So I may hear the whisper of my soul.

When doubt clouds my mind,
Let me return to stillness.
When fear tries to lead me,
Remind me of the deep knowing within.

My soul speaks with love.
My intuition guides with truth.
I trust the wisdom that rises in the quiet.

May I walk in alignment with my inner voice,
Moving with faith, clarity, and peace.
I am always guided, always supported,
And I am never alone.

DAY 19:

Walking with Grace

Lesson for the Day

Grace is the quiet strength that carries us through life's challenges with dignity, compassion, and trust. It is not about perfection but about moving through the world with an open heart—responding with kindness, even when faced with difficulty, and offering love, even when it is not returned. Walking with grace means choosing peace over reaction, patience over frustration, and faith over fear.

There will be moments when life feels heavy, when frustration, doubt, or disappointment arise. In those times, grace is the gentle reminder that you are not alone, that you do not have to have all the answers, and that you can trust in something greater than yourself. Grace allows you to release what is beyond your control and move forward with confidence and serenity.

Today, choose to walk with grace. Speak with kindness, even when it is difficult. Extend patience, even when you feel rushed. Trust that you are supported in ways unseen. Grace is not something you must earn—it is something that flows through you when you allow it.

Meditative Prayer

Divine Grace,
Fill my heart with Your presence.
Help me walk through this day
With patience, wisdom, and peace.

When challenges arise,
Let me respond with kindness.
When I feel overwhelmed,
Remind me that I am carried by Your love.

May I speak with gentleness,
Act with compassion,
And trust that I am always supported.

Grace flows through me effortlessly.
Grace carries me forward with strength.
Grace is the gift I receive,
And the gift I give to the world.

DAY 20:

The Sacred Pause

Lesson for the Day

In the rush of life, we often forget the power of the pause—the sacred space between action and reaction, between one breath and the next. It is in these pauses that clarity emerges, that peace is found, and that we reconnect with ourselves and the Divine. The sacred pause is not empty. It is full of presence.

Pausing does not mean inaction. It is an intentional choice to slow down, to listen, and to align with what is true. When we pause before speaking, we choose words with love. When we pause before reacting, we choose understanding over impulse. When we pause to breathe, we invite calm into our hearts. The world tells us to keep moving, but wisdom tells us to pause and find balance.

Today, embrace the sacred pause. Before you rush to respond, to judge, or to decide—breathe. Give yourself space to listen deeply, to reflect, and to trust. Within the pause, there is wisdom. Within the stillness, there is grace.

Meditative Prayer

Divine Presence,
Teach me the power of the pause.
Help me embrace stillness,
So that I may listen before I speak,
Breathe before I react,
And trust before I fear.

When I feel rushed, slow my steps.
When I feel scattered, center my spirit.
Let me rest in the sacred stillness
Where Your wisdom speaks.

I do not need to force or chase.
All that is meant for me
Will come in perfect time.

In the pause, I find clarity.
In the pause, I find peace.
In the pause, I find You.

DAY 21:

Embracing Your Inner Wisdom

Lesson for the Day

Within you lies a well of wisdom deeper than you realize. This wisdom is not found in the opinions of others or in the endless search for external validation. It is the quiet knowing, the intuition that nudges you forward, the deep truth that has always been a part of you. When you trust your inner wisdom, you step into alignment with your soul's path.

Too often, we second-guess ourselves, ignoring the voice within because it seems quieter than the noise around us. But wisdom does not shout—it whispers. It is felt in moments of clarity, in the peace that comes when a decision feels right, in the way your spirit expands when you are in harmony with your truth.

Today, trust in yourself. Honor the wisdom that rises within you. Instead of seeking answers outside, turn inward. You already hold what you seek. Your soul knows the way—all you need to do is listen.

Meditative Prayer

Divine Wisdom,
Awaken within me the knowing that has always been there.
Help me trust my intuition,
To hear its whispers above the noise of the world.

When I doubt myself, remind me
That You have placed truth within me.
When I seek direction, guide me inward,
Where clarity and peace reside.

I release the need for external validation.
I embrace the wisdom already within me.
I walk with confidence, knowing
That my soul is aligned with divine truth.

I am wise. I am guided. I am enough.

Day 22:

The Power of Gratitude

Lesson for the Day

Gratitude is more than a feeling—it is a powerful force that transforms the way we see the world. When we choose gratitude, we shift our focus from what is missing to what is already present. We begin to see blessings where we once saw burdens, opportunities where we once saw obstacles. Gratitude is the key that opens our hearts to joy, abundance, and divine presence in all things.

Life will always bring moments of challenge, but even in difficult times, there is something to be thankful for—a lesson, a moment of grace, the simple gift of breath. Gratitude does not deny struggle, but it reminds us that we are never without light. The more we practice gratitude, the more we create space for peace, healing, and deeper connection with the Divine.

Today, take a moment to reflect on your blessings. Notice the small things—a kind word, a warm cup of tea, the beauty of the sky. Let gratitude fill your heart, and watch how it changes the energy of your day. Gratitude is not just something we feel—it is something we live.

Meditative Prayer

Divine Giver of All,
Thank You for the blessings that surround me,
Both seen and unseen.
Help me to open my heart to gratitude,
So that I may see life's goodness more clearly.

When I focus on what is lacking,
Gently remind me of all I have.
When I face struggles,
Let me find the hidden gifts within them.

May I walk through this day
With a heart full of appreciation.
May my words and actions
Reflect the gratitude within me.

With every breath, I give thanks.
With every step, I choose joy.
Gratitude is my prayer, and today, I live it.

DAY 23:
Trusting in Divine Timing

Lesson for the Day

There are moments when we want things to happen faster—when we feel impatient, uncertain, or frustrated by delays. But everything unfolds in its perfect time. Just as the seasons change in their own rhythm, our lives follow a divine order that we may not always understand. Trusting in divine timing means believing that what is meant for you will arrive when you are ready to receive it.

When we try to force outcomes, we often create unnecessary stress and struggle. But when we surrender to divine timing, we allow life to unfold with grace. Delays are not denials; they are often divine redirections, guiding us toward something even better than we imagined. Every step, even the waiting, has purpose.

Today, release the need to control the timing of your life. Trust that things are working in your favor, even if you cannot yet see how. Have faith that what is meant for you will never pass you by. Breathe deeply, be present, and know that divine timing is always right on time.

Meditative Prayer

Divine Keeper of Time,
Help me trust in Your perfect plan.
When I feel impatient,
Remind me that everything unfolds
At the right moment, in the right way.

Teach me to release control,
To surrender my timeline to Yours.
Let me find peace in the waiting,
Knowing that delays are not denials,
But divine alignment in motion.

May I walk with faith instead of fear,
With trust instead of doubt.
I know that what is meant for me
Will arrive at the perfect time.

I trust. I release. I surrender.

DAY 24:
Holding Space for Yourself

Lesson for the Day

You spend so much time showing up for others, offering kindness, support, and understanding. But how often do you hold that same space for yourself? Holding space for yourself means allowing rest when you are weary, offering grace when you fall short, and embracing yourself with the same love you so freely give to others.

This is not selfish—it is necessary. Just as a well must be replenished to continue flowing, your spirit needs care and nurturing to thrive. Taking time to reflect, to breathe, and to honor your emotions is an act of self-respect. When you hold space for yourself, you remind your soul that it is seen, valued, and deeply loved.

Today, give yourself permission to pause. Whether through quiet reflection, deep breathing, or simply saying no to what drains you, take time to honor your own needs. You are worthy of the love, care, and kindness you so often extend to others.

Meditative Prayer

Divine Nurturer,
Help me hold space for myself today.
Let me release guilt for resting,
And embrace the truth that I, too, am worthy of care.

When I feel weary,
Remind me that I am allowed to pause.
When I doubt my worth,
Let me see myself through Your loving eyes.

May I nourish my soul,
As I so often nourish others.
May I offer myself grace,
Knowing that I do not need to be perfect to be loved.

Today, I choose to honor myself.
I make space for my healing,
My growth, and my peace.
And in doing so, I walk in divine love.

DAY 25:
A Mind Anchored in Peace

Lesson for the Day

The mind is a powerful force—capable of creating calm or chaos, clarity or confusion. When left untended, it can easily become overwhelmed with worries, distractions, and fears. But just as an anchor steadies a ship in the midst of waves, we can choose to anchor our minds in peace, even when life feels uncertain.

True peace is not found in the absence of difficulty but in the ability to remain centered despite it. It comes from trusting that no matter what unfolds, you are supported, guided, and held in divine grace. When we quiet the noise within, we create space for wisdom, clarity, and serenity to rise.

Today, choose peace. Each time a stressful thought arises, gently redirect it. Breathe deeply, remind yourself that you are safe, and let peace settle within you. You do not have to control everything—you only need to trust. A mind anchored in peace creates a life anchored in faith.

Meditative Prayer

Divine Source of Peace,
Steady my mind when it wavers.
Let me release the worries I cannot control,
And trust in the unfolding of my path.

When fear rises,
Fill me with calm.
When my thoughts become restless,
Anchor me in stillness.

May I choose peace over worry,
Faith over fear,
And presence over distraction.

I am held in divine love.
I am grounded in truth.
I am anchored in perfect peace.

Day 26:
The Beauty of Small Beginnings

Lesson for the Day

Every great journey begins with a single step. Every strong tree started as a tiny seed. Often, we hesitate to start something new because we think our efforts must be grand, our progress must be immediate, or our path must be fully clear. But there is beauty in small beginnings—the quiet, humble moments where growth takes root.

Small beginnings teach us patience, faith, and trust. They remind us that what matters is not how fast we move but that we move at all. The Divine does not measure success by speed or size but by the willingness to begin. Even the smallest step forward is an act of courage, and each step builds upon the last, leading us toward something greater.

Today, embrace the beauty of beginning. Do not let fear or doubt stop you from planting the seeds of your dreams. Trust that what starts small will grow in its perfect time. Move forward, even if it is just one step. The path ahead is unfolding—one small beginning at a time.

Meditative Prayer

Divine Creator,
Thank You for the gift of new beginnings.
Help me trust that even the smallest step
Holds purpose, meaning, and growth.

When doubt whispers that I am not ready,
Remind me that I do not need to be perfect.
I only need to begin.

May I have faith in what is unfolding,
Patience in what is growing,
And courage to take the next step,
No matter how small.

I release the need to rush.
I trust in divine timing.
I honor the beauty of small beginnings,
Knowing they are the foundation of great things.

DAY 27:

Silence as a Teacher

Lesson for the Day

Silence is often misunderstood. In a world filled with constant noise, we may fear silence, mistaking it for emptiness or loneliness. But silence is a sacred teacher. In its stillness, we find clarity. In its quiet, we hear the wisdom that is often drowned out by the busyness of life.

Silence invites us to listen—not just to the world around us, but to the voice within. It teaches us patience, deepens our intuition, and reconnects us with the presence of the Divine. When we embrace silence, we create space for peace, for reflection, and for the answers that cannot be forced but must instead be received.

Today, welcome silence as a companion. Take a moment to sit in stillness, without distraction or expectation. Breathe deeply, let go of the need to fill the space with words or thoughts, and simply be. In silence, there is wisdom. In silence, there is presence. In silence, you are never truly alone.

Meditative Prayer

Divine Presence,
Teach me to welcome silence.
Help me quiet my mind,
So I may hear the whispers of wisdom within.

When I seek answers,
Let me find them in stillness.
When I feel restless,
Let silence bring me peace.

May I embrace the quiet as sacred.
May I learn from its wisdom.
May I find comfort in its presence,
Knowing that You are always near.

I do not fear silence.
I embrace it as a gift.
In the stillness, I listen.
In the stillness, I receive.

DAY 28:

Becoming Who You Are Meant to Be

Lesson for the Day

You are constantly evolving, growing into the person you were always meant to become. Your journey is not about becoming someone else—it is about uncovering the truth of who you already are. The more you embrace your authenticity, the more you step into your highest purpose.

Becoming who you are meant to be requires courage. It means releasing old identities that no longer serve you, letting go of fear, and trusting in the divine unfolding of your life. It is not about perfection but about alignment—walking in truth, listening to your inner wisdom, and honoring the unique gifts within you.

Today, take a step toward your most authentic self. Speak your truth with confidence, follow the path that calls to your soul, and trust that you are exactly where you need to be. You are not lost—you are becoming. And in that becoming, you are whole.

Meditative Prayer

Divine Creator,
Guide me as I step into my truth.
Help me release the fears and doubts
That keep me from embracing who I am.

When I question my path,
Remind me that I am being shaped
With wisdom, purpose, and love.
When I feel unworthy,
Show me the light within me
That has always been enough.

I trust in my journey.
I trust in my becoming.
I trust that I am exactly where I need to be.

With each step, I grow.
With each breath, I align.
With each moment, I become
Who I was always meant to be.

DAY 29:
The Healing Power of Presence

Lesson for the Day

So much of life is spent dwelling on the past or worrying about the future, but healing happens in the present moment. When we are fully here—fully aware, fully engaged, fully open—we allow ourselves to receive the peace and renewal that can only be found in the now.

Presence is a gift we give ourselves and others. When we truly listen, when we observe the beauty around us, when we breathe deeply and let go of distractions, we align with divine energy. In presence, we release anxiety, quiet the mind, and reconnect with the wisdom of our soul. The present moment is where love, healing, and transformation reside.

Today, choose to be present. Slow down. Breathe. Notice the way light filters through the trees, the way your body feels as it moves, the way your spirit expands when you surrender to this moment. Let presence be your healer. Everything you need is right here, right now.

Meditative Prayer

Divine Presence,
Help me rest in this moment.
Calm my mind,
That I may release the weight of the past.
Steady my heart,
That I may let go of worries for the future.

Teach me to be fully here,
To listen with my whole spirit,
To see the beauty in each breath,
To trust that this moment is enough.

In presence, I find healing.
In presence, I find peace.
In presence, I am whole.

I embrace the now,
And in doing so, I embrace You.

DAY 30:
Finding Your Sacred Rhythm

Lesson for the Day

Life moves in cycles, much like the rising and setting of the sun, the ebb and flow of the tides, and the changing of the seasons. There is a natural rhythm to all things, including your own life. When you try to force yourself into a pace that is not your own—rushing when you need rest or waiting when you are meant to move—you feel disconnected and unsettled. But when you honor your sacred rhythm, you find balance, flow, and peace.

Your sacred rhythm is unique to you. It is the pace at which your soul thrives, the energy that aligns with your purpose, the timing that feels natural to your spirit. The more you listen to your inner guidance, the more you will recognize when it is time to act, when it is time to pause, and when it is time to simply be. Trusting this rhythm allows you to walk in harmony with life, rather than resisting its flow.

Today, take a deep breath and tune into your own rhythm. Are you moving too fast or holding back when you are ready to step forward? Release the pressure to match the pace of others and instead align with the rhythm of your soul. When you honor your sacred flow, you walk with grace, trust, and ease.

Meditative Prayer

Divine Flow,
Help me align with my sacred rhythm.
When I move too fast,
Slow my steps and bring me back to presence.
When I hesitate out of fear,
Give me the courage to move forward.

May I trust the pace of my journey,
Knowing that I am always in divine timing.
May I honor the cycles of rest and renewal,
Of action and stillness,
Of learning and becoming.

I release the need to force,
And instead surrender to flow.
I am in harmony with life.
I am walking in rhythm with my soul.

Day 31:

The Strength of Surrender

Lesson for the Day

Surrender is often misunderstood as giving up, but in truth, it is one of the greatest acts of strength. To surrender is to trust—to release the need to control every outcome and instead open your heart to divine guidance. It is an act of courage to let go of what is not meant for you and to believe that something greater is unfolding beyond what you can see.

There will be moments when holding on feels safer, but resistance creates struggle. Surrender allows flow. It does not mean you stop moving forward—it means you release the weight of worry, the pressure of forcing things into place, and the fear of the unknown. When you surrender, you align with the rhythm of life, allowing grace, wisdom, and divine timing to lead the way.

Today, choose to surrender what burdens you. Breathe deeply and let go of the need to have all the answers. Trust that what is meant for you will not pass you by. Strength is not about controlling everything—it is about having faith that you are held, supported, and guided in ways beyond your understanding.

Meditative Prayer

Divine Wisdom,

Help me find strength in surrender.

I release my need to control,

And trust that Your plan is greater than mine.

When I hold on too tightly,

Remind me that I am safe in letting go.

When fear rises within me,

Fill me with the peace of knowing I am guided.

I surrender my worries,

I surrender my doubts,

I surrender the weight I was never meant to carry.

May I walk forward in trust,

With open hands and an open heart.

In surrender, I find strength.

In surrender, I find peace.

Day 32:
Walking by Faith, Not by Sight

Lesson for the Day

There will be times in life when the path ahead is unclear—when you cannot see how things will unfold or when uncertainty fills your heart with doubt. In these moments, faith becomes your guide. Walking by faith means trusting that even when you cannot see the full picture, the Divine is leading you toward your highest good.

Faith is not about having all the answers, it is about knowing that you are not alone. It is choosing to take the next step, even when you do not know where the road will lead. It is believing in the unseen, in the wisdom that works beyond your understanding, in the love that surrounds you at all times.

Today, take a deep breath and release the need for certainty. Choose to walk forward with faith, trusting that you are exactly where you need to be. The way will become clear as you move forward, step by step, held by the Divine.

Meditative Prayer

Divine Guide,
When the path is unclear,
Help me walk by faith, not by sight.
When doubt clouds my heart,
Remind me that I am always supported.

I do not need to see every step ahead,
For I trust that You are leading me.
I release the need for control,
And surrender to Your divine wisdom.

May I walk with courage,
Even when I do not know what lies ahead.
May I trust in Your perfect timing,
Knowing that all things are unfolding for my highest good.

With faith, I step forward.
With trust, I embrace the unknown.
With love, I walk the path before me.

DAY 33:

The Unseen Blessings

Lesson for the Day

Not all blessings are immediately visible. Some arrive in disguise—hidden within challenges, delays, or unexpected changes. It is easy to recognize blessings when they come in the form of joy, abundance, or answered prayers. But often, the greatest blessings are those we do not yet understand, the ones that shape us in ways beyond our current awareness.

When something does not go as planned, it does not mean you are being denied—it may mean you are being redirected. When a door closes, it does not mean you have lost your way—it may mean something greater is waiting for you. The Divine is always working behind the scenes, weaving together blessings that you may not see until the time is right.

Today, trust in the unseen blessings. Even if you do not yet recognize them, know that they are unfolding in perfect alignment with your journey. Have faith that what is happening now is preparing you for something far greater than you can imagine.

Meditative Prayer

Divine Giver of Blessings,
Help me trust in the unseen gifts
That are unfolding in my life.
Even when I do not understand,
Let me walk forward with faith.

When a door closes,
May I trust that another is opening.
When life does not go as I planned,
Let me believe that Your plan is even greater.

I release doubt and fear,
And embrace the unknown with a peaceful heart.
I trust that unseen blessings surround me,
Guiding me in ways beyond my understanding.

Thank You for the gifts I have yet to see.
Thank You for the blessings already on their way.
I receive them with faith, with gratitude, and with love.

DAY 34:

Holding onto Hope

Lesson for the Day

Hope is the light that carries us through even the darkest of times. It is the quiet assurance that no matter what we face today, tomorrow holds the possibility of something new. Hope does not deny the hardships of life—it strengthens us to endure them. It reminds us that even when we cannot yet see the way, there is still a path unfolding before us.

There will be days when hope feels distant, when challenges seem too great, and when the weight of uncertainty presses heavily upon you. In those moments, do not let go. Even the smallest spark of hope is enough to keep moving forward. The Divine is always working in unseen ways, preparing new opportunities, new healing, and new beginnings.

Today, hold onto hope. Let it fill your heart with possibility. Trust that the storm will pass, that better days are ahead, and that the Divine is guiding you toward something greater than you can yet imagine. Hope is not just a wish—it is a promise that life continues to unfold in miraculous ways.

Meditative Prayer

Divine Light,
Fill my heart with hope,
Even in moments of uncertainty.
Let me trust that beyond this moment,
New blessings await.

When I feel weary,
Remind me that hope is never lost.
When I struggle to see the way,
Help me trust that You are already making a way.

I choose hope over fear.
I choose faith over doubt.
I choose to believe that
Something beautiful is still ahead.

Hope is my anchor.
Hope is my guide.
Hope is the light that leads me forward.

DAY 35:
The Light That Guides You

Lesson for the Day

No matter how uncertain life may feel, there is always a light guiding you forward. This light may not always be visible, but it is always present—shining through moments of clarity, divine timing, and the quiet whispers of intuition. It is the presence of the Divine, walking with you, illuminating the way even when the path ahead seems unclear.

There will be times when doubt creeps in, when you feel lost or unsure of your next step. In those moments, do not fear the darkness. Instead, trust that the light is still there, waiting to be noticed. Sometimes it comes as a small flicker, other times as a bright and undeniable force. Either way, it is enough to lead you forward.

Today, trust in the light that guides you. Even if you do not see the full path ahead, take one step in faith. The Divine is always with you, revealing the way, shining hope into the unknown. You are never walking alone.

Meditative Prayer

Divine Light,
Be my guide when the path is unclear.
Help me trust that even in the darkness,
Your presence is leading me forward.

When doubt fills my heart,
Remind me that I am never alone.
When fear clouds my vision,
Let Your wisdom shine through.

I walk in faith,
Knowing that Your light will always find me.
I step forward with trust,
Believing that You are making a way.

No matter what lies ahead,
I know that I am guided,
I am supported,
And I am held in love.

DAY 36:
When Doors Close, Windows Open

Lesson for the Day

Not every door is meant to stay open. Some close to protect you, to redirect you, or to make space for something greater. It can be painful when a door closes—when an opportunity fades, a relationship ends, or a path you envisioned no longer seems possible. But trust that when one door closes, a window of new possibility is waiting to be found.

The Divine is always working on your behalf, even when you do not see it. What seems like an ending may be a sacred turning point. Sometimes, what you thought you wanted was not truly meant for you, and something far greater is waiting ahead. If you spend too much time looking at the closed door, you might miss the open window inviting you into something new.

Today, shift your perspective. Instead of focusing on what has ended, open your heart to what is beginning. Trust that the Divine is guiding you toward something better than you imagined. Have faith that your path is unfolding perfectly, even when it takes an unexpected turn.

Meditative Prayer

Divine Guide,
Help me trust in Your greater plan.
When a door closes,
Let me not be discouraged,
But instead, open my heart to new possibilities.

When I feel lost,
Remind me that You are leading me.
When I grieve what is ending,
Fill me with hope for what is beginning.

May I walk forward in faith,
Believing that what is meant for me
Will never pass me by.
I trust that the windows You open
Will lead me to exactly where I need to be.

With gratitude, I embrace the new.
With courage, I step forward.
With faith, I welcome what is to come.

DAY 37:

Trusting the Unknown

Meditative Prayer

DAY 38:

Resting in Divine Love

Lesson for the Day

There is a love that asks nothing of you—a love that does not need to be earned, proven, or chased. This is divine love, an eternal presence that surrounds and fills you at all times. No matter where you are on your journey, no matter what burdens you carry, this love remains steady, constant, and unconditional.

Too often, we believe we must strive for love, that we must be perfect or worthy before we can receive it. But divine love is not given as a reward, it is simply there, waiting for us to rest in its embrace. When we stop resisting, stop questioning, and simply allow ourselves to receive, we find the peace and healing that only love can bring.

Today, let yourself rest in divine love. Release the need to prove yourself. Let go of any doubts that whisper you are not enough. You are already held, already loved, already whole. Allow yourself to simply be, knowing that love is your foundation, your strength, and your home.

Meditative Prayer

Divine Love,
I open my heart to Your presence.
Help me release the need to strive,
And allow myself to simply rest in Your embrace.

When I feel unworthy,
Remind me that Your love is unconditional.
When I feel lost,
Let Your love be the light that guides me home.

May I trust that I am enough,
Exactly as I am in this moment.
May I rest in the comfort of knowing
That I am seen, known, and deeply loved.

I do not need to chase love,
For love is already within me.
I do not need to be perfect,
For love accepts me as I am.

I am held. I am cherished.
I am forever wrapped in divine love.

DAY 39:
Embracing the Sacred Flow

Lesson for the Day

Life is not meant to be forced. Like a river flowing effortlessly toward the ocean, there is a natural rhythm to all things—a sacred flow that carries us exactly where we need to be. When we resist, we create struggle. When we force, we exhaust ourselves. But when we surrender to the divine flow, we find ease, alignment, and unexpected blessings.

Embracing the sacred flow does not mean being passive; it means trusting the journey. It means listening to the quiet guidance of your soul, knowing when to move forward and when to be still. It means releasing fear and trusting that the Divine is always guiding you, even when the path unfolds in ways you did not expect.

Today, let go of the need to control. Instead of fighting the current, allow yourself to flow with it. Trust that you are being carried exactly where you need to go. The more you surrender to the sacred flow, the more you will realize that life is always unfolding in perfect harmony.

Meditative Prayer

Divine Flow,
Teach me to trust the rhythm of life.
Help me release resistance,
And embrace the path unfolding before me.

When I try to force my way,
Remind me that Your way is greater.
When I fear the unknown,
Let me rest in the knowing that I am guided.

May I move with grace and ease,
Trusting that every twist and turn has purpose.
May I find peace in surrender,
Knowing that all is aligning for my highest good.

I release control.
I surrender to the sacred flow.
I trust in the divine unfolding of my journey.

DAY 40:
Finding Strength in Stillness

Lesson for the Day

Strength is often associated with action, movement, and perseverance. But there is also great power in stillness. When we pause, when we allow ourselves to simply be, we tap into a deeper source of strength—one that is not rushed, not forced, but steady and unshaken.

Stillness is where clarity is found. It is in the quiet moments that we reconnect with ourselves, hear the whispers of the Divine, and allow our spirit to be restored. When the world feels chaotic, when your mind is filled with noise, stillness becomes a refuge—a sacred space where peace replaces worry and trust overcomes fear.

Today, take time to be still. Let go of the need to always do, fix, or figure things out. Instead, breathe deeply and rest in the present moment. Know that strength is not just in movement but also in the quiet surrender of simply being. In stillness, you will find the strength you seek.

Meditative Prayer

Divine Presence,
Teach me the strength of stillness.
When life feels rushed,
Let me find peace in the pause.
When my mind is restless,
Quiet my thoughts and bring me back to center.

May I trust that I do not need to have all the answers.
May I rest in the knowing
That clarity comes in its own time.

Help me embrace the power of stillness,
The calm within the storm,
The wisdom in the quiet,
The peace that surpasses all understanding.

I do not need to force or chase.
I only need to be.
And in that being, I am strong.

Day 41:

The Art of Letting Go

Lesson for the Day

Letting go is not a sign of weakness. It is an act of trust. We often hold on tightly to people, outcomes, and expectations, fearing that releasing them will leave us empty or lost. But true freedom comes when we learn to let go with grace, making space for new growth, new blessings, and new beginnings.

Letting go does not mean forgetting or giving up. It means surrendering the weight of what no longer serves you. It is a release of control, a softening of resistance, and a deep trust that the Divine is guiding you toward something greater. What is meant for you will never be lost, and what leaves your life was never meant to stay.

Today, practice the art of letting go. Breathe deeply and release old fears, past hurts, and attachments to what no longer aligns with your path. Trust that in letting go, you are making space for something even more beautiful to unfold.

Meditative Prayer

Divine Presence,
Help me let go with grace.
When I cling to what is no longer meant for me,
Remind me that release is not loss, but freedom.

Teach me to trust the unfolding of my life.
When I fear the unknown,
Fill my heart with faith.
When I resist change,
Show me the beauty in surrender.

May I open my hands and heart,
Releasing the past with gratitude,
Welcoming the future with hope.

I let go of what no longer serves me.
I make space for what is meant to be.
I walk forward in trust,
Knowing that all is well.

DAY 42:
Your Soul's Inner Compass

Lesson for the Day

Within you, there is an inner compass—your intuition, your soul's deep knowing, the quiet voice that whispers truth. This compass is always guiding you, pointing you toward alignment, peace, and purpose. Yet, in the noise of the world, it is easy to ignore, second-guess, or doubt its direction.

Your soul's wisdom does not shout. It speaks in gentle nudges, in feelings of resonance, in moments of clarity that seem to arise from nowhere. When you trust this inner guidance, you step into flow, making decisions not out of fear or pressure, but from a place of deep inner truth. The more you listen, the stronger your compass becomes.

Today, tune into your inner wisdom. Before seeking answers outside of yourself, pause and listen within. Trust that your soul knows the way. Even if the path ahead is unclear, your inner compass will always lead you in the right direction—one step at a time.

Meditative Prayer

Divine Guide,
Help me trust the wisdom within me.
When the world is loud,
Quiet my mind so I may hear my soul's truth.

When I feel uncertain,
Remind me that I already hold the answers.
When doubt creeps in,
Strengthen my faith in my own knowing.

May I follow the path that feels aligned,
That brings me peace,
That expands my spirit and deepens my joy.

I trust my inner compass.
I trust the voice within.
I walk forward in confidence,
Knowing that I am always guided.

DAY 43:

A Foundation of Trust

Lesson for the Day

Trust is the foundation upon which peace, faith, and inner strength are built. Without trust, fear takes hold, doubt clouds our vision, and worry becomes our constant companion. But when we trust—trust in ourselves, in the Divine, in the unfolding of life—we step into a space of surrender and deep assurance that we are held.

Trust does not mean having all the answers. It does not mean that life will always go as planned. It means believing that no matter what happens, you are not alone, and that all things are working together for your highest good. It is the quiet confidence that even when you cannot see the way, the path is still being laid before you.

Today, build your foundation on trust. Release the need for certainty. Let go of the fear of the unknown. Stand firmly in the belief that you are guided, supported, and exactly where you need to be. Trust is not just something you give—it is something you live.

Meditative Prayer

Divine Source,
Help me build my life on trust.
When I feel uncertain,
Let me rest in the knowing that I am guided.

When fear whispers in my heart,
Fill me with faith.
When doubt clouds my mind,
Clear the way for truth.

May I trust in divine timing.
May I trust in my own strength.
May I trust that all is unfolding for my highest good.

I stand on a foundation of trust.
I walk in faith, not fear.
I surrender, knowing that I am always held.

DAY 44:
Releasing the Need for Control

Lesson for the Day

There is a part of us that longs to control—to shape outcomes, to plan every step, to hold tightly to what feels certain. But control is often an illusion, and the more we grasp, the more we struggle. True peace comes when we release the need to control and instead trust in the divine flow of life.

Letting go does not mean giving up. It means surrendering the weight of trying to force things into place. It means believing that you do not have to figure everything out on your own. When you loosen your grip, you make space for miracles, for unexpected blessings, for the Divine to move in ways greater than you could have imagined.

Today, take a deep breath and release what you cannot control. Let go of the pressure to have all the answers. Trust that what is meant for you will come, and what is not will fall away. When you surrender, you do not lose—you gain freedom, peace, and a heart open to divine guidance.

Meditative Prayer

Divine Presence,
Help me release my need for control.
When I cling too tightly,
Remind me that I am safe in surrender.

Teach me to trust in Your wisdom,
To believe that all things unfold in perfect timing.
When I feel anxious about the unknown,
Fill me with peace and assurance.

I release my worries.
I let go of the need to force my way.
I open my heart to divine flow,
Knowing that I am always guided.

I do not have to control everything.
I only need to trust.
And in that trust, I find peace.

Day 45:

The Call to Surrender

Lesson for the Day

Surrender is not about giving up—it is about letting go of resistance and allowing the Divine to guide your path. It is the sacred act of releasing the need to control every outcome and instead trusting that life is unfolding exactly as it should. Surrender is a deep invitation to rest in faith rather than struggle in fear.

When we resist surrender, we create unnecessary tension. We hold onto plans, expectations, and fears, believing that we must carry everything alone. But the call to surrender is a reminder that we are never meant to bear life's burdens by ourselves. There is a greater force at work, one that sees the full picture even when we cannot.

Today, answer the call to surrender. Release what is heavy on your heart. Trust that the Divine is working on your behalf, even in ways you do not yet understand. When you surrender, you make space for peace, clarity, and grace to enter your life.

Meditative Prayer

Divine Presence,
I answer the call to surrender.
I release my grip on what I cannot control,
And place my trust in Your perfect plan.

When I hold on too tightly,
Remind me that I am safe in Your hands.
When I feel uncertain,
Let me rest in the knowing that all is unfolding for my highest
good.

I surrender my worries.
I surrender my fears.
I surrender my need to control the outcome.

May I walk in faith, not resistance.
May I trust in divine timing.
May I rest in the peace that surrender brings.

I am guided. I am supported.
I am free.

Day 46:
Faith Beyond Understanding

Lesson for the Day

Faith is easy when life makes sense—when prayers are answered, when doors open, when the path ahead is clear. But true faith is tested in the moments when we do not understand, when things do not go as planned, when we are called to trust without visible proof. Faith is not about having all the answers, it is about believing even in uncertainty.

There will be times when life unfolds in ways you did not expect. When you are faced with delays, disappointments, or detours, faith reminds you that the Divine sees what you cannot. What seems like a setback may be a setup for something greater. What feels like an unanswered prayer may be divine protection or redirection.

Today, lean into faith beyond understanding. Instead of seeking control, choose trust. Instead of demanding answers, choose surrender. Even in the unknown, you are held. Even when you cannot see the way, the Divine is leading you forward.

Meditative Prayer

Divine Source,
Help me trust beyond what I can see.
When life is unclear,
Let my faith be my foundation.

When I long for answers,
Remind me that I do not need to understand
To know that You are guiding me.
When fear rises,
Fill my heart with the peace of surrender.

I release the need for certainty.
I walk forward in faith,
Knowing that all things are unfolding
In divine perfection.

Even when I do not understand,
I trust.
Even when I cannot see the way,
I believe.

Day 47:
Being Held by the Divine

Lesson for the Day

No matter where you are on your journey, you are never alone. You are always being held by the Divine—wrapped in love, guided by wisdom, and supported in ways seen and unseen. Even in moments of struggle, doubt, or uncertainty, the Divine presence remains steady, offering comfort and strength.

Too often, we carry our burdens alone, believing we must be strong enough to handle everything ourselves. But the greatest strength comes in surrender—trusting that we are supported, allowing ourselves to rest in divine love, and remembering that we do not have to walk this path alone. The Divine is always holding you, always carrying you, always working on your behalf.

Today, allow yourself to rest in this truth. Let go of the need to figure everything out on your own. Release your worries, your fears, and your need for control. You are held, you are loved, and you are deeply cared for.

Meditative Prayer

Divine Presence,
Thank You for holding me in love.
When I feel weak,
Remind me that I do not have to carry everything alone.

When life feels heavy,
Lift my burdens and fill me with peace.
When I struggle to trust,
Let me feel Your steady presence guiding me.

I surrender my fears,
I release my worries,
I open my heart to Your grace.

I am safe in Your hands.
I am supported in ways beyond my understanding.
I am held by the Divine, now and always.

DAY 48:
The Power of Divine Alignment

Lesson for the Day

When you are in alignment with the Divine, life flows with a sense of ease and purpose. It does not mean that challenges disappear, but it does mean that you move with clarity, guided by something greater than yourself. Divine alignment happens when you trust the path unfolding before you, when your heart, mind, and spirit are centered in faith rather than fear.

There may be times when things feel out of sync, when plans fall apart, or when uncertainty clouds your vision. These moments are not signs of failure but invitations to realign—to step back, reconnect with your inner wisdom, and allow the Divine to guide you. True alignment is not about controlling every outcome, but about walking in faith, knowing that the right doors will open at the right time.

Today, focus on alignment rather than control. Surrender what is not yours to carry. Trust in divine timing. Open yourself to the flow of grace, and let the presence of the Divine lead you. When you are in alignment, you will always find your way.

Meditative Prayer

Divine Guide,
Align my heart with Your wisdom.
Help me release resistance,
And trust the path unfolding before me.

When I feel lost,
Realign me with my highest purpose.
When I try to control,
Remind me that Your way is always greater.

I surrender to divine flow.
I walk in trust,
Knowing that I am always guided,
Always supported,
Always where I am meant to be.

May I move in harmony with life,
May I embrace the doors You open,
May I walk forward with grace,
In perfect divine alignment.

Day 49:

A Heart Open to Miracles

Lesson for the Day

Miracles are not always grand or dramatic. They often arrive in quiet, unexpected ways—a kind word, a moment of clarity, a door opening when you least expect it. The Divine is always at work, orchestrating blessings in ways beyond our understanding. But to receive these gifts, we must first open our hearts to them.

A heart open to miracles is a heart that trusts, that believes in possibilities beyond what is seen, that welcomes the unexpected with faith rather than doubt. When we release the need to control how things unfold, we create space for divine intervention, for synchronicities, and for blessings we never could have planned.

Today, open your heart to miracles. Expect goodness, look for beauty, and trust that unseen forces are working in your favor. The more you believe in miracles, the more you will see them unfolding all around you.

Meditative Prayer

Divine Giver of Miracles,
Open my heart to receive the unexpected.
Help me release doubt,
And trust that blessings are always on their way.

When I feel uncertain,
Remind me that miracles come in many forms.
When I try to control,
Let me surrender to divine timing.

May I walk in faith,
With eyes open to wonder,
With a heart ready to receive,
With a spirit filled with gratitude.

I welcome miracles into my life.
I trust in divine surprises.
I believe in the unseen blessings unfolding before me.

Day 50:
The Path Revealed in Time

Lesson for the Day

There are moments in life when the path ahead feels unclear, when you long for direction but can only see a few steps forward. In these times, it is easy to feel lost or uncertain, but the truth is, the path is always unfolding—even when you cannot yet see where it leads.

Divine timing is never rushed, yet it is never late. What you need to know will be revealed at the right moment. Trust that each step you take, no matter how small, is guiding you toward something greater. The Divine does not require you to know every answer—only to walk in faith, trusting that clarity will come when it is meant to.

Today, release the need to have it all figured out. Trust that the way forward will become clear in time. Walk with faith, knowing that every turn, every delay, and every detour is part of a greater plan. The path is not lost—it is simply waiting to be revealed.

Meditative Prayer

Divine Guide,
Help me trust in the unfolding of my journey.
When I cannot see the way,
Remind me that each step is leading me forward.

Teach me patience in the unknown,
Faith in divine timing,
And peace in the journey itself.

I do not need to see the full picture.
I only need to trust that clarity will come.
I surrender my need for certainty,
And open my heart to divine guidance.

The path is unfolding.
I am exactly where I need to be.
And in time, all will be revealed.

DAY 51:
Resting in Unshakable Peace

Lesson for the Day

Peace is not found in a life without challenges, but in the ability to remain steady within them. True peace is unshakable—not dependent on circumstances, external validation, or the absence of difficulty. It is rooted in trust, in surrender, and in the deep knowing that no matter what happens, you are held by the Divine.

The world may shift around you, uncertainties may arise, and storms may come, but peace remains available to you at all times. When you center yourself in divine presence, when you release the need to control, when you allow yourself to simply be, you enter into a space of stillness that no external force can disrupt.

Today, choose peace. Let go of the worries that pull you away from the present moment. Breathe deeply, knowing that you are safe, guided, and deeply loved. The peace you seek is already within you—rest in it.

Meditative Prayer

Divine Presence,
Fill my heart with unshakable peace.
Let me rest in the knowing
That I am held, safe, and always guided.

When the world feels uncertain,
Let my spirit remain steady.
When fear rises,
Quiet my heart with the calm of Your presence.

May I carry peace within me,
A refuge no storm can disturb.
May I trust that all things are unfolding
Exactly as they are meant to.

I release worry.
I embrace stillness.
I rest in the deep and unshakable peace of the Divine.

DAY 52:
Finding Strength in Uncertainty

Lesson for the Day

Uncertainty is a part of life—there will always be moments when the future feels unclear, when answers do not come easily, and when you are asked to walk forward without knowing exactly where the path leads. In these moments, strength is not found in controlling every detail but in trusting that you are strong enough to navigate the unknown.

Strength in uncertainty comes from faith. It is the willingness to take the next step even when you cannot see the full road ahead. It is the choice to believe that even in confusion, the Divine is guiding you. Uncertainty is not a sign that you are lost—it is an invitation to trust, to surrender, and to lean into the wisdom unfolding in divine timing.

Today, instead of fearing uncertainty, embrace it as a space of growth and possibility. Let go of the need to have all the answers. Trust that you are strong enough for this season, and that the path will become clear in time. You are never walking alone.

Meditative Prayer

Divine Strength,
In moments of uncertainty,
Help me find peace in the unknown.
When I seek control,
Remind me that I am safe in surrender.

When the path is unclear,
Let me trust in divine timing.
When fear whispers doubt,
Fill my heart with courage.

I do not need to have all the answers.
I do not need to see the full picture.
I only need to take the next step,
Knowing that I am always guided.

I am strong, even in uncertainty.
I am held, even in the unknown.
I trust in the unfolding of my path.

DAY 53:
The Divine Works Through You

Lesson for the Day

You are not separate from the Divine—you are an instrument of its love, wisdom, and healing. Every act of kindness, every word of encouragement, every moment you extend love to another is the Divine working through you. You are not here by accident. Your presence, your gifts, and your spirit are part of something greater.

Too often, we underestimate the impact we have. We think our actions are too small to matter, but even the gentlest ripple can create waves of change. The Divine moves through you in ways you may never fully see—the comforting words you offer, the hope you inspire, the light you bring simply by being yourself.

Today, open yourself to be a vessel for love. Let the Divine flow through your thoughts, your words, and your actions. Trust that you are being used for a greater purpose. The more you align with love, the more you allow the Divine to shine through you.

Meditative Prayer

Divine Presence,
Work through me today.
Let my thoughts be filled with wisdom,
My words be filled with kindness,
And my actions be filled with love.

When I doubt my impact,
Remind me that even the smallest act of love
Is a reflection of Your presence in the world.
When I feel unworthy,
Let me remember that I was created with purpose.

May I be a vessel for healing,
A light in the darkness,
A source of peace in a restless world.
Use me, guide me, and move through me,
So that I may walk in alignment with You.

I am here to love.
I am here to serve.
I am here to shine.

DAY 54:
Leaning into the Mystery

Lesson for the Day

There are aspects of life, of the Divine, and of your journey that are beyond human understanding. We often long for certainty, for answers that bring a sense of control, but some things are meant to remain a mystery—unfolding in divine timing, revealing wisdom only when we are ready to receive it.

Leaning into the mystery is an act of trust. It is accepting that not everything needs to be known right now. It is embracing the beauty of the unknown rather than fearing it. The Divine does not ask us to have all the answers, only to have faith in the unfolding. Some of the most profound moments of growth happen when we surrender to what we cannot yet see.

Today, release the need for certainty. Instead of seeking control, seek trust. Let go of the pressure to figure everything out, and allow yourself to rest in the mystery of what is still becoming. The unknown is not something to fear—it is a sacred space where miracles take shape.

Meditative Prayer

Divine Mystery,
Teach me to embrace the unknown.
When I long for certainty,
Remind me that faith is found in trust.

Help me release my need for answers,
And rest in the beauty of what is still unfolding.
Let me find peace, not in knowing,
But in believing that all is happening in perfect time.

I surrender my doubts.
I embrace the sacred mystery.
I trust that even in the unseen,
I am guided, held, and loved.

The unknown is not empty—
It is filled with divine possibilities.
And I welcome them with an open heart.

DAY 55:
Becoming a Vessel for Love

Lesson for the Day

Love is the most powerful force in existence, and you are meant to be a vessel for it. Every time you offer kindness, extend compassion, or speak words of encouragement, you allow divine love to flow through you. Love is not something to be hoarded or earned—it is meant to be shared freely, healing both the giver and the receiver.

Being a vessel for love does not require grand gestures. It is found in the way you listen with an open heart, in the way you uplift those around you, in the way you show up for yourself and others with grace. The more you embody love, the more you align with the Divine, for love is the language of the sacred.

Today, let love be your intention. Let it shape your words, your actions, and your thoughts. Ask yourself, *How can I be a vessel for love today?* The more you give, the more love expands within you, touching lives in ways you may never fully see.

Meditative Prayer

Divine Love,
Flow through me today.
Let my heart be open,
My words be gentle,
And my actions be filled with kindness.

When I feel unworthy,
Remind me that I was created from love.
When I feel hesitant to give,
Show me that love multiplies when it is shared.

May I be a source of light in the world,
A reflection of divine love in every moment.
Use me as a vessel,
That I may uplift, heal, and inspire.

I choose love.
I embody love.
I am a vessel for love.

DAY 56:
Walking with the Sacred

Lesson for the Day

The sacred is not distant. It is woven into every moment of your life. It is in the quiet of the morning, the kindness of a stranger, the rhythm of your breath. When you walk with the sacred, you move through life with awareness, reverence, and deep connection to the Divine.

Walking with the sacred does not mean escaping the ordinary—it means seeing the Divine within it. It is recognizing that each step, each encounter, each breath is an opportunity to be present with the holy. When you slow down, when you notice the beauty around you, when you choose gratitude and love, you are walking in sacred alignment.

Today, let yourself walk with the sacred. Be mindful of the small miracles surrounding you. Speak with kindness, listen with presence, and move through your day as if each moment is a prayer. The Divine is not just above or beyond—you carry the sacred within you.

Meditative Prayer

Divine Presence,
Help me walk with the sacred today.
Let me see the holiness in small moments,
The beauty in the ordinary,
The light in all things.

When I rush, slow my steps.
When I feel disconnected,
Remind me that You are always near.

May my words be a prayer,
May my actions reflect love,
May my spirit move in harmony
With the sacred presence within and around me.

I walk with awareness.
I walk with gratitude.
I walk with the Divine.

DAY 57:
The Deep Roots of Faith

Lesson for the Day

Faith is like a tree with deep roots—grounded, strong, and unwavering. It does not depend on perfect circumstances, nor is it shaken by passing storms. True faith remains steady, even when the winds of uncertainty blow, because it is rooted not in what is seen, but in trust in the Divine.

There will be moments when doubt tries to pull you away, when fear tempts you to question your path. But faith is not about never experiencing doubt—it is about choosing to stand firm despite it. It is about believing that even in the unknown, you are supported, guided, and never alone. When your faith has deep roots, nothing can uproot your peace.

Today, nourish your faith. Spend time in stillness, in prayer, in trust. Let your heart be strengthened by the knowing that you are always held. The deeper your faith grows, the stronger you become, and the more resilient your spirit will be through every season of life.

Meditative Prayer

Divine Source,
Anchor me in deep and unshakable faith.
Let my trust be rooted in You,
Steady and strong, no matter the storms I face.

When doubt arises,
Fill me with quiet assurance.
When fear tempts me to waver,
Remind me that I am always held.

May my faith grow deeper each day,
Grounded in truth,
Strengthened by love,
Nourished by the presence of the Divine.

I am rooted in faith.
I am steady in trust.
I am held in divine grace.

DAY 58:
Knowing You Are Enough

Lesson for the Day

You do not have to prove your worth. You do not have to earn love, chase validation, or become someone else to be accepted. You are enough—exactly as you are, in this moment, without condition or exception. The Divine created you in love, and that love is not based on achievements, perfection, or external approval.

Too often, we measure ourselves against impossible standards, believing that we must do more or be more to deserve happiness and peace. But the truth is, your worth has never been in question. You are already whole. You are already loved. Nothing you do can add to or take away from the divine light that already exists within you.

Today, release the pressure to be anything other than yourself. Rest in the knowing that you are enough. Let go of self-doubt and embrace the truth that you are already worthy, already loved, already complete.

Meditative Prayer

Divine Creator,
Help me remember that I am enough.
Not because of what I do,
But because of who I am.

When I doubt my worth,
Remind me that I am loved beyond measure.
When I feel like I am not enough,
Fill my heart with the truth of my divine essence.

May I release the need to prove myself.
May I walk in confidence,
Knowing that I am already whole.

I am worthy.
I am loved.
I am enough.

DAY 59:
Love as the Ultimate Truth

Lesson for the Day

At the core of all things, beneath every fear, every doubt, and every struggle, there is love. Love is the foundation of existence, the force that breathes life into the universe, and the truth that transcends all illusion. When we align with love—when we choose it, embody it, and share it—we return to the deepest truth of who we are.

Love is not just an emotion, it is a way of being. It is found in the way we speak, the way we listen, the way we extend kindness even when it is difficult. The more we choose love over fear, the more we invite peace, healing, and connection into our lives. Love does not need to be earned, nor does it run out—it is infinite, abundant, and always available.

Today, let love be your truth. Speak words of love, act with love, and receive love with an open heart. The Divine is love, and you are a reflection of that love in this world. Return to love, and you will always find your way home.

Meditative Prayer

Divine Love,
Let me remember that love is my truest nature.
Help me to see love in all things,
And to choose love in all moments.

When fear tries to guide me,
Let love be my compass.
When anger or doubt arise,
Let love be my response.

May I be a vessel of love,
A light that brings warmth and healing.
May I see others through the eyes of love,
And know that I, too, am deeply loved.

Love is the foundation.
Love is the way.
Love is the ultimate truth.

Day 60:

A Soul Aligned with the Divine

Lesson for the Day

There is a deep sense of peace that comes when your soul is aligned with the Divine. In this alignment, you are not striving, forcing, or questioning—you are simply in harmony with the flow of life, trusting that you are exactly where you need to be. Alignment is not about perfection, it is about living in connection with your highest truth, walking in faith, and allowing divine wisdom to guide you.

When your soul is aligned with the Divine, you begin to see life differently. Challenges become lessons, delays become divine timing, and even the unknown feels sacred. The more you align with love, trust, and inner peace, the more your life unfolds with grace. You no longer need to control every outcome because you trust in the greater plan that is unfolding for you.

Today, take a deep breath and realign with the Divine. Release what pulls you away from your truth, and return to a state of faith and flow. The more you align with the sacred, the more you will feel at home within yourself and at peace with the journey ahead.

Meditative Prayer

Divine Presence,
Align my soul with Your wisdom.
Let my heart beat in rhythm with Your love,
And my steps move in harmony with Your plan.

When I feel lost,
Guide me back to truth.
When I try to force my way,
Remind me that Your way is always greater.

May I trust in divine timing,
May I walk in faith instead of fear,
May I surrender what no longer serves me,
So that I may fully embrace my sacred path.

I am aligned with peace.
I am aligned with trust.
I am aligned with the Divine.

DAY 61:

The Light of a New Dawn

Lesson for the Day

Each new day is a gift—an opportunity to begin again, to release the past, and to step forward with renewed hope. No matter what yesterday held, today is a fresh start, a blank canvas waiting to be filled with light, love, and possibility. The rising sun is a reminder that no darkness lasts forever, and that each dawn brings new energy, new clarity, and new grace.

The Divine offers us constant renewal, not just in the turning of the days but in the shifting of our hearts. When we choose to embrace the light of a new dawn, we welcome transformation. We release what no longer serves us, forgive what needs to be forgiven, and walk forward with trust that something beautiful is unfolding.

Today, breathe in the promise of a new beginning. Let the light of this day fill you with gratitude. No matter what has come before, you are here now, standing in the dawn of a new possibility. Step forward with faith, knowing that the Divine walks with you into this day.

Meditative Prayer

Divine Light,
As the sun rises, so do I.
I step into this new day
With an open heart and a spirit renewed.

Help me release the burdens of yesterday,
And embrace the fresh possibilities before me.
Let Your light fill my soul,
Guiding me with wisdom, love, and grace.

May I walk through this day
With gratitude, peace, and purpose.
May I trust that each moment
Is a chance to begin again.

The light of a new dawn is upon me.
I welcome it with faith.
I walk forward with joy.

Divine Creator,
Thank You for the gift of new beginnings.
Help me release the past with grace,
And step into this moment with faith.

DAY 62:

The Power of New Beginnings

Lesson for the Day

Every moment holds the possibility of a new beginning. No matter where you have been, what choices you have made, or what challenges you have faced, you are never stuck. The Divine offers renewal at every turn, inviting you to step forward with faith and embrace the life that is waiting for you.

New beginnings are not about forgetting the past but about learning from it and moving forward with greater wisdom. They require courage—to release what no longer serves you, to trust in the unknown, and to believe that something beautiful is unfolding, even when you cannot yet see the full picture.

Today, embrace the power of a new beginning. Let go of what weighs you down and walk forward with hope. Trust that every step you take brings you closer to the life meant for you. The past does not define you—the choices you make today do.

Meditative Prayer

Divine Creator,
Thank You for the gift of new beginnings.
Help me release the past with grace,
And step into this moment with faith.

When I feel afraid to start again,
Fill me with courage.
When I doubt my ability to move forward,
Remind me that You are guiding my steps.

I welcome transformation.
I embrace renewal.
I trust that my journey is unfolding perfectly.

With every breath, I begin again.
With every step, I walk in faith.
With every moment, I am made new.

DAY 63:

Your Healing is Unfolding

Lesson for the Day

Healing is not always instant. It is a journey, a sacred unfolding that takes time, patience, and trust. There may be days when you feel progress, and others when old wounds resurface. But no matter how slow it seems, know this—your healing is happening. The Divine is working within you, restoring what was broken, strengthening what was weary, and bringing peace where there was pain.

Healing does not mean forgetting the past or pretending struggles never existed. It means allowing yourself to grow beyond them. It means giving yourself grace in the process, trusting that even when you cannot see the full transformation, it is already underway. Each step, no matter how small, is a step forward.

Today, trust that your healing is unfolding in perfect time. Release the pressure to have it all figured out. Breathe deeply and know that every moment of reflection, forgiveness, and self-care is a part of the divine restoration happening within you.

Meditative Prayer

Divine Healer,
I trust in the unfolding of my healing.
Even when I cannot see the full picture,
I know that You are restoring me.

When I feel impatient,
Remind me that healing is a journey.
When old wounds resurface,
Fill me with the grace to keep moving forward.

May I release the need to rush,
And instead embrace the process.
May I trust that each day, each breath,
Brings me closer to wholeness.

I am healing.
I am growing.
I am being renewed.

DAY 64:
Trusting the Process of Growth

Lesson for the Day

Growth is not always easy. It stretches you, challenges you, and sometimes places you in uncomfortable spaces. But just like a seed buried in the soil, you are not stuck—you are growing. Even when you cannot see the progress, trust that transformation is taking place beneath the surface.

The Divine is always working within you, guiding you toward your highest self. Growth requires patience, faith, and the willingness to release what no longer serves you. It is not about rushing to the next stage but embracing where you are, knowing that every experience— every success, every challenge—is shaping you in divine timing.

Today, trust the process of your growth. Do not compare your journey to others. You are exactly where you need to be. Allow yourself to expand, evolve, and step into the fullness of who you are becoming.

Meditative Prayer

Divine Gardener,
Nurture the growth within me.
Help me trust the process,
Even when I do not see the full picture.

When I feel impatient,
Remind me that all things bloom in their time.
When I doubt my progress,
Let me feel Your presence guiding me forward.

May I embrace this season of growth,
With trust, with patience, with faith.
I release the need to control,
And surrender to the unfolding of my becoming.

I am growing.
I am evolving.
I am exactly where I need to be.

Day 65:
Shedding the Layers of the Past

Lesson for the Day

Growth often requires letting go—shedding old beliefs, patterns, and identities that no longer align with who you are becoming. Like the trees that release their leaves in autumn, you, too, are meant to release what no longer serves you. This is not a loss but a sacred transformation, making space for new beginnings.

The past has shaped you, but it does not define you. Every experience, every lesson, and every challenge has brought you to this moment. But you are not meant to carry the weight of what has been forever. There is freedom in releasing, in trusting that what you let go of was never meant to stay.

Today, give yourself permission to shed the layers of the past. Breathe deeply and let go of any burdens, regrets, or fears that hold you back. Step forward lighter, freer, and open to the new season ahead. You are not who you were—you are who you are becoming.

Meditative Prayer

Divine Light,
Help me release what no longer serves me.
Let me shed the weight of the past,
So that I may walk freely into what is next.

When I cling to old wounds,
Remind me that healing is found in letting go.
When I fear change,
Fill my heart with trust in the path before me.

I embrace this transformation.
I step forward with courage.
I release the old and welcome the new,
Knowing that I am always growing.

I am lighter.
I am freer.
I am ready.

DAY 66:
Walking the Path of Transformation

Lesson for the Day

Transformation is a journey, not a single moment. It is the continuous unfolding of your soul's growth, the shedding of old layers, and the stepping into a new, truer version of yourself. At times, transformation may feel uncertain or even uncomfortable, but trust that every step you take is leading you closer to alignment with your highest self.

The Divine is guiding you through this process, even when you cannot see the full picture. Growth does not always happen in great leaps—it happens in small, steady shifts, in quiet realizations, in the willingness to keep moving forward even when the road feels unfamiliar. True transformation requires trust, patience, and a heart open to change.

Today, embrace the path of transformation. Walk forward with faith, knowing that every lesson, every challenge, and every moment of growth is shaping you. You are not who you once were, and you are not yet who you will become—but you are exactly where you need to be.

Meditative Prayer

Divine Guide,
Walk with me on this path of transformation.
Help me trust in the changes unfolding within me.
When I feel uncertain,
Remind me that I am growing in divine timing.

When the journey feels slow,
Let me find patience in the process.
When fear tries to hold me back,
Fill my heart with courage to move forward.

I surrender to the unfolding.
I embrace my evolution.
I trust that I am being shaped into the person I am meant to be.

I walk in faith.
I walk in purpose.
I walk in transformation.

Day 67:

The Energy of Renewal

Lesson for the Day

Just as the earth renews itself with the changing seasons, so too are you constantly being renewed. Every breath, every sunrise, every moment is an opportunity to begin again. Renewal is not about erasing the past—it is about embracing the present with fresh energy, clarity, and purpose.

There may be times when you feel weary, as though you have given all you have to give. But the Divine is always offering restoration, pouring new strength into your spirit. Renewal comes when you release what drains you and open yourself to what revitalizes you—whether through rest, reflection, or reconnection with your purpose.

Today, welcome the energy of renewal. Let go of what no longer serves you and invite in what uplifts your spirit. Trust that you are always being refreshed, restored, and prepared for the next chapter of your journey.

Meditative Prayer

Divine Source,
Fill me with the energy of renewal.
Let each breath bring fresh strength,
Each moment awaken new possibility.

When I feel weary,
Revive my spirit.
When I feel burdened,
Lighten my heart with Your grace.

I release what drains me,
And embrace what restores me.
I am renewed in mind, body, and soul.

With every breath, I begin again.
With every step, I move forward.
I welcome the energy of renewal.

ALEX McCANN JOHNSON

DAY 68:

Embracing Your Authentic Self

Lesson for the Day

You were created to be exactly who you are—unique, radiant, and filled with divine purpose. Yet, the world often teaches us to shrink, to conform, or to hide parts of ourselves in fear of judgment. Embracing your authentic self is an act of courage, a declaration that you are enough just as you are.

Your true self is not something you need to create—it is something you need to uncover. Beneath layers of doubt, expectations, and old stories, your soul knows who you are meant to be. The more you step into your truth, the more you align with your purpose, and the more you allow your light to shine in the world.

Today, release any fear of being fully seen. Honor your strengths, your gifts, your voice. Walk confidently in the truth of who you are, knowing that you are a divine creation, exactly as you are meant to be.

Meditative Prayer

Divine Creator,
Help me embrace my authentic self.
Let me release fear,
And stand boldly in my truth.

When I doubt my worth,
Remind me that I am already enough.
When I feel pressure to change,
Guide me back to the wisdom of my soul.

May I walk in confidence,
Unapologetic in my light.
May I trust that I was made with purpose,
And that my authenticity is a gift to the world.

I am seen.
I am worthy.
I am exactly who I am meant to be.

DAY 69:

Strength in the Shadows

Lesson for the Day

It is easy to embrace the light—the moments of clarity, joy, and success. But true strength is often forged in the shadows, where uncertainty, fear, and challenge reside. It's in those darker seasons of life that your resilience is tested and your spirit deepens. The shadows are not your enemy. They are sacred spaces where growth takes root and truth is revealed.

The Divine is not only found in the light but walks with you through the shadow. These moments are invitations to face what has been hidden, to heal what has been avoided, and to rise stronger and more grounded than before. Your courage in the dark makes your light even brighter.

Today, do not fear the shadows. Honor them as part of your sacred journey. Know that even here—especially here—you are not alone. Strength is rising within you, and the light you carry will always be enough to guide you through.

Meditative Prayer

Divine Light,
Be with me in the shadows.
When I walk through uncertainty,
Let me feel Your steady presence.

When fear whispers in the dark,
Remind me of the strength within me.
When I feel lost,
Shine Your light on the truth I need to see.

May I not run from the shadows,
But face them with courage and grace.
May I trust that even in the dark,
You are working within me.

I rise from the shadows,
Wiser, braver, and more whole.
In the dark, I find my light.

DAY 70:

Seeing Through the Eyes of Love

Lesson for the Day

When you choose to see the world through the eyes of love, everything changes. Judgment softens. Compassion deepens. The ordinary becomes sacred. Love is not just a feeling—it is a lens through which you can view yourself, others, and the journey you're on. It transforms your perspective, allowing you to respond rather than react, to forgive rather than hold on, to heal rather than harm.

To see through the eyes of love is to look past fear, past wounds, past defenses, and into the heart of truth. It doesn't mean ignoring pain or pretending all is well—it means choosing kindness even in the midst of conflict, and recognizing the Divine in every soul you encounter, including your own.

Today, ask yourself, *How would love see this moment?* Whether you're looking in the mirror or at someone who challenges you, practice viewing them with love. It will not only change how you see the world—it will change how you walk through it.

Meditative Prayer

Divine Love,
Teach me to see through Your eyes.
Let me look at myself with compassion,
And at others with understanding.

When judgment rises,
Let love speak louder.
When fear closes my heart,
Open it again with grace.

Help me to notice beauty in the ordinary,
To find light in the hidden corners,
To honor the sacred in everyone I meet.

I choose to see with love.
I choose to lead with love.
I choose to live in love.

DAY 71:

The Journey Back to Yourself

Lesson for the Day

Life has a way of pulling you in many directions—toward expectations, responsibilities, and roles that sometimes feel far from who you truly are. But underneath it all, your true self is still there, waiting patiently for your return. The journey back to yourself is not about becoming someone new—it's about remembering who you've always been.

This journey is one of gentle reconnection. It invites you to listen to your heart, honor your soul's truth, and reclaim the parts of yourself that were quieted or forgotten. It requires honesty, vulnerability, and grace. And while the path may feel winding, every step taken in self-love brings you closer to alignment and inner peace.

Today, take time to come home to yourself. Breathe deeply. Listen inward. Let go of who you think you're supposed to be, and embrace the beauty of who you are. The Divine lives in your authenticity—and your soul has always known the way.

Meditative Prayer

Divine Presence,
Guide me back to my true self.
Help me release the masks I've worn,
And return to the truth of who I am.

When I feel lost in the noise,
Lead me back to the quiet voice within.
When I feel pulled away,
Call me home with compassion.

May I walk this path of self-return
With courage, softness, and grace.
May I honor the light within me,
And trust that I am enough.

I am remembering.
I am returning.
I am home.

DAY 72:

The Sacred Fire of Change

Lesson for the Day

Change can feel like a wildfire—unpredictable, consuming, and often uncomfortable. But within that fire lies a sacred power. The energy of transformation, purification, and rebirth. Just as fire clears away the old to make room for new growth, change invites you to release what no longer serves and step into who you are becoming.

The sacred fire of change does not destroy your essence—it refines it. It burns away the illusions, fears, and limitations that keep you small, and illuminates the strength, wisdom, and purpose within. To resist change is to resist your own evolution. To welcome it is to say yes to expansion, to freedom, and to divine alignment.

Today, honor the changes in your life. Even if they feel challenging, trust that they are part of your sacred becoming. Let the fire of transformation cleanse your spirit and reignite your passion. You are not being broken—you are being reborn.

Meditative Prayer

Sacred Flame,
Burn away what no longer serves me.
Clear the old patterns and fears,
So I may rise renewed and free.

When change feels overwhelming,
Remind me that transformation is holy.
When I resist,
Fill me with courage to surrender.

Let Your fire refine my soul,
Illuminate my path,
And spark within me
A new vision of who I am becoming.

I welcome change.
I honor transformation.
I rise from the sacred fire,
Stronger, clearer, and more alive.

DAY 73:

Awakening to Your Purpose

Lesson for the Day

Your life holds meaning far beyond what you may currently see. Within you is a unique purpose—a sacred calling placed in your heart by the Divine. Awakening to your purpose isn't about striving to become someone else. It's about remembering why your soul came here and aligning with the truth of who you are.

Purpose reveals itself in quiet nudges, moments of inspiration, and the things that light you up from within. It may not come all at once, but piece by piece, it unfolds as you say yes to the things that feel true. Trust that your gifts, your voice, and your presence matter. When you live in alignment with your purpose, you become a vessel for healing, love, and transformation.

Today, pause and listen to your soul's whisper. What brings you alive? What feels sacred when you do it? Be open to the signs, the stirrings, and the passions that rise within you. The world needs what only you can offer—your purpose is already within you, waiting to be awakened.

Meditative Prayer

Divine Source of Purpose,
Awaken within me the reason I am here.
Clear away the doubt and confusion,
So I may hear the call of my soul.

When I question my worth,
Remind me that my presence matters.
When I feel lost,
Guide me back to what makes me come alive.

May I follow the path of joy and meaning,
Trusting each step as sacred.
Let my purpose unfold with grace,
And let my life reflect the love I came to share.

I am open.
I am listening.
I am ready to awaken to my purpose.

Day 74:
Honoring Your Healing Journey

Lesson for the Day

Healing is not a straight line—it's a winding, sacred path filled with moments of growth, release, stillness, and renewal. To honor your healing journey is to recognize that every part of it is meaningful. The pain, the breakthroughs, the pauses, and the steps backward are all part of your becoming. You are not behind. You are right on time.

Too often we compare our progress to others, forgetting that healing is personal and deeply individual. Your journey is not meant to look like anyone else's. What matters is that you keep showing up for yourself with compassion, patience, and love. The fact that you are healing—choosing growth over stagnation—is a powerful act of courage.

Today, honor your path. Celebrate how far you've come, even if you still feel tender in places. You are doing sacred work, tending to your soul with care. Trust that every breath, every tear, and every act of self-love is a step toward deeper wholeness.

Meditative Prayer

Divine Healer,
Thank You for walking with me on this journey.
Help me honor each step I've taken,
Even the ones that felt heavy.

When I'm hard on myself,
Remind me that healing takes time.
When I feel lost,
Guide me back with gentleness and grace.

May I celebrate my progress,
Even when it's quiet and unseen.
May I offer myself compassion,
Knowing that I am doing the work of the soul.

I honor my healing.
I trust my pace.
I am becoming whole.

Day 75:

A Spirit Unshaken

Lesson for the Day

Life can bring storms—times of uncertainty, loss, and unexpected change. But within you, there is a deep, unshakable spirit. It is the part of you that endures, that knows peace even in chaos, and that stands firm in faith when the winds of life try to pull you off course.

This unshakable spirit isn't loud or showy—it's steady, quiet, and deeply rooted in the Divine. It grows stronger each time you choose to rise, each time you choose love over fear, faith over doubt, and hope over despair. You are far more resilient than you know, not because you never fall, but because you always get back up.

Today, anchor yourself in that unshakable place within. Let your breath steady you, your heart ground you, and your spirit remind you that no matter what comes, you cannot be broken. You are supported by the Divine, and your soul is made of strength.

Meditative Prayer

Divine Strength,
Anchor me in unshakable peace.
When life feels uncertain,
Let me stand firm in faith.

When fear surrounds me,
Fill me with calm.
When I feel weary,
Renew me with Your presence.

May I remember the power within me,
The steady light that cannot be dimmed.
I am not defined by the storm,
But by the strength that rises in me.

I am grounded.
I am strong.
I am a spirit unshaken.

Day 76:

Finding Peace in Every Season

Lesson for the Day

Life moves in seasons—times of growth, rest, loss, and renewal. Some seasons are full of light and momentum, while others invite you to slow down, reflect, or release. Each one holds its own sacred purpose. Peace isn't found in trying to rush through or resist the season you're in—it's found in embracing it with grace and trust.

When you learn to flow with life instead of fighting it, you begin to experience peace no matter what is happening around you. The Divine is present in every season—guiding your growth in spring, sustaining you in summer, supporting your release in fall, and holding you gently in winter's stillness. You are never alone in your process.

Today, take a moment to ask, *What season am I in?* Then honor it. Lean into what it's teaching you. Find peace not by wishing for something else, but by being fully present in what is. Every season has its beauty, its wisdom, and its blessings.

Meditative Prayer

Divine Presence,
Help me find peace in the season I'm in.
When I want to rush ahead,
Slow me down with grace.

When I resist what is unfolding,
Remind me that each season has its purpose.
In growth or stillness,
In joy or letting go,
Let me feel Your presence beside me.

May I trust the rhythm of life,
And embrace the lessons of now.
I release the need to force,
And open to the flow of divine timing.

In every season,
I am guided.
In every season,
I am at peace.

DAY 77:
Becoming Light in the Darkness

Lesson for the Day

There will be times when the world feels heavy—when pain, fear, or uncertainty cloud your view. But even in the darkest moments, you carry a light within you that cannot be extinguished. This light is your hope, your faith, your love—it is the Divine presence shining through your spirit.

You don't have to have all the answers or fix everything around you. Sometimes, simply being a presence of kindness, stillness, or quiet strength is enough. When you choose compassion over judgment, love over fear, and truth over silence, you become a beacon of light for yourself and others.

Today, let your light shine—even if it flickers, even if it feels small. The darkest night cannot put out the tiniest flame. You are a vessel of Divine light, and by choosing to shine, you help others remember that they can, too.

Meditative Prayer

Divine Light,
Shine through me today.
When the world feels heavy,
Let me be a bearer of hope.

When I feel overwhelmed,
Remind me that even a small light matters.
When darkness surrounds me,
Let my spirit shine with truth and love.

May I be a comfort to others,
A reminder that peace is still possible.
May I lead with love,
And walk with grace.

I am not afraid of the dark,
Because I carry the light.
I am light.
I am love.
I am here to shine.

DAY 78:

The Strength of Your Spirit

Lesson for the Day

There is a strength within you that goes deeper than muscle or willpower—it is the quiet, steady force of your spirit. This strength shows up not in moments of ease, but in how you rise through difficulty, how you keep going when it would be easier to give up, and how you continue to love, trust, and hope despite life's challenges.

The strength of your spirit is not loud or boastful. It is the calm in the storm, the resilience in your soul, the courage to keep showing up as yourself. It is the Divine moving through you, reminding you that you are never truly alone in what you face. Every trial you've come through has revealed just how powerful your spirit truly is.

Today, honor that strength. Reflect on how far you've come and how deeply you've grown. You don't need to do more or be more to be strong—you already are. Let that inner strength guide you today with confidence, peace, and grace.

Meditative Prayer

Divine Presence,
Thank You for the strength within me.
Even when I feel weak,
My spirit remains steady and true.

When I face challenges,
Remind me of the power I carry.
When I feel discouraged,
Lift me with Your presence.

I trust the resilience in my soul.
I honor the courage in my heart.
I walk forward knowing
That my spirit is strong and unbreakable.

May I carry this strength with humility,
And share it with those who need a reminder of their own.
My spirit is strong.
My spirit is sacred.
My spirit is enough.

DAY 79:
The Power of Divine Healing

Lesson for the Day

Healing is not something you must do alone. Divine healing is always available—gentle, powerful, and deeply transformational. It moves through the body, mind, and spirit, reaching places words cannot. It knows where you've been wounded, where you've held pain, and where light needs to return.

Sometimes healing is immediate, and other times it unfolds over weeks, months, or years. But in every moment, the Divine is working within you—restoring, renewing, and returning you to wholeness. Your only task is to open your heart, trust the process, and allow that sacred energy to move through you.

Today, invite Divine healing into your life. Whether you seek physical, emotional, or spiritual restoration, trust that the healing has already begun. You are not broken—you are being made whole. Let grace do its work.

Meditative Prayer

Divine Healer,
I open my heart to Your loving presence.
Touch the places within me
That need renewal, comfort, and peace.

Where there is pain,
Bring relief.
Where there is sorrow,
Bring peace.
Where there is fear,
Bring Your calming light.

I surrender to Your healing hands.
I trust that You know exactly what I need.
May Your energy flow through me,
Restoring me on every level.

I am open.
I am ready.
I am being healed.

DAY 80:

Resting in the Arms of Grace

Lesson for the Day

There is a sacred stillness that comes when you stop striving and allow yourself to rest in the arms of grace. Grace is the Divine's unconditional love—freely given, not earned. It meets you exactly where you are, offering compassion when you fall, strength when you're weary, and peace when you're overwhelmed.

You don't have to prove yourself to be worthy of grace. You don't need to have it all together. Grace whispers, *"Come as you are."* It invites you to let go of perfection, to exhale your burdens, and to simply receive. Resting in grace is not giving up—it's trusting that you are already enough and held by something greater than yourself.

Today, allow yourself to rest. Let grace carry what you cannot. Let it remind you that even in your most vulnerable moments, you are deeply loved. You are safe here—in the stillness, in the softness, in the arms of grace.

Meditative Prayer

Divine Grace,
Hold me in Your gentle embrace.
When I am tired from striving,
Let me find rest in You.

When I feel I am not enough,
Remind me that Your love is unconditional.
When I cannot carry my burdens alone,
Lift them from my heart with tenderness.

May I release the need to perform,
And simply be held in Your presence.
May I trust that grace surrounds me,
Even when I cannot feel it.

I rest in You now.
I surrender to Your peace.
I am enough, just as I am.

DAY 81:

The Truth That Sets You Free

Lesson for the Day

Truth is not something to be feared—it is a light that brings freedom. When you live in truth, you release the weight of pretending, hiding, or trying to be someone you're not. You begin to live with authenticity, clarity, and alignment with your soul. The truth that sets you free is not just external—it's the inner truth of who you are, why you're here, and what you truly need.

Facing the truth can be uncomfortable, but it is always liberating. It clears away illusion and makes room for healing. The Divine does not ask for perfection, only honesty. When you are willing to see things clearly—with compassion, not judgment—you open yourself to transformation and peace.

Today, ask yourself, *What truth am I ready to embrace?* Let it rise with grace. Speak it gently. Honor it deeply. The more you walk in truth, the more lightness and freedom you will feel in your body, your mind, and your spirit.

Meditative Prayer

Divine Truth,
Shine Your light within me.
Help me see clearly,
And speak honestly with love.

When I am tempted to hide,
Give me the courage to be seen.
When I fear the truth,
Surround me with Your peace.

May I live with integrity,
Aligned with who I truly am.
May truth be my compass,
And love be my guide.

I choose truth.
I choose freedom.
I choose to walk in light.

DAY 82:

A New Chapter Awaits

Lesson for the Day

Life is a series of chapters—some joyful, some painful, some full of growth, and others filled with rest. No chapter lasts forever, and each one prepares you for the next. As one season closes, another quietly opens. Even if you can't yet see what's ahead, trust that a new chapter awaits you—one filled with possibilities, purpose, and peace.

Turning the page can be bittersweet. You may grieve what is ending while still feeling unsure of what's to come. But the Divine invites you forward—not to forget the past, but to carry its wisdom with you. You are being called into a new beginning, one only you can live.

Today, open your heart to the new. Release any fear of the unknown. Let curiosity, faith, and hope guide you into this next chapter. You don't need to know every detail—just trust that what's waiting for you is exactly what your soul is ready for.

Meditative Prayer

Divine Author of Life,
Help me turn the page with grace.
Thank You for the chapters behind me,
And for the promise of what lies ahead.

When I fear change,
Remind me that every ending is a beginning.
When I feel uncertain,
Steady me with faith in Your plan.

I open my heart to new beginnings,
To the unfolding of a sacred story
Written in love, guided by You.

I trust the journey.
I welcome the unknown.
A new chapter awaits, and I am ready.

DAY 83:
Embracing the Fullness of Life

Lesson for the Day

Life is a rich, beautiful tapestry of light and shadow, joy and sorrow, beginnings and endings. To truly live is to embrace all of it—not just the moments that feel easy or joyful, but also the ones that stretch and shape you. The fullness of life is found in allowing yourself to feel, to be present, and to participate in the sacred unfolding of your journey.

When you open yourself to the fullness of life, you say yes to growth. You begin to see that even the hard days carry purpose, and that every experience holds something for your soul. The Divine walks with you through every emotion, every shift, and every season. Nothing is wasted.

Today, allow yourself to be fully present with what is. Whether you're in a season of blooming or a time of shedding, trust that this too is part of the sacred whole. Embrace your life with open hands and an open heart—because this moment is worthy of your presence.

Meditative Prayer

Divine Presence,
Help me embrace the fullness of life.
Let me be open to every moment,
Knowing that each one is sacred.

When joy visits,
Let me dance with gratitude.
When sorrow comes,
Let me sit with it in compassion.

May I not run from the hard places,
Nor cling too tightly to the easy ones.
Instead, may I live with courage,
Trusting that all is part of Your design.

I open myself to this moment.
I receive life in all its fullness.
And I walk forward in wonder,
Guided by love.

Day 84:

Renewal in Every Breath

Lesson for the Day

Each breath you take is a quiet miracle—an invitation to begin again. In the space between inhale and exhale, there is an opening, a chance to release what no longer serves you and to draw in peace, clarity, and life. Renewal isn't always found in dramatic change. Often, it begins in something as simple and sacred as your breath.

When the world feels overwhelming or you feel disconnected from yourself, return to your breath. Let it ground you, center you, and remind you that in this moment, you are alive, you are held, and you have the power to choose again. The Divine meets you here, breath by breath, with grace that renews you from the inside out.

Today, let your breath be your anchor. Slow down. Breathe deeply. With every inhale, receive. With every exhale, release. Know that you don't have to wait for a new season to find renewal—it's available to you now, in this very breath.

Meditative Prayer

Divine Breath of Life,
Breathe through me today.
With every inhale, fill me with peace.
With every exhale, carry away my burdens.

When I feel scattered,
Bring me back to the present moment.
When I feel tired,
Let my breath restore my strength.

May I find renewal in this sacred rhythm,
This quiet miracle happening within me.
Let each breath remind me
That I can begin again.

I breathe in grace.
I breathe out fear.
I am made new in every breath.

DAY 85:

Learning to Trust Again

Lesson for the Day

Trust can be one of the hardest things to rebuild after it's been broken—whether by life's disappointments, painful relationships, or unexpected loss. But trust is also one of the most powerful gifts you can reclaim. Learning to trust again doesn't mean forgetting the past. It means allowing yourself to believe in goodness, in healing, and in the possibility of love and grace once more.

The Divine understands the tenderness of your heart and walks gently with you through your healing. You don't have to force trust—it can grow slowly, like a flower reaching for the sun after a long winter. As you listen to your inner wisdom, honor your boundaries, and open your heart one step at a time, trust begins to return.

Today, give yourself permission to trust again. Trust yourself. Trust the timing of your journey. Trust that the Divine is not only with you, but working for your highest good. You are safe to open your heart again—to life, to love, to hope.

Meditative Prayer

Divine Presence,
Help me learn to trust again.
Where I have been hurt,
Pour healing into my heart.

Where I have doubted,
Restore my faith gently.
Where I have closed myself off,
Invite me to open with grace.

May I trust myself again,
Trust the path I'm on,
And trust in the love
That flows from Your heart into mine.

I release the fear of being hurt.
I embrace the courage of vulnerability.
I choose to trust again.

DAY 86:

The Wisdom of Your Soul

Lesson for the Day

Within you lies a wellspring of wisdom—deep, ancient, and always available. Your soul carries the quiet knowing that transcends logic and fear. It speaks in gentle nudges, inner peace, and quiet clarity. When you slow down and listen, you'll hear the guidance that is already within you.

The world may be loud, full of opinions, distractions, and expectations, but your soul will never lead you astray. It is your connection to the Divine, your compass in the unknown, and your source of truth when everything else feels uncertain. Trusting your soul's wisdom is not about having all the answers—it's about being willing to listen and follow what feels aligned, even if it doesn't yet make sense.

Today, return to your inner knowing. Be still. Ask, *What is my soul trying to tell me?* Then listen with your heart. The answers you seek are already inside you, waiting to be heard. You are wise, guided, and deeply connected to something greater.

Meditative Prayer

Divine Source of Wisdom,
Help me hear the voice of my soul.
In the stillness,
Let Your guidance rise within me.

When I feel uncertain,
Remind me to trust my inner knowing.
When the world pulls me in many directions,
Lead me back to center.

May I honor the truth that lives within me,
And walk in alignment with who I really am.
May I follow my soul's wisdom
With courage, peace, and grace.

I am listening.
I am guided.
I am wise beyond words.

Day 87:
Love's Ever-Present Light

Lesson for the Day

Love is not fleeting, and it is never far away. It is the steady, ever-present light that continues to shine—through every season, every struggle, every moment of uncertainty. Love does not abandon you in the dark. It becomes your beacon. It does not weaken when life feels heavy, it grows stronger, surrounding you in comfort and warmth.

This love comes from the Divine, but it also lives within you. You carry it in your breath, in your kindness, in the way you show up when it's hard. Love is what you return to when everything else fades. Even when you feel disconnected, love is still there—waiting, patient, unshaken.

Today, rest in love's light. Let it heal what is wounded, soften what is hardened, and awaken what is sleeping. Let it remind you that no matter what is happening around you, love is with you, in you, and guiding you always.

Meditative Prayer

Divine Love,
Shine Your light upon me today.
When I feel lost,
Lead me gently back to love.

When my heart feels heavy,
Wrap me in warmth and peace.
When I forget my worth,
Let Your love remind me who I am.

May I carry love into each moment,
Into each word, each breath, each choice.
May I become a reflection of Your light,
Even in the shadows.

Love is here.
Love is constant.
Love is the light that leads me home.

Day 88:

A Heart Reawakened

Lesson for the Day

There are seasons when your heart feels closed—guarded by pain, exhaustion, or disappointment. But your heart was never meant to stay hidden. It was made to feel deeply, to give freely, and to love without fear. When your heart reawakens, it doesn't erase the past—it honors it while opening again to the beauty of life.

Reawakening is not sudden. It comes in quiet moments of trust, in small acts of courage, in the decision to try again. It's the breath you take before forgiving, the warmth you feel when hope returns, the gentle yes that whispers, *I'm ready.* Your heart is resilient. And with each beat, it calls you back to connection, presence, and joy.

Today, honor your heart. Let it soften. Let it breathe. Let it awaken to the love that still surrounds you and the life that's still unfolding. The Divine is gently calling you back—not to what was, but to what can now become.

Meditative Prayer

Divine Healer of Hearts,
Awaken my heart with Your love.
Where I have gone numb,
Bring me back to feeling.

Where I have closed myself off,
Open me gently, with grace.
Where I have been afraid to love,
Fill me with courage to try again.

Let my heart remember joy.
Let it beat with new hope and soft strength.
May I love with freedom,
And receive love with trust.

My heart is awakening.
My spirit is opening.
And I am ready to feel again.

Day 89:
Walking into the Unknown with Courage

Lesson for the Day

The unknown can be intimidating. It holds no guarantees, no clear signs, no neatly drawn map. Yet, it is often in the spaces we do not understand that the greatest transformations occur. Walking into the unknown is not about having certainty—it's about having courage. It's choosing to move forward with faith, even when you can't see the full path ahead.

Courage doesn't mean you're without fear. It means you listen to the whisper of your soul over the noise of your doubt. It means you trust that the Divine is walking beside you, even when the way feels unclear. Every brave step you take opens the door to new possibilities and deeper wisdom.

Today, let courage lead you. Don't wait until everything makes sense. Choose to step forward with an open heart, knowing that you are supported, guided, and never alone. The unknown is not empty—it is filled with sacred potential.

Meditative Prayer

Divine Guide,
Walk with me into the unknown.
When I feel afraid,
Remind me that courage lives within me.

When the path is unclear,
Be the light at my feet.
When I want to turn back,
Strengthen my spirit to move forward.

May I trust in the unfolding,
Even when I do not understand.
May I walk with faith,
Knowing that each step is sacred.

I am not alone.
I am guided.
I walk into the unknown with courage and grace.

DAY 90:

Your Spirit is Rising

Lesson for the Day

No matter how heavy the past has been, no matter how long you've sat in the shadows—your spirit is rising. With each new breath, each small act of love, each moment of trust, something within you lifts. You may not notice it right away, but deep within, a light is growing stronger. This is your spirit returning to life, reconnecting with purpose, and reclaiming its voice.

You were never meant to stay in the valley. The climb may have been steep, and the journey long, but every step has built a deeper resilience in you. Your rising is not a return to who you were—it's an emergence into who you truly are. The Divine is lifting you, breath by breath, into new beginnings, new strength, and new light.

Today, feel that rising. Let it stir in your chest, let it awaken your hope, let it move you to stand taller. You are not just surviving—you are ascending. Your spirit is rising, and nothing can hold back the soul that remembers its light.

Meditative Prayer

Divine Light,
Thank You for the rising within me.
When I felt low,
You stayed beside me.
When I felt lost,
You held my light until I could see it again.

Now, I feel the lift in my soul,
The quiet strength returning,
The hope rising like dawn.

May I move forward with grace,
Rooted in love,
Lifted by faith,
And awakened to my own sacred power.

I rise in truth.
I rise in peace.
I rise in You.

DAY 91:

A Season of New Life

Lesson for the Day

There comes a time when the old falls away and something fresh begins to stir. This is the season of new life—a time of renewal, awakening, and quiet blossoming. You may feel it in your heart, your thoughts, or your spirit, like a gentle breeze whispering, *It's time.* Time to begin again. Time to plant new dreams. Time to rise with purpose.

New life doesn't always arrive with a grand entrance. Sometimes, it begins softly—with a new perspective, a shift in energy, or a simple decision to let the past stay in the past. As you align with the rhythms of renewal, you begin to walk in harmony with the Divine. There is magic in beginnings, and this moment holds the promise of something beautiful taking root.

Today, embrace the energy of new life. What do you feel called to grow, create, or become? Let hope rise within you. The soil of your spirit is fertile. Trust that what is blooming now is aligned with your highest good.

Meditative Prayer

Divine Creator,
I welcome this season of new life.
Let the light of renewal
Shine in every corner of my being.

Where there was dormancy,
Let growth begin.
Where I once felt lost,
Plant seeds of hope and direction.

Help me trust the timing of this rebirth,
And nurture what You are growing within me.
May I walk gently,
Honoring both what has been and what is becoming.

I am ready to begin again.
I am open to what is new.
I step forward into the beauty of this season.

DAY 92:

Planting Seeds of Hope

Lesson for the Day

Hope is a sacred act of planting—placing belief in what has not yet come, trusting in growth that you cannot yet see. Like a seed buried in the earth, hope begins quietly. It requires faith, nurturing, and patience. Even when the soil looks still, transformation is happening beneath the surface.

To plant hope is to believe that tomorrow can be better, that healing is possible, and that your dreams still have a place in this world. You may not always feel hopeful, but every small action taken in faith—every prayer, every kind word, every choice to keep going—is a seed. And in divine time, those seeds bloom.

Today, plant seeds of hope with intention. Speak life into your dreams. Water them with love and trust. Even if you cannot yet see the garden, know that something beautiful is already growing.

Meditative Prayer

Divine Gardener,
Help me plant seeds of hope today.
Let my words be filled with belief,
And my actions with gentle faith.

Where fear has taken root,
Replace it with the promise of new growth.
Where doubt lingers,
Sow trust deep within my heart.

I may not see the bloom yet,
But I trust in the unseen work of Your hands.
May hope rise in me,
Quiet but strong, steady and alive.

I plant with love.
I wait with faith.
I believe in what is becoming.

DAY 93:

The Beauty of Renewal

Lesson for the Day

Renewal is a sacred invitation to begin again—not as who you once were, but as who you are becoming. It's a return to your essence, a releasing of what has grown heavy, and a reawakening of the light within you. Renewal doesn't erase the past—it integrates its lessons while offering a fresh, grace-filled path forward.

There is beauty in allowing yourself to be renewed. In letting go of what no longer fits. In shedding old layers so your spirit can breathe more freely. Like the earth after a gentle rain, your soul becomes soft and fertile, ready to welcome new growth, new clarity, and new peace.

Today, embrace the beauty of renewal. Let yourself be made new—not by force, but by trust. Let the Divine restore what's been tired, renew what's been forgotten, and remind you of the sacred strength that still lives within.

Meditative Prayer

Divine Source of Life,
Breathe renewal into my spirit today.
Wash away the heaviness I no longer need,
And awaken the light that still burns within me.

When I feel worn,
Remind me that I can begin again.
When I feel stuck,
Let Your grace move gently through me.

I welcome this season of renewal,
In my thoughts, in my heart, in my soul.
Let each breath restore me.
Let each step renew my purpose.

I am open.
I am ready.
I am beautifully becoming.

Day 94:
Embracing Change with Joy

Lesson for the Day

Change is often met with resistance, because it asks us to step away from the familiar and into the unknown. But when you begin to see change as a gift—not a threat—you open the door to joy. Change is the Divine's way of creating space for new growth, deeper wisdom, and unexpected blessings.

Embracing change with joy doesn't mean pretending it's easy. It means trusting that something beautiful is unfolding, even if you can't yet see the full picture. Joy can be found in the little things along the way—the freedom in letting go, the curiosity of new experiences, and the grace of discovering who you are becoming.

Today, welcome change with an open heart. Celebrate the ways you're evolving. Let joy meet you in the transition. The more you trust the process, the more you'll see that every change carries within it the seed of something wonderful.

Meditative Prayer

Divine Creator,
Help me embrace change with joy.
Let me trust the flow of life,
Even when I don't know where it's leading.

When fear rises,
Fill me with courage and light.
When I cling to the past,
Remind me of the blessings to come.

May I meet this season with open arms,
Seeing beauty in the new,
And peace in the unfolding.

I release resistance.
I choose joy.
I walk forward with a heart full of faith.

DAY 95:
Trusting the Growth Process

Lesson for the Day

Growth doesn't always look like progress. Sometimes it feels like standing still, unraveling, or being pulled backward. But beneath the surface, your spirit is expanding, your roots are deepening, and the Divine is gently preparing you for your next chapter. Growth is not instant—it's a sacred process that unfolds in its own time.

Trusting the growth process means honoring where you are without judgment. It means being patient with your unfolding, even when you can't see the full picture. The transformation you're undergoing is meaningful, even if it's quiet. Your willingness to show up for the journey is enough.

Today, release the need to rush. Trust that your soul knows what it's doing. Breathe deeply into the present moment and know that the Divine is working in and through you. Every step, every pause, every lesson is part of the beautiful, living story of your growth.

Meditative Prayer

Divine Gardener,
Thank You for the process of growth.
Help me trust what I cannot yet see,
And be patient with what is still becoming.

When I feel discouraged,
Remind me that I am still growing.
When I want to give up,
Whisper truth and strength to my soul.

May I honor this season,
Even in its stillness,
Even in its mystery.
May I trust that I am exactly where I need to be.

I release the rush.
I choose the rhythm of grace.
I am growing,
And that is enough.

DAY 96:
The Light That Awakens You

Lesson for the Day

There is a light within you that never goes out—a spark placed there by the Divine, always ready to guide you home to yourself. Sometimes, this light feels like a sudden illumination, a moment of clarity or inspiration. Other times, it stirs slowly, like the rising sun casting away the shadows of doubt, fear, or forgetfulness.

This light awakens you not only to your purpose but also to your beauty, your worth, and your connection to all things sacred. It is what nudges you toward healing, growth, and truth. When you feel lost, this light remains constant. When you are ready to rise, it's already shining the way.

Today, welcome the light that awakens you. Let it fill your spirit with hope. Let it gently lift you from heaviness and remind you of who you are. You were never meant to stay asleep to your potential— your light is ready to shine.

Meditative Prayer

Divine Light,
Awaken me with Your presence.
Let Your love rise in me
Like the dawn after a long night.

When I feel dimmed,
Fan the flame within me.
When I forget who I am,
Shine truth into my soul.

May I rise in Your light,
Awake to my calling,
Alive to the beauty of this life.
Let me carry this light forward,
And become a beacon for others.

I am waking.
I am shining.
I am one with the light.

Day 97:

Every Step is Sacred

Lesson for the Day

It's easy to honor the big moments—the breakthroughs, the celebrations, the milestones. But the truth is, every step of your journey is sacred. Even the quiet ones. Even the ones filled with doubt, rest, or uncertainty. The Divine doesn't just dwell at the destination—it walks with you through the process.

Each choice you make with intention, each breath taken in faith, each act of love—these are holy. Even the days you feel like you're merely surviving, you are still moving forward. The sacred is not reserved for perfection. It lives in the ordinary, in the effort, and in the grace of your becoming.

Today, pause and honor your path. Know that wherever you are, whatever step you're on, it matters. You are not behind. You are not lost. You are walking a sacred path, guided by love, and your every step is worthy of reverence.

Meditative Prayer

Divine Companion,
Walk with me today,
And help me see the sacred
In each step I take.

When I feel small or unsure,
Remind me that this moment matters.
When I long to be further ahead,
Let me honor where I am.

May I move with intention,
Grounded in love,
Guided by faith.
May I know that You are with me,
In every breath,
In every step.

This journey is holy.
My steps are sacred.
And I am never alone.

DAY 98:

Seeing Life with New Eyes

Lesson for the Day

Sometimes the greatest shift doesn't come from changing your circumstances, but from changing how you see them. When you choose to view life through fresh eyes—through the lens of wonder, gratitude, and presence—you awaken to beauty that was always there, waiting to be noticed.

Seeing life with new eyes means letting go of old assumptions, softening your judgments, and becoming curious again. It means seeing yourself with compassion, others with kindness, and your journey with reverence. The Divine is constantly offering new perspectives—little reminders that each day, each breath, and each experience carries meaning.

Today, open your heart and allow your vision to be renewed. Look at your life not through the eyes of what's missing, but through the eyes of what's possible. Let the world surprise you. Let your spirit be refreshed by the simple joy of seeing things anew.

Meditative Prayer

Divine Vision,
Help me see my life with new eyes.
Wash away the filters of fear and doubt,
And open me to wonder.

Where I've grown weary,
Let me see renewal.
Where I've been critical,
Let me see with compassion.

May I witness the beauty of this moment,
And recognize the sacred all around me.
Refresh my spirit,
So I may see with clarity,
With softness,
With love.

I open my eyes anew.
I welcome what is.
And I give thanks for the gift of this view.

Day 99:
Becoming Who You Were Meant to Be

Lesson for the Day

You are not here by accident. Within you is a sacred design, a unique light, and a divine purpose waiting to be fully expressed. Becoming who you were meant to be is not about striving to meet external expectations—it's about coming home to your truest self. It is a journey of remembering, revealing, and rising into the fullness of your soul.

This becoming is not rushed. It unfolds in layers, through experiences, through healing, through love. Every time you choose authenticity over approval, courage over fear, and truth over comfort, you align more deeply with who you truly are. The Divine is not asking you to be someone else—only to become more of *you.*

Today, honor the sacred process of your becoming. Trust that even now, you are being shaped with intention. Let go of who you were told to be, and embrace who you truly are. You are not behind. You are blossoming right on time.

Meditative Prayer

Divine Shaper of Souls,
Thank You for the journey of becoming.
Guide me back to my essence,
And help me release all that is not mine.

When I doubt my path,
Remind me I am unfolding with purpose.
When I feel small,
Show me the light that lives within me.

May I walk in truth,
Speak with love,
And live in alignment with my spirit.

I am becoming who I was always meant to be.
I trust the process.
I embrace the journey.

Day 100:

The Blossoming of Your Spirit

Lesson for the Day

There comes a time in your journey when the quiet inner work begins to show—when all the seeds you've planted, the healing you've embraced, and the faith you've held onto begin to bloom. This is the blossoming of your spirit, and it is as natural as it is sacred. You may not have noticed the growth while it was happening, but now, you feel it. It comes as a lightness, a strength, a clarity that wasn't there before.

Your blossoming doesn't need to be loud or visible to others. It might be a gentle peace, a new sense of self-worth, or a deeper connection with the Divine. Whatever it looks like, it is the result of your courage to keep showing up, even when it was hard. You've watered your soul with hope, and now the beauty of your becoming is unfolding.

Today, honor how far you've come. Celebrate the ways your spirit has bloomed. Trust that there is more growth to come, more light to share, and more love to give. You are a living garden of grace, and your soul is in full bloom.

Meditative Prayer

Divine Gardener,
Thank You for the blossoming of my spirit.
I feel the quiet joy of growth,
The soft unfolding of who I truly am.

When I doubted, You held me.
When I struggled, You nourished me.
Now, I rise in beauty and truth,
Rooted in Your love.

May I honor this season of blooming,
Without rushing or holding back.
Let my life be a reflection
Of the grace that has brought me here.

I am blooming.
I am radiant.
I am the blossoming of Divine light.

Day 101:

The Strength Found in Growth

Lesson for the Day

Growth is not always gentle. Sometimes it stretches you in uncomfortable ways, asks you to let go of what feels familiar, and brings you face to face with your own limitations. But within this sacred process lies great strength—the kind that is built slowly, deeply, and with purpose.

True strength doesn't come from avoiding difficulty but from moving through it with intention and grace. Every lesson, every challenge, every season of change shapes you into someone wiser, more compassionate, and more aligned with your soul's truth. The Divine walks with you in every growing season, planting courage where fear once lived.

Today, honor the strength you've found in your growth. Reflect on all you've moved through and how it has shaped you. Let it remind you that even when things feel hard, you are never going backward— you are becoming stronger, steadier, and more whole.

Meditative Prayer

Divine Presence,
Thank You for the strength that grows within me.
Even when the journey is hard,
You are shaping me with love.

When I feel stretched or uncertain,
Remind me that growth is sacred.
When I feel weary,
Renew me with Your grace.

May I trust the process,
Honor the lessons,
And celebrate the strength I've discovered
On this unfolding path.

I am growing.
I am learning.
And I am stronger than I've ever been.

DAY 102:
Finding Joy in the Journey

Lesson for the Day

Joy is not just a destination—it is a companion that walks with you, if you allow it. Too often we postpone joy, waiting for everything to be perfect before we let ourselves feel it. But joy is found in the little things, in the present moment, in the sacred pauses along the way. The journey itself is full of treasures waiting to be noticed.

Finding joy in the journey doesn't mean pretending everything is easy. It means choosing to notice beauty even in the midst of challenge, to laugh when you can, and to celebrate small victories. It is an act of presence and of faith—trusting that life is not only about where you're going, but also about how you get there.

Today, open your heart to joy. Let yourself feel the warmth of a quiet morning, the kindness in a smile, the peace in a breath. The Divine is with you on this journey, and joy is one of the greatest gifts along the way.

Meditative Prayer

Divine Joy,
Walk with me on this journey.
Open my heart to delight
In the simple and sacred moments.

When I get lost in striving,
Bring me back to presence.
When I forget to smile,
Surprise me with joy.

Help me to find beauty in the process,
Not just in the destination.
Let my journey be filled with laughter,
Lightness, and love.

I welcome joy.
I choose joy.
I carry joy with me.

Day 103:
Embracing Divine Timing

Lesson for the Day

There is a rhythm to life that is wiser than our own—an unseen flow that carries us forward, even when we can't feel it. Divine timing is not always aligned with our schedules or expectations, but it is always perfect. When we surrender to that timing, we open ourselves to receive what is truly meant for us, exactly when we're ready for it.

Impatience often comes from fear—the fear that we're falling behind, missing out, or not doing enough. But the Divine is never late. What is meant for you cannot be lost. Every delay, every pause, every redirection is part of a larger tapestry being woven with care and love.

Today, release the need to force or rush. Breathe deeply and trust that everything is unfolding as it should. You are not behind—you are right on time. Rest in the knowing that the Divine is orchestrating every detail for your highest good.

Meditative Prayer

Divine Timekeeper,
Help me trust in Your perfect timing.
When I grow restless,
Calm my spirit with peace.

When I try to control,
Remind me that surrender is strength.
When I fear missing my moment,
Let me feel Your steady hand guiding me.

May I embrace the pauses,
The waiting, the unfolding.
May I remember that what is for me
Will arrive right on time.

I release the rush.
I trust the process.
I align with Divine timing.

DAY 104:

Opening Your Heart to Love

Lesson for the Day

Love is the most powerful force in the universe—and the most healing. When you open your heart to love, you align with the Divine. Love softens what's been hardened, mends what's been broken, and brings light to the darkest places. But love also requires courage. The courage to be vulnerable, to receive, and to give without condition.

Your heart may have been guarded by pain or disappointment, but it was never meant to stay closed. Opening your heart doesn't mean ignoring past wounds—it means trusting that love is still worth the risk. The more you open, the more freely love flows to you and through you. It is endless, abundant, and already within you.

Today, gently open your heart. Let love in—from a smile, a moment of stillness, a kind word. And let love out—in your thoughts, your presence, your actions. You are worthy of love. You are made of love. And the world is brighter when you share it.

Meditative Prayer

Divine Love,
Help me open my heart today.
Soften the walls I've built in fear,
And fill me with the courage to love again.

Where I've been wounded,
Bring healing.
Where I've been guarded,
Bring peace.

Let love flow to me freely,
And through me generously.
May my heart be a sanctuary
For compassion, connection, and grace.

I am open.
I am loved.
I am love.

DAY 105:

A Soul in Full Bloom

Lesson for the Day

There is a moment in your journey when all the inner work, quiet healing, and sacred surrender begins to radiate outward—this is the blooming of your soul. It doesn't happen all at once, and it rarely looks perfect, but it is powerful, beautiful, and true. A soul in full bloom reflects the Divine light it carries and offers that light freely to the world.

To bloom is to live fully—honoring your truth, embracing your path, and allowing your spirit to be seen. It means no longer shrinking to fit old stories or hiding behind fear. You are meant to be fully alive, fully present, fully you. The petals of your purpose are unfolding now, one by one, in grace and divine timing.

Today, celebrate the ways your soul is blooming. Even if it feels quiet or subtle, your light is shining. Stand tall in your truth. Root yourself in love. And trust that your blossoming is a sacred gift to this world.

Meditative Prayer

Divine Gardener,
Thank You for the blooming of my soul.
Help me open fully to who I am becoming,
Without fear, without apology.

Where I once held back,
Let me now shine.
Where I once felt hidden,
Let me now be seen.

May my life reflect Your beauty,
May my spirit radiate Your love.
I am blooming with purpose,
Anchored in truth and grace.

I am ready.
I am radiant.
I am a soul in full bloom.

Day 106:

The Lessons of the Past, The Hope of the Future

Lesson for the Day

Your past has shaped you, but it does not define you. Each moment you've lived—every joy, every heartbreak, every detour—has offered wisdom and strength. When you choose to learn from the past instead of reliving it, you open the door to healing and growth. The past becomes a teacher, not a weight.

Equally important is the hope that lives ahead of you. The future is unwritten, and within it lies infinite possibility. You are not bound to repeat old patterns. You are free to dream again, to hope again, and to walk forward with faith in the goodness that is still coming. The Divine is already preparing the way ahead.

Today, honor what the past has taught you, but don't linger there. Carry its lessons, not its pain. Let your eyes look forward with expectancy. A new chapter is beginning, and it is filled with grace, purpose, and hope.

Meditative Prayer

Divine Teacher,
Thank You for the lessons of my past.
Help me carry wisdom forward,
And leave behind what no longer serves me.

Where I once felt regret,
Plant peace.
Where I once felt broken,
Shine healing light.

Let hope rise within me for all that is still to come.
May I walk into the future with courage,
Rooted in grace,
And open to miracles.

I honor where I've been.
I trust where I'm going.
And I live in the promise of what's possible.

DAY 107:
Holding onto Faith in the Unknown

Lesson for the Day

The unknown can feel overwhelming—a vast space filled with uncertainty and questions. Yet, within that mystery lies a powerful invitation to trust. Holding onto faith in the unknown means accepting that not every detail needs to be understood for your journey to be purposeful. It is the willingness to step forward, even when the path isn't clear, trusting that the Divine is orchestrating each moment with perfect wisdom.

In the midst of uncertainty, faith becomes your anchor. It reassures you that even if you can't see the whole picture, every step is guided by love. When you hold onto faith, you open yourself to growth, transformation, and the miracles that emerge when you let go of control. The unknown is not empty. It is filled with potential waiting for you to embrace it with an open heart.

Today, choose to hold onto faith. Surrender your need for immediate answers and trust that each moment is unfolding for your highest good. Embrace the mystery as a sacred space where new opportunities, lessons, and blessings are quietly taking shape.

Meditative Prayer

Divine Guide,
In the midst of the unknown, help me hold fast to faith.
When uncertainty clouds my vision,
Let Your love shine a path before me.

When I am tempted to seek control,
Teach me to trust in Your greater plan.
Fill my heart with the courage to step forward,
Even when the way is not fully revealed.

May I lean into the mystery with confidence,
Knowing that every moment is divinely orchestrated.
I choose faith over fear,
And trust in the unfolding of my journey.

I hold onto faith.
I surrender to the unknown.
And I walk forward with love.

DAY 108:

Letting the Light In

Lesson for the Day

There are moments when we unknowingly close ourselves off—guarding our hearts, dimming our hope, and shielding our spirit from the light we long for. But healing, joy, and transformation begin the moment we open. Letting the light in means softening the barriers we've built, and allowing love, truth, and grace to flow freely through us once again.

The light you are letting in is not just from the world around you—it is the Divine presence that has been gently waiting for your permission to enter. This light brings warmth to the cold places, clarity to confusion, and renewal to what's been weary. It doesn't force its way in. It responds to your invitation.

Today, choose to let the light in. Open the windows of your heart. Welcome healing, peace, and truth. No matter how long you've lived in the shadows, it's never too late to invite the light back home.

Meditative Prayer

Divine Light,
I open my heart to You.
Shine into the places I've hidden,
And fill them with peace.

Where I've closed myself off,
Let warmth return.
Where I've been afraid to feel,
Let love break through.

May Your light bring healing,
Restoring what has been dimmed.
May I allow joy to enter,
And hope to rise again.

I welcome Your light.
I receive Your love.
I am open, I am ready, I am whole.

DAY 109:

Dancing with the Winds of Change

Lesson for the Day

Change is inevitable, but how we move with it defines the experience. Resisting change can leave us feeling fearful or stuck, while embracing it with openness allows us to grow, evolve, and discover new parts of ourselves. When you learn to dance with the winds of change, you become fluid, trusting, and responsive to the rhythm of life.

There is a sacred freedom in surrendering to what is shifting. It doesn't mean you lose your footing—it means you choose to move with grace, knowing the Divine is leading the dance. Even when the steps are unfamiliar, your spirit knows how to follow. Every gust of change carries with it the potential for beauty, clarity, and renewal.

Today, instead of bracing against the winds, stretch your arms wide and let them carry you. Let change become a dance—a movement of trust, joy, and possibility. You are not being swept away, you are being lifted into something new.

Meditative Prayer

Divine Mover of All Things,
Teach me to dance with the winds of change.
When life shifts around me,
Help me move with grace, not fear.

Let me trust in the rhythm of Your will,
Even when the music feels unfamiliar.
May I bend, not break,
Flow, not freeze.

Guide my steps with courage and peace.
Let change become an invitation,
A sacred dance of becoming more of who I am.

I do not resist.
I rise.
I dance with the winds of change.

DAY 110:

The Power of Gentle Transformation

Lesson for the Day

Transformation doesn't always arrive with thunder and lightning—it often comes quietly. Like the soft unfolding of a flower or the slow warming of dawn, gentle transformation reshapes us in sacred, subtle ways. It invites us to evolve through kindness, compassion, and steady grace rather than force or urgency.

Gentle change honors the pace of the soul. It allows room for breath, reflection, and healing. It reminds us that growth doesn't have to be dramatic to be powerful. Each moment of awareness, each choice to respond with love, and each step forward in truth is a holy act of transformation.

Today, embrace the gentle shifts taking place within you. Celebrate the quiet victories and the healing that happens in stillness. Trust that even when the change feels small, it is sacred—and the Divine is guiding every part of your unfolding.

Meditative Prayer

Divine Presence,
Thank You for the gift of gentle transformation.
Teach me to honor the slow,
The quiet,
The sacred unfolding within me.

When I feel the urge to rush,
Remind me that Your timing is perfect.
When I overlook my progress,
Show me the beauty in each small step.

Let my heart soften into change.
Let my soul rise in peace.
May I grow with grace,
Becoming more of who You created me to be.

I am changing,
I am healing,
And I am gently becoming.

Day III:

The Beauty of Starting Again

Lesson for the Day

There is something profoundly sacred about beginning again. Whether it's a fresh start after a setback, a new perspective after a moment of clarity, or simply choosing hope again after disappointment—starting over is a courageous and beautiful act. It's not a sign of failure, but of resilience and faith.

Each time you begin again, you honor your growth. You say, *I am not stuck—I am still unfolding.* The Divine offers endless grace for new beginnings, and your soul holds the wisdom to know when it's time to release the old and step into the new. No matter how many times you've had to start over, there is beauty in your willingness to rise.

Today, embrace the beauty of your fresh start. Whether you're taking a small step or a bold leap, know that you are supported. The past has prepared you, and the future welcomes you. You are not starting from scratch—you're starting from strength.

Meditative Prayer

Divine Creator of New Beginnings,
Thank You for the grace to start again.
Wash over me with renewal,
And fill me with the courage to rise.

Where I have stumbled,
Let forgiveness flow.
Where I have paused,
Let movement return.

I release shame,
I release fear,
And I embrace the fresh unfolding of this day.

May I begin again with trust,
With love,
And with joy in the journey ahead.

I am not behind.
I am becoming.
This is the beauty of starting again.

DAY 112:
Walking Through Open Doors

Lesson for the Day

Life is full of invitations—opportunities that gently nudge you forward, beckoning you to grow, to trust, and to step into something new. Sometimes these doors open wide, and sometimes they appear quietly, almost unnoticed. But when you have the courage to walk through them, you step into alignment with the Divine's greater plan for your life.

Open doors often require you to leave something behind—comfort, fear, old identities. They ask you to trust that what lies ahead is greater than what's been. Walking through them is an act of faith, of saying yes to the unknown and believing in the promise of what's unfolding.

Today, notice the doors that are opening in your life. They may come in the form of a conversation, a decision, or a sudden shift. Trust your intuition, listen deeply, and if the door feels aligned with your soul—walk through it. The Divine has already gone before you.

Meditative Prayer

Divine Guide,
Thank You for the doors You are opening before me.
Give me eyes to see the path,
And a heart willing to say yes.

When I hesitate out of fear,
Fill me with courage.
When I grieve what I'm leaving behind,
Comfort me with peace.

May I walk through new doors with trust,
Knowing You have prepared the way.
Let each step I take be sacred,
And each opportunity a gift.

I walk forward with faith.
I follow where You lead.
And I welcome what's waiting on the other side.

DAY 113:

The Call of Your Soul

Lesson for the Day

There is a quiet voice within you that speaks with deep knowing—the call of your soul. It doesn't shout or demand, but gently nudges you toward truth, alignment, and purpose. This call may come as a persistent longing, a sense of restlessness, or a quiet pull toward something more meaningful.

Your soul's call is the Divine whispering through your inner wisdom, inviting you to live with authenticity and intention. It is a call back to yourself—your dreams, your gifts, your deepest truths. Answering it doesn't require you to have it all figured out. It only asks for your willingness to listen and take the next small, brave step.

Today, pause and tune in. What is your soul asking of you? What part of you is ready to be expressed or reclaimed? Trust what you hear. The Divine planted this longing within you for a reason. You are being called into a life that is fully yours.

Meditative Prayer

Divine Voice Within,
Help me hear the call of my soul.
Let me be still enough to listen,
And brave enough to respond.

Where I have ignored my truth,
Gently guide me back.
Where I have feared my purpose,
Strengthen me with courage.

May I walk the path of authenticity,
Rooted in who I truly am.
Let every step I take
Be a response to the sacred call within me.

I am listening.
I am open.
I am ready to answer.

DAY 114:
Choosing to Bloom Where You Are Planted

Lesson for the Day

Sometimes we long for different circumstances, believing that growth or joy will come once we're somewhere else—another job, another place, another season of life. But the truth is, the soul can bloom anywhere. Choosing to bloom where you are planted is a sacred decision to thrive, to trust, and to grow in the here and now.

You don't need perfect conditions to begin unfolding. The Divine can meet you in the ordinary, the messy, the unexpected. Every moment holds the potential for beauty when you choose to nurture your spirit with presence, gratitude, and intention. Blooming isn't about your surroundings—it's about your willingness to be fully alive where you are.

Today, honor the place you stand. Water your soul with love, and stretch toward the light available to you now. Trust that even here, especially here, you are being invited to flourish.

Meditative Prayer

Divine Gardener,
Help me bloom where I am planted.
Even if this place feels unfamiliar or imperfect,
Let me trust that I am here for a reason.

When I feel restless or stuck,
Remind me of the growth that's already happening.
When I long for somewhere else,
Bring me back to the gifts of this moment.

May I root deeply in faith,
And rise in beauty and strength.
Let me thrive in the here and now,
Fully alive, fully present, fully me.

I choose to bloom.
I choose to trust.
I choose to grow where I am.

DAY 115:

Grace in the Growing Season

Lesson for the Day

The growing season is often filled with both beauty and discomfort. It asks you to stretch, to shed, to reach for more than you thought possible. In the midst of this expansion, it's easy to be hard on yourself—to wish you were further along, more "together," or already transformed. But what your spirit needs most during this time is grace.

Grace reminds you that growth is not linear. It allows space for stumbles, detours, and rest. It says, *You are still worthy, even as you are becoming.* The Divine doesn't rush your process, and you don't need to either. Grace offers a gentle, steady hand as you navigate your transformation, encouraging you to trust the unfolding.

Today, breathe deeply and offer yourself grace. Honor your effort, your courage, and your willingness to grow. Let grace soften your inner voice and nourish your journey. You are blooming in sacred timing, and that is enough.

Meditative Prayer

Divine Presence,
Thank You for meeting me in the growing season.
When I feel stretched or uncertain,
Wrap me in Your grace.

Teach me to be patient with my process,
To trust the slow and sacred unfolding.
When I'm tempted to push or perfect,
Remind me that I am already enough.

May grace fill the spaces where doubt lingers,
And peace steady my spirit as I grow.
I choose compassion over pressure,
And love over judgment.

I am growing.
I am learning.
I am held in grace.

DAY 116:
The Strength of Tender Beginnings

Lesson for the Day

Beginnings are often quiet, fragile things. They rarely come with certainty or clarity—but within them lies immense strength. There is courage in taking the first step, in trying again after disappointment, and in allowing something new to take root even when the outcome is unknown. Tender beginnings carry the sacred energy of hope.

You don't have to be fully ready to begin. You only need to be willing. The Divine honors even the smallest step toward healing, love, or purpose. What starts out as a whisper of desire can become a bold unfolding when nurtured with faith and patience. Every beautiful journey begins with a moment of bravery, no matter how soft it may seem.

Today, trust the power in your new beginning. Let your tenderness be your strength. You are not weak for starting small—you are powerful for choosing to start at all. The Divine is walking beside you, cheering you on with every breath.

Meditative Prayer

Divine Source of All New Things,
Thank You for the gift of beginning again.
Even when my steps are small,
Let them be filled with purpose.

When I feel unsure,
Anchor me in Your steady love.
When I doubt my strength,
Remind me of the courage it takes to start.

Bless this tender beginning,
This moment of saying yes to growth,
To healing,
To becoming more of who I truly am.

I trust this first step.
I honor my courage.
And I walk forward in faith.

DAY 117:

A Time to Rise

Lesson for the Day

There comes a moment when your spirit knows it's time to rise—not because everything is perfect, but because something deep within you is ready. Ready to shed old layers. Ready to step into truth. Ready to live more fully, more freely, more aligned with who you really are. Rising isn't about rushing forward—it's about honoring your readiness to stand tall in your own light.

You may have spent a long season resting, healing, or waiting—and that, too, was sacred. But now, the energy is shifting. Your soul feels the stirrings of purpose calling you forward. The Divine is lifting you, inviting you to take your place, not above others but in full alignment with your unique path and power.

Today, say yes to the invitation to rise. Let go of hesitation. Rise in your truth. Rise in your voice. Rise in your worth. This is not just a moment—it is a calling. And you are ready.

Meditative Prayer

Divine Light,
Thank You for this moment to rise.
Lift me from the weight of fear,
And awaken me to my strength.

Where I once stayed small,
Let me now expand.
Where I once stayed silent,
Let me now speak with truth.

Help me rise in love,
In courage,
In purpose.
Let my rising be a blessing
To the world around me.

I am ready.
I am rising.
I am becoming.

Day 118:
The Breath of Fresh Possibilities

Lesson for the Day

Every new day brings with it a breath of fresh possibilities—an invitation to step into something new, think differently, or feel more deeply. Just as a deep breath clears the mind and resets the body, the energy of possibility can shift your perspective and renew your spirit. You are never stuck where you are. The Divine is constantly opening new paths, even when you can't yet see them.

Fresh possibilities don't always come in big, dramatic ways. Sometimes they appear in a new thought, a conversation, a gentle nudge in your heart. When you create space—through stillness, curiosity, and hope—you allow new energy to enter. You begin to see beyond the limitations of yesterday and into the vast potential of today.

Today, take a deep breath. Let it clear away what is heavy or stagnant. Inhale faith, exhale fear. Trust that something beautiful is possible. Let the breath of newness fill you with excitement, clarity, and openness. The world is full of fresh beginnings—and one of them belongs to you.

Meditative Prayer

Divine Source of Newness,
Thank You for the gift of today.
Let each breath I take
Remind me of the possibilities before me.

Where I've felt stuck,
Clear the way.
Where I've been afraid to dream,
Awaken my courage.

Open my eyes to opportunities,
And my heart to new beginnings.
Let hope rise with every inhale,
And peace settle with every exhale.

I welcome the fresh winds of change.
I believe in what's possible.
I breathe in life,
And I begin again.

DAY 119:

Trusting the Unfolding of Your Path

Lesson for the Day

You don't need to have every answer to take the next step. Your path is not a straight line—it's a living, breathing journey that reveals itself one moment at a time. Trusting the unfolding of your path means allowing the mystery, being patient with the process, and choosing faith even when clarity is just out of reach.

It's natural to want certainty, but the beauty of the path is in its unfolding. The Divine is always guiding, even in silence. What feels delayed may be preparation. What feels like a detour may be sacred redirection. You don't have to see the whole road to keep moving—you only need to trust the One who walks beside you.

Today, release the pressure to have it all figured out. Rest in the knowing that your path is unfolding exactly as it should. Trust the timing, trust the process, and most of all, trust the quiet wisdom of your soul. You are on your way.

Meditative Prayer

Divine Guide,
I surrender to the unfolding of my path.
Even when I can't see what's ahead,
Help me trust that I am being led with love.

When I grow impatient,
Remind me that every step holds purpose.
When I doubt the way,
Surround me with Your steady peace.

May I walk in faith,
Open to the journey,
And willing to grow in the unknown.
I trust the pauses, the progress,
And the promise of what's to come.

My path is sacred.
My journey is guided.
And I trust the unfolding.

Day 120:

Honoring the Journey of Becoming

Lesson for the Day

You are not who you were yesterday, and you are not yet who you will be tomorrow—you are in the sacred space of becoming. This journey is not about reaching a final version of yourself, but about growing, evolving, and deepening into the truth of who you are. Every moment, every experience, every emotion is shaping you into something beautiful.

It can be tempting to rush the process or judge yourself for not being "there" yet. But the journey itself is holy. Your becoming is not a race—it's a dance of soul and spirit, woven with grace, trial, joy, and transformation. The Divine honors the unfolding of your story just as it is.

Today, pause and honor the journey you're on. Reflect on how far you've come. Give thanks for the lessons, the progress, and even the detours. You are becoming more of your truest self with every breath, and that is something worth celebrating.

Meditative Prayer

Divine Creator,
Thank You for the sacred journey of becoming.
Help me release comparison and embrace my path.
Let me honor who I am today,
While holding space for who I am still becoming.

When I feel behind,
Remind me that I am right on time.
When I feel unsure,
Anchor me in Your loving presence.

May I walk this journey with grace,
Gratitude,
And faith in the unfolding.
I honor the steps, the shifts, and the soul that is growing.

I am becoming.
I am enough.
And I am beautifully on my way.

DAY 121:

Strength in Every Season

Lesson for the Day

Life moves in seasons—each with its own rhythm, challenges, and beauty. There are times of growth and blooming, of rest and reflection, of release and rebuilding. It's easy to feel strong in the vibrant seasons, but true strength is found in embracing them all. Every season serves a purpose, and within each one, your soul is learning how to stand, soften, and trust.

The Divine does not favor one season over another. Your winter is as holy as your spring. Your pauses are as sacred as your progress. Strength isn't about always pushing forward—it's about honoring where you are, listening to what your spirit needs, and showing up with presence and love.

Today, recognize the season you're in and celebrate the strength it takes to be there. Whether you're blooming or resting, grieving or growing, know that your courage is seen. You are strong—not because you do it all, but because you keep going with grace.

Meditative Prayer

Divine Sustainer,
Thank You for the strength that rises in every season.
Teach me to honor the rhythm of my life,
And trust the wisdom in each phase.

When I am growing,
Give me roots.
When I am resting,
Give me peace.
When I am releasing,
Give me courage.

May I find strength in stillness,
And grace in the unknown.
I am not behind—I am becoming.
And every season is shaping me in love.

I walk in strength.
I rest in faith.
I live with purpose in every season.

DAY 122:

Embracing the Lessons of Growth

Lesson for the Day

Growth is not always comfortable, but it is always meaningful. It stretches your heart, challenges your perspective, and often invites you to let go of what no longer serves your highest good. Every growing season brings with it sacred lessons—lessons that are not meant to punish you, but to shape you into a fuller version of who you are becoming.

Some lessons come gently, others arrive with force. But each one holds a gift of greater self-awareness, deeper compassion, stronger faith. When you choose to embrace these lessons, rather than resist them, you invite transformation. You become more grounded, more open, and more aligned with your soul's path.

Today, reflect on the lessons that have found you lately. What are they teaching you about who you are and what you're ready to release or reclaim? Trust that each one is a stepping stone placed with love. Growth is not just happening to you—it's happening for you.

Meditative Prayer

Wise and Loving Presence,
Thank You for the lessons that shape me.
Even when they are hard to hold,
Help me embrace them with grace.

When I want to resist,
Soften my heart.
When I fear what's changing,
Fill me with faith in what's becoming.

May I see growth not as a burden,
But as a gift.
Let every lesson lead me closer
To truth, healing, and wholeness.

I welcome the wisdom.
I honor the process.
I grow in love.

Day 123:
Patience in the Process

Lesson for the Day

Growth takes time. Healing takes time. Becoming who you truly are is not an overnight transformation, but a lifelong unfolding. Patience in the process is an act of love toward yourself and trust in the Divine. It means giving yourself permission to move slowly, to rest when needed, and to believe that progress is still being made— even when you can't see it yet.

Impatience often comes from the fear of not being enough, fast enough, or good enough. But the truth is, you are already enough— even in your becoming. The Divine does not rush your journey. Every pause, every small step, every moment of stillness holds purpose. You are growing in exactly the way you're meant to.

Today, breathe into patience. Release the pressure to be further along. Celebrate where you are, and know that your timing is sacred. You don't need to hurry—your soul knows the way.

Meditative Prayer

Divine Timekeeper,
Teach me the beauty of patience.
When I feel rushed or restless,
Center me in peace.

Help me trust the process,
Even when it feels slow.
Remind me that growth is not a race,
And that You are never late.

May I honor each moment of becoming,
Knowing that transformation takes time.
Let patience bloom within me
Like a quiet, steady light.

I release the need to rush.
I embrace the unfolding.
And I trust in the sacred timing of it all.

Day 124:

Trusting the Journey Even When You Can't See the Path

Lesson for the Day

There will be moments when the road ahead is unclear, when the next step feels uncertain, and the future seems wrapped in fog. These are the moments that call for deep trust—not in the visible path, but in the One who walks beside you. Trusting the journey doesn't mean always knowing where you're going—it means believing that each step is guided by love, even when the map is hidden.

It's okay to not have all the answers. You don't need to see the whole picture to keep moving forward. Faith is choosing to walk with an open heart, even when clarity hasn't arrived. It's leaning into the unknown with the quiet confidence that the Divine is unfolding something beautiful, even now.

Today, release your grip on certainty. Take a breath, take a step, and know that you are being led with care. The path will reveal itself in time. You are not lost—you are on sacred ground.

Meditative Prayer

Divine Guide,
Help me trust this journey,
Even when I cannot see the road ahead.

When doubt clouds my vision,
Shine Your light in my heart.
When fear grips my soul,
Steady me with Your peace.

May I walk forward in faith,
Believing that each step is enough.
Let my trust rise above my questions,
And my heart stay open to Your guidance.

I am not alone.
I am not lost.
I am being led by love.

DAY 125:
Growing Through What You Go Through

Lesson for the Day

Every experience in your life—whether joyful or painful—holds the potential to help you grow. Even the moments that feel like breaking points are often sacred turning points. When you choose to grow through what you go through, you allow your spirit to be shaped by wisdom, resilience, and grace rather than fear or regret.

You are not defined by what happens to you, but by how you choose to rise from it. Growth doesn't mean avoiding hardship. It means allowing your challenges to deepen your understanding, compassion, and strength. The Divine doesn't waste any part of your story—all of it can become soil for transformation.

Today, look at what you're moving through with fresh eyes. Ask, *What is this here to teach me?* Then open your heart to the lesson, the healing, and the light that is trying to reach you. You are not just surviving—you are evolving.

Meditative Prayer

Divine Teacher,
Thank You for walking with me through all things.
Even in the hardest moments,
Help me grow with grace.

When I feel overwhelmed,
Anchor me in trust.
When I question the purpose of my struggle,
Show me the wisdom rising within it.

May I not simply endure,
But expand.
May I not just move on,
But rise transformed.

I am learning.
I am healing.
I am growing through what I go through.

Day 126:
Finding Peace in the Waiting

Lesson for the Day

Waiting can be one of the hardest parts of the journey. It challenges your patience, tests your faith, and brings to the surface all the doubts and fears you thought you had laid to rest. But waiting is not a void—it is a sacred space where the unseen work is being done. In the stillness, your spirit is being strengthened, your trust is being deepened, and your heart is being prepared.

Peace in the waiting doesn't come from knowing the outcome—it comes from trusting that something meaningful is unfolding, even in the silence. The Divine is never inactive, even when it feels like nothing is moving. There is purpose in the pause, and grace in the delay.

Today, release the urgency to have everything now. Let peace settle into the space where answers haven't arrived. Trust that this waiting season is not wasted. It is making you ready for what is already making its way to you.

Meditative Prayer

Divine Presence,
Meet me in the waiting.
Still my anxious thoughts,
And quiet my restless heart.

When I grow weary of the silence,
Whisper Your peace into my soul.
When I long to move forward,
Help me trust that I am exactly where I need to be.

Let this waiting time be holy,
A space of preparation,
Of deepening trust,
Of sacred rest.

I surrender to Your timing.
I trust in Your plan.
And I find peace in the pause.

DAY 127:

The Power of a Faith-Filled Heart

Lesson for the Day

Faith isn't always loud. Sometimes, it's the quiet decision to believe when everything in you wants to give up. A faith-filled heart doesn't require perfect circumstances—it simply chooses to trust, to hope, and to keep moving forward even when the path is uncertain. This kind of faith is powerful. It anchors you in storms, lifts you when you're weary, and connects you to something greater than yourself.

A heart filled with faith becomes a vessel of light. It radiates strength, compassion, and peace—not because it never struggles, but because it knows where to return when struggle comes. The Divine meets you in your faith, not because it's flawless, but because it's real. Faith is not about never doubting, it's about believing even with the doubt present.

Today, nurture your faith. Speak life into your heart. Remember the times when trust carried you through, and know it will again. A faith-filled heart is never empty—it is filled with divine power, infinite love, and unstoppable hope.

Meditative Prayer

Divine Sustainer,
Fill my heart with unwavering faith.
When fear rises,
Let trust rise higher.

When the way feels uncertain,
Anchor me in Your presence.
Even in doubt,
Let my heart believe in Your goodness.

May my faith be gentle and bold,
Quiet and steady.
Let it be my strength,
My guide, my light.

I choose to trust.
I choose to believe.
My heart is filled with faith.

DAY 128:

Divine Guidance in Every Step

Lesson for the Day

You are never walking alone. Even when the way seems unclear or the journey feels heavy, Divine guidance is with you—steady, subtle, and faithful. Sometimes it comes as a gentle nudge, a moment of clarity, or a deep inner peace. Other times, it whispers through intuition, synchronicity, or the quiet reassurance that you're on the right path.

Trusting Divine guidance doesn't mean you'll always know what's next. It means believing that every step, even the uncertain ones, is being held by something greater than yourself. The more you listen and align with that sacred guidance, the more confident and centered your steps become.

Today, pause and ask, *What is being shown to me right now?* Trust the answer, even if it comes in stillness. Walk with awareness, knowing that the Divine is not just ahead of you, but beside you, within you, and in every step you take.

Meditative Prayer

Divine Guide,
Thank You for walking with me.
In every step I take,
Let me feel Your gentle presence.

When I feel unsure,
Illuminate my path.
When I wander,
Lead me home with grace.

May I be open to Your whispers,
Attuned to Your wisdom,
And trusting in Your perfect timing.

I walk in faith.
I walk in trust.
I walk in Divine guidance,
With every sacred step.

DAY 129:
Nurturing the Soul's Garden

Lesson for the Day

Your soul is like a sacred garden. What you plant, water, and tend within will grow and shape the way you experience the world. Just as a garden needs sunlight, rest, and care, your soul needs moments of stillness, love, and reflection to flourish. Growth doesn't happen by force—it happens through gentle nurturing and consistent presence.

The seeds of peace, joy, compassion, and wisdom are already within you. But they need attention. They need you to slow down, to notice what needs to be released like weeds, and to nourish what wants to bloom. When you care for your inner life, your outer world begins to reflect that same harmony.

Today, tend to your soul with intention. Create space for rest. Speak to yourself with kindness. Let your spirit breathe. With every loving choice, you are nurturing the sacred garden within—and the Divine is smiling with every bloom.

Meditative Prayer

Divine Gardener,
Help me care for the garden of my soul.
Show me what needs to be released,
And what longs to grow in love.

When I've neglected my spirit,
Bring me back to stillness.
When I've rushed past my needs,
Slow me with grace.

Plant peace in my thoughts,
Joy in my heart,
And trust in my journey.
Let my soul bloom with beauty,
Tended by Your love.

I nurture my inner world,
And I watch it flourish.

DAY 130:
The Beauty of Trusting Yourself

Lesson for the Day

There is a quiet, powerful beauty in learning to trust yourself. Not just your decisions, but your intuition, your voice, your truth. Trusting yourself means honoring the wisdom you carry, the lessons you've lived, and the sacred connection between your soul and the Divine.

Self-trust is not arrogance—it's alignment. It's knowing that you are worthy of listening to, that your inner guidance is valid, and that you are capable of navigating your path with clarity and grace. When you trust yourself, you walk with greater confidence, gentleness, and peace.

Today, listen within. Hear the still, small voice that's been there all along. Let your choices reflect your inner knowing. The more you trust yourself, the more you align with the life you were created to live. The Divine has always trusted you—now it's time you do the same.

Meditative Prayer

Divine Wisdom Within,
Help me trust myself today.
Quiet the voices of doubt,
And awaken the truth I carry inside.

Remind me that I am guided,
That my intuition is sacred,
And that my heart knows the way.

When I hesitate,
Fill me with calm and confidence.
When I question,
Anchor me in love.

I honor my voice.
I trust my path.
And I believe in the beauty of who I am.

DAY 131:

Learning to Surrender to Growth

Lesson for the Day

Growth is not always comfortable. It asks you to release the familiar, stretch beyond your limits, and trust what is becoming—even when you don't fully understand it yet. Surrendering to growth is not about giving up. It's about giving in to the process of becoming. It's choosing to trust that what is unfolding in you is sacred, even if it feels messy or uncertain.

True transformation requires surrender. It invites you to soften your resistance and let go of the need to control the outcome. When you surrender to growth, you partner with the Divine. You stop pushing against what is, and instead, begin to flow with what is meant to be.

Today, release the pressure to figure it all out. Surrender to the truth that you are evolving in perfect timing. Allow yourself to be changed by love, by truth, and by the quiet, persistent movement of your spirit rising.

Meditative Prayer

Divine Source of Transformation,
I surrender to the growth unfolding within me.
Even when it feels uncertain,
I trust that You are leading me forward.

Help me release my grip,
And soften into the sacred unknown.
Let me welcome the changes,
And find strength in surrender.

May I grow with grace,
Rooted in Your presence,
Open to the lessons,
And trusting in the journey.

I am becoming.
I am evolving.
And I surrender with faith and peace.

Day 132:
Becoming Rooted in Faith

Lesson for the Day

Faith is more than belief—it is an anchor, a foundation, a steady presence beneath life's ever-changing surface. To become rooted in faith means to ground yourself in trust, even when the winds of uncertainty blow. It is the quiet strength that reminds you. *You are held. You are guided. You are never alone.*

Roots grow in the unseen. They take time to deepen. The same is true for your faith—it often strengthens in the stillness, in the waiting, in the places where you choose to believe even without evidence. And just like a tree that draws nourishment through its roots, your spirit draws peace, courage, and hope through faith.

Today, return to what grounds you. Breathe deep into trust. Let your faith go deeper than fear. No matter what you face, you are firmly planted in the Divine—strong, steady, and unshaken.

Meditative Prayer

Divine Anchor,
Root me in faith today.
When the world feels uncertain,
Let my soul rest in Your steady love.

Grow my trust deeper than fear,
And my peace stronger than doubt.
Help me stand tall,
Even when I cannot see what lies ahead.

I plant myself in Your promises,
And draw strength from Your truth.
May I bend, but never break.
May I grow, but never drift.

I am rooted.
I am grounded.
I am held in faith.

DAY 133:
The Balance Between Action and Stillness

Lesson for the Day

Life invites us into a rhythm—a dance between doing and being, movement and rest, action and stillness. Both are necessary. Action propels us forward, helps us create and respond. Stillness grounds us, restores our energy, and reconnects us to our inner wisdom. The balance between the two is where peace and purpose meet.

Sometimes, we feel the pressure to constantly move, to produce, to prove our worth through effort. But there is sacred power in pausing. In stillness, we hear Divine guidance more clearly. In rest, our spirit is nourished. When we learn to honor both the drive to act and the need to be still, we walk in harmony with ourselves and the Divine.

Today, ask yourself, *Is this a moment for action or stillness?* Honor the answer. Let your actions come from alignment, not urgency. And let your stillness be as intentional and holy as any movement.

Meditative Prayer

Divine Rhythm,
Teach me the sacred balance of life.
Help me know when to move,
And when to be still.

In moments of action,
May I move with purpose,
Grounded in Your wisdom.
In moments of stillness,
May I find peace,
And listen for Your gentle voice.

Let my doing be led by love,
And my rest be filled with grace.
Align my heart with Your rhythm,
That I may live in harmony with my soul.

I honor the stillness.
I trust the action.
I walk in balance with You

DAY 134:
A Season of Divine Alignment

Lesson for the Day

There are seasons in life when everything begins to shift into place—not through force, but through flow. Divine alignment is the unfolding of your life in harmony with your soul's truth. It doesn't mean everything is perfect, but that you are moving with intention, clarity, and trust in the Divine orchestration that is guiding you.

Alignment is not found in doing more—it's found in returning to what matters most. It's choosing presence over pressure, peace over performance, and purpose over perfection. When you are aligned, life feels less like a struggle and more like a sacred conversation between your heart and Spirit.

Today, open yourself to this season of alignment. Ask, *What feels true for me right now?* Follow that. Release what pulls you out of balance. Trust that the Divine is arranging the pieces, and you are exactly where you're meant to be.

Meditative Prayer

Divine Architect,
Thank You for aligning my life with Your love.
In this season,
Help me move with grace,
Not resistance.

Guide my thoughts,
My choices,
My energy,
So that they reflect my highest truth.

Where I've been out of rhythm,
Bring me back to center.
Where I've felt lost,
Realign me with purpose and peace.

I am in flow.
I am in harmony.
I am in divine alignment.

DAY 135:
Knowing When to Let Go and When to Hold On

Lesson for the Day

Life often brings us to sacred crossroads where we must decide, *Is it time to release or time to remain?* Letting go and holding on are both acts of courage. One requires the strength to release with trust, and the other asks us to stay rooted with faith. The wisdom lies in knowing the difference—and listening to the quiet truth within.

Letting go is not giving up. It's making space for something new to grow. Holding on is not clinging. It's honoring what still serves your soul. The Divine gently guides you in these choices, not through pressure, but through peace. When you feel peace in your release or your commitment, you'll know the path is aligned.

Today, pause and ask, *What in my life needs to be released with love? What still deserves my devotion?* Trust your heart to show you the way. Both letting go and holding on can be sacred, when led by truth.

Meditative Prayer

Divine Wisdom,
Help me discern with clarity and grace.
Show me what it's time to release,
And what it's time to hold close.

When I'm afraid to let go,
Give me courage.
When I'm unsure what to keep,
Give me peace.

May I honor my soul's knowing,
And trust that You guide every decision.
Let my hands open with love,
To release, to receive, to remain.

I trust the rhythm of surrender and strength.
I choose with love.
And I follow the truth within.

DAY 136:
Trusting Your Inner Voice

Lesson for the Day

Your inner voice is the sacred whisper of your soul—calm, wise, and steady. It's the part of you connected deeply to the Divine, guiding you toward truth, peace, and alignment. Trusting your inner voice means honoring your intuition, even when it goes against logic, expectation, or the noise of the outside world.

This voice often speaks in stillness, in gentle nudges, in the quiet knowing that lingers after the world has fallen silent. It does not shout for attention, but it remains—faithful and clear when you are willing to listen. The more you trust it, the more confident you become in your choices, your path, and your purpose.

Today, take a moment to listen within. Ask your inner voice what it wants you to know right now. Then trust what arises. You are wiser than you think. The Divine is not far away—it's speaking through the truth already living inside you.

Meditative Prayer

Divine Voice Within,
Help me listen to the wisdom of my soul.
Quiet the noise around me,
And calm the doubt within me.

When I question myself,
Remind me that truth already lives inside.
When I feel pulled in many directions,
Guide me back to my center.

May I trust the soft nudges,
The sacred whispers,
The peaceful knowing that leads me home.

I honor my intuition.
I trust my inner voice.
I follow the guidance of my soul.

DAY 137:
The Strength Found in Stillness

Lesson for the Day

In a world that moves fast and praises constant motion, stillness can feel uncomfortable or even unproductive. But there is profound strength found in stillness—the kind that anchors your soul, sharpens your awareness, and reconnects you to what truly matters. Stillness is not the absence of movement. It is the presence of peace.

When you choose to pause, you allow space for clarity, healing, and Divine connection. In the quiet, you remember who you are without the noise. You return to your breath, your heart, your center. This is where deep wisdom rises and where your spirit is renewed. Stillness doesn't slow your journey—it strengthens you for it.

Today, choose stillness as a sacred practice. Even just a few moments of intentional quiet can shift your energy, calm your mind, and steady your steps. You are not falling behind by being still—you are rising in power.

Meditative Prayer

Divine Presence,
Meet me in the stillness today.
Quiet the rush around me,
And bring peace to the storm within.

When I feel pulled in many directions,
Help me return to center.
When I feel weak,
Let stillness restore my strength.

May I trust the quiet,
Honor the pause,
And listen to the wisdom that lives in silence.

I am grounded.
I am centered.
I am strong in stillness.

DAY 138:
Growth is Not Always Comfortable

Lesson for the Day

Growth often begins where comfort ends. It stretches you beyond the familiar, asks you to release old habits, and brings you face-to-face with parts of yourself that are ready to transform. Though uncomfortable, these seasons are sacred. They are where strength is built, truth is revealed, and the soul steps more fully into its purpose.

Discomfort doesn't mean you're doing something wrong—it often means you're doing something meaningful. Growth may look like confusion, stillness, or struggle before it takes shape as clarity, movement, and peace. The Divine is present in every part of this process, lovingly guiding you through each layer of becoming.

Today, honor the discomfort if you're feeling it. Let it be a sign not of failure, but of transformation. You are not being broken—you are being reshaped. Trust that what feels hard now is helping you grow into the next, truer version of yourself.

Meditative Prayer

Divine Refiner,
Thank You for walking with me through this growing season.
Even when it feels uncomfortable,
Help me trust that I am being shaped with love.

When I feel resistance,
Remind me that I am being expanded.
When I feel weary,
Breathe strength into my soul.

May I surrender to the process,
Knowing that You are with me in every stretch,
Every lesson,
Every sacred shift.

I embrace the discomfort.
I welcome the growth.
I trust the transformation.

DAY 139:

Expanding Beyond Your Comfort Zone

Lesson for the Day

Your comfort zone is a place of safety, but it is not a place of growth. Real transformation begins when you stretch beyond what's familiar and step into the unknown. It's in that space—beyond predictability— where your courage deepens, your confidence strengthens, and your soul expands into its greater potential.

Leaving your comfort zone doesn't mean abandoning yourself. It means trusting yourself enough to explore what's possible. You were not created to stay small. The Divine invites you to rise, to reach, to discover new parts of who you are by embracing new experiences, perspectives, and challenges.

Today, take one step beyond what feels safe. Say yes to something that stretches you. It doesn't have to be dramatic—small acts of bravery are just as sacred. Each time you move beyond your comfort zone, you open the door to a more empowered, aligned version of yourself.

Meditative Prayer

Divine Encourager,
Help me step beyond my comfort zone today.
When fear whispers stay,
Let Your voice call me forward.

Give me courage to grow,
Strength to try,
And trust to take the next bold step.

I release the need to play small,
And open to the life that's waiting for me.
Expand my heart,
Stretch my vision,
And anchor me in faith as I rise.

I am not afraid to grow.
I am not afraid to begin.
With You, I can move beyond what I thought possible.

DAY 140:

The Power of Hope in Difficult Times

Lesson for the Day

Hope is a quiet but powerful force. It does not deny the pain or pretend the struggle isn't real—it simply dares to believe that something good is still possible. In difficult times, hope becomes a lifeline, a flicker of light that reminds you that this moment is not the end of your story.

Holding onto hope doesn't mean you always feel strong. It means you allow yourself to believe in healing, in new beginnings, in the presence of the Divine even when circumstances feel heavy. Hope does not require proof—only a willing heart. And from that small flame, courage, peace, and transformation can grow.

Today, lean into hope. Let it be your anchor and your guide. Speak hope into your heart, into your situation, into your future. The storm may rage, but hope will hold you steady until the skies begin to clear.

Meditative Prayer

Divine Source of Hope,
In my darkest moments,
Let hope rise within me.
Not as denial, but as light,
A steady flame that guides me through the storm.

When I feel weary,
Whisper the promise of a new day.
When I want to give up,
Remind me that You are still working,
Still loving,
Still present.

May hope be my strength,
My comfort,
And my prayer.
I hold on. I believe.
I rise in hope.

DAY 141:

Trusting Life's Divine Plan

Lesson for the Day

There is a greater plan at work in your life—one woven with love, wisdom, and purpose. Even when the pieces don't seem to fit, even when the path feels uncertain, the Divine is moving on your behalf. Trusting life's divine plan doesn't mean you'll always understand it. It means you believe that something meaningful is unfolding beyond what you can see.

This trust calls you to surrender your need for control and lean into faith. It asks you to believe that your life is not random, that every experience is part of your becoming, and that nothing is wasted. When you release the pressure to figure everything out, you make space for grace to guide you.

Today, breathe deeply and surrender into trust. Let go of what you can't control and rest in the assurance that your life is held in divine hands. You are being led with love, and each step is part of something sacred.

Meditative Prayer

Divine Architect,
Thank You for the plan You are unfolding in my life.
Even when I cannot see the full picture,
Help me trust that every moment has purpose.

When I feel unsure,
Anchor me in faith.
When I want to take control,
Remind me that You are already guiding the way.

Let my heart be at peace in the unknown.
Let my soul rest in Your timing.
I trust in Your wisdom,
In Your love,
In Your divine plan for me.

DAY 142:

Embracing the Flow of Change

Lesson for the Day

Change is one of life's constants—an ever-moving current that invites you to grow, shift, and evolve. Resisting it can create tension, but embracing the flow of change allows grace to carry you forward. When you stop clinging to what was and open your heart to what is becoming, you find yourself aligned with the rhythm of the Divine.

Change can be uncomfortable, uncertain, and even painful. But it is also the birthplace of transformation. When you trust the flow, you stop fighting the river and start moving with its wisdom. You realize that change isn't happening *to* you—it's happening *for* you, and ultimately, *through* you.

Today, release the need to hold everything still. Let go of your grip and allow yourself to move with the current of life. Trust that what's shifting is sacred and what's emerging is beautiful. The Divine is in every turn of the tide.

Meditative Prayer

Divine Flow,
Help me embrace the changes before me.
When I resist,
Soften my heart.
When I fear the unknown,
Fill me with trust.

Let me move with grace,
Even when the waters feel deep.
Let me surrender to what is shifting,
And find peace in the unfolding.

I trust the current of life.
I release the need to control.
I flow with You,
Guided, carried, and free.

DAY 143:
Finding Strength in Surrender

Lesson for the Day

Surrender is not weakness—it is the deepest form of trust. It is choosing to release your grip on what you cannot control and placing your faith in something greater than yourself. True strength is found not in forcing, but in yielding. Not in holding tight, but in letting go with grace.

When you surrender, you make space for the Divine to move. You invite clarity where confusion once reigned, and peace where there was once striving. Surrender doesn't mean you've given up—it means you've handed over the weight of worry and chosen alignment instead. It is a courageous, sacred act of releasing your will to embrace divine timing and guidance.

Today, allow yourself to let go. Lay down the pressure, the need to fix or figure it all out. In your surrender, you are not alone. You are supported, loved, and strengthened beyond measure.

Meditative Prayer

Divine Love,
I surrender today.
Not from defeat,
But from faith.

I lay down my worries,
My plans,
My need to control.
And I open my hands to Your will.

Where I've struggled,
Bring peace.
Where I've resisted,
Bring softness.

Let my surrender be my strength,
And my trust be my anchor.
I let go.
I trust.
I am held.

Day 144:
A Heart That Trusts in the Unseen

Lesson for the Day

There is a quiet bravery in trusting what you cannot see. It means believing in the goodness of what's coming, even when it hasn't yet arrived. It means holding hope in your heart when the path ahead is foggy, and listening for the voice of the Divine even when it whispers through the silence.

A heart that trusts in the unseen is a heart anchored in faith. It surrenders the need for proof and instead leans into peace, knowing that not everything needs to be visible to be real. Some of the most sacred things—love, grace, purpose, and transformation—begin in the unseen and bloom in time.

Today, let your heart rest in trust. Even if you can't see the full picture, believe that the Divine is at work behind the scenes, preparing the way for something beautiful. Your faith is a light that guides you forward, one step at a time.

Meditative Prayer

Divine Mystery,
Teach me to trust what I cannot see.
When doubt creeps in,
Anchor me in quiet faith.

Let me believe in Your promises,
Even when they haven't yet arrived.
Let me walk in confidence,
Even when the path is hidden.

Strengthen my heart with unseen hope.
Fill me with peace beyond understanding.
I trust the invisible threads of grace
That are weaving my story in love.

I walk by faith, not by sight.
I trust in the unseen.
And I know You are with me always.

DAY 145:
Walking in the Light of Grace

Lesson for the Day

Grace is the quiet gift that meets you where you are, not where you think you should be. It wraps around you in your imperfections, lifts you when you're weary, and whispers love when you feel unworthy. Walking in the light of grace means choosing to move through life with compassion—for yourself and for others—trusting that you are enough, even in your becoming.

Grace is not something you earn. It is something you allow. It flows freely from the Divine, offering renewal, forgiveness, and peace. When you walk in its light, you begin to see yourself and the world through softer, kinder eyes. You no longer strive to prove your worth—you simply live it.

Today, let grace be your guide. Let it color your words, your actions, your thoughts. Receive it fully and extend it freely. The path of grace is not about perfection—it is about presence, love, and walking gently in the light.

Meditative Prayer

Divine Grace,
Shine Your light on my path today.
Help me walk gently,
With love in my heart
And compassion in my steps.

When I judge myself harshly,
Remind me of Your mercy.
When I feel unworthy,
Let Your grace lift me up.

May I see others through the eyes of grace,
And offer kindness where it is needed most.
Let my journey be one of gentleness,
Anchored in truth and love.

I walk in grace.
I live in light.
And I am held by a love that never fades.

DAY 146:
The Beauty of a Resilient Spirit

Lesson for the Day

Resilience is not the absence of struggle—it is the strength to rise through it. A resilient spirit bends but does not break. It learns, heals, adapts, and continues forward even when the path has been hard. There is incredible beauty in the soul that has faced darkness and still chooses light.

You may not always feel strong, but your spirit carries wisdom born from experience. Every challenge you've moved through has added to your resilience. The Divine has walked with you through it all, gently shaping you into someone stronger, softer, and more compassionate.

Today, honor your resilience. Reflect on how far you've come and how many times you've risen. Even in your tender places, you are strong. You are a living testament to the quiet, sacred power of the human spirit held in divine love.

Meditative Prayer

Divine Strength,
Thank You for the resilience within me.
Even when I've fallen,
You have helped me rise again.

When I feel worn down,
Remind me of all I've overcome.
When I question my strength,
Let me feel Your steady presence beside me.

May I carry my scars as symbols of strength,
And walk forward with courage and grace.
Let my spirit shine,
Not because it has never been tested,
But because it has never stopped rising.

I am resilient.
I am radiant.
I am held in divine strength.

DAY 147:
Trusting Yourself as You Evolve

Lesson for the Day

You are not the same person you were a year ago, a month ago, or even yesterday. Evolution is part of your soul's journey—a natural unfolding into deeper truth, love, and purpose. As you grow and change, it's important to trust yourself in the process. You are allowed to become someone new, and still be fully you.

With each layer you shed and each truth you claim, your inner compass becomes more attuned to your authentic self. Trusting yourself as you evolve means listening to your heart, honoring your growth, and allowing your identity to expand without guilt or apology. The Divine is guiding your transformation from within.

Today, give yourself permission to grow beyond who you've been. Trust your inner wisdom. Trust your voice. Trust the new version of yourself that is emerging—it is not a departure, but a return to who you've always been beneath it all.

Meditative Prayer

Divine Creator of Change,
Thank You for the gift of growth.
As I evolve,
Help me trust the journey within.

When I feel unsure of who I'm becoming,
Remind me that I am held in love.
When I feel distant from my past self,
Anchor me in truth.

Let me walk with confidence
As I embrace the new parts of me.
May I trust my voice,
My choices,
And the unfolding of my soul.

I honor my evolution.
I trust who I am becoming.
And I walk forward in faith.

DAY 148:
Every Season Has Its Purpose

Lesson for the Day

Life flows in seasons—each one holding its own wisdom, rhythm, and purpose. There are seasons of blossoming and breakthrough, and others of stillness and release. Some seasons bring joy and celebration, while others ask you to grieve, reflect, or wait. None of them are wasted. Each is a sacred part of your journey.

It can be tempting to resist the seasons that feel heavy or quiet, but even those are necessary. They offer rest for the soul, deeper clarity, and a chance to reconnect with the Divine. Just like nature, your spirit knows how to rise again—stronger and more rooted—when it has honored the process of each phase.

Today, embrace the season you are in. Ask what it is here to teach you. Trust that the Divine is at work, whether things feel full of life or stripped bare. You are never outside the flow of sacred timing.

Meditative Prayer

Divine Keeper of Seasons,
Thank You for the rhythm of my life.
Help me honor the season I'm in,
Even if I don't yet understand its purpose.

When I long for spring in the middle of winter,
Give me patience.
When I resist the quiet,
Teach me to rest in You.

Let each season grow something beautiful in me,
Compassion, wisdom, joy, or strength.
I trust the timing.
I trust the unfolding.

I am rooted in purpose.
I am guided by grace.
And I welcome the gifts of this season.

DAY 149:
The Peace That Comes with Trust

Lesson for the Day

Trust is a gateway to peace. When you let go of the need to control every outcome, when you surrender the weight of worry, and when you place your heart in the care of the Divine, a calm begins to settle over your soul. Trust doesn't mean you won't face uncertainty—it means you're anchored in something greater than fear.

Peace doesn't always come from circumstances aligning just right. True peace comes from knowing that, no matter what unfolds, you are supported, loved, and guided. The more you practice trust, the more you discover an inner stillness that holds steady, even in the storms.

Today, choose trust. When your thoughts begin to spiral, gently bring them back to faith. Speak to your heart with kindness. Let peace rise—not from having all the answers, but from believing that everything is unfolding as it should.

Meditative Prayer

Divine Anchor,
I choose to trust You today.
When fear rises,
Let peace rise higher.

When I don't know what's ahead,
Remind me You already do.
When I'm tempted to worry,
Still my heart with Your presence.

Let trust be the soil where peace can grow.
Let faith be the light that calms my mind.
I surrender control,
And I rest in Your care.

I am safe.
I am held.
I am at peace.

DAY 150:
Walking Forward in Faith

Lesson for the Day

Faith isn't always a grand leap—it's often a steady, quiet step taken in trust. Walking forward in faith means moving even when you can't see the full picture, believing even when the outcome is uncertain, and trusting that the Divine is guiding you through every unknown.

There may be fear or hesitation, but faith gently reminds you that you are not walking alone. With each step, you are being supported by something greater—by love, by grace, by a purpose unfolding with intention. Faith is not the absence of uncertainty. It is the courage to continue anyway.

Today, take one step forward. It doesn't have to be big. What matters is that you are moving in trust, allowing your heart to lead and your soul to follow. Let each step be an offering of hope, and know that the Divine walks with you.

Meditative Prayer

Divine Guide,
Thank You for walking beside me.
Today, I choose to move forward,
Even when I cannot see the whole path.

Strengthen my steps with courage,
And quiet my doubts with Your peace.
Let my faith be stronger than my fear,
And my hope brighter than my hesitation.

I trust the way You lead me.
I follow where You call.
Step by step,
I walk forward in faith.

Day 151:
Awakening to Your Purpose

Lesson for the Day

There is a sacred reason you are here—something uniquely yours to offer the world. Your purpose isn't always loud or obvious. Often, it awakens slowly, through moments of clarity, curiosity, and quiet recognition. It's not just something you do—it's who you are when you live in alignment with your soul.

Awakening to your purpose requires listening to your heart, paying attention to what brings you alive, and trusting that the Divine placed gifts within you for a reason. Your path may not look like anyone else's, and that's the beauty of it. You are not here to copy—you are here to shine in your own light.

Today, open yourself to the truth that your life has meaning. Ask the Divine to show you what lights you up, and be willing to follow where it leads. You don't have to have it all figured out—you just have to begin.

Meditative Prayer

Divine Creator,
Thank You for the purpose You've planted within me.
Help me awaken to it fully,
With open eyes and a willing heart.

Where I feel lost,
Bring clarity.
Where I feel afraid,
Bring courage.

Show me the gifts I carry,
And how to use them with love and intention.
Let my life reflect Your light,
And my steps align with my soul's calling.

I am open.
I am ready.
I am here to live my purpose.

DAY 152:
The Light That Leads the Way

Lesson for the Day

There is a light that never fades—a sacred, guiding presence that leads you even when the path seems dim. This light is not always external. It shines within your heart, fueled by faith, love, and the quiet whisper of the Divine. It illuminates your next step, even when you cannot see the full road ahead.

When you feel lost or uncertain, turn toward the light. It may appear as inner peace, a sense of knowing, a sign, or a moment of stillness. Trust that this light has always been with you, even in the shadows. It does not demand attention—it invites trust. And when you follow it, you walk not in fear, but in sacred alignment.

Today, pause and seek the light. Let it rise in you and guide you gently forward. You are not walking in darkness—you are being led by a love that knows the way.

Meditative Prayer

Divine Light,
Shine upon my path today.
When I feel unsure,
Let Your presence guide me forward.

Illuminate my heart
With peace, clarity, and courage.
Remind me that I am never alone,
And that Your light walks before me.

Let me follow where You lead,
With faith as my compass,
And love as my guide.
Even in the unknown,
I trust the light that leads the way.

I am guided.
I am safe.
I am walking in Your light.

DAY 153:

A Season of Expansion

Lesson for the Day

There are times in life when you feel yourself stretching—beyond old patterns, beyond former limits, and into a wider, more authentic version of yourself. These are seasons of expansion, when the soul is ready to grow, not only inward but outward, expressing its light more fully in the world.

Expansion is not always easy. It can come with discomfort, vulnerability, and the need to release what no longer fits who you are becoming. But it is also exhilarating. It is the Divine saying, *You are ready for more.* More truth, more purpose, more presence. Trust that as you expand, the universe expands with you.

Today, lean into your season of growth. Say yes to the opportunities that stretch you. Trust your capacity to hold more love, more vision, more light. You were not made to stay small—this is your time to rise.

Meditative Prayer

Divine Source of Growth,
I open myself to this season of expansion.
Stretch me with love,
And guide me with grace.

Help me release what no longer serves,
So I may step into what is calling me forward.
When I feel afraid to grow,
Anchor me in trust.

Let my spirit rise with purpose,
And my heart widen with joy.
May I expand with courage,
Becoming more of who I truly am.

I am growing.
I am rising.
I am expanding into light.

DAY 154:
Letting Your Soul Shine

Lesson for the Day

You were not meant to hide your light. The truth, beauty, and love that live within you are not accidents—they are sacred gifts meant to be shared. Letting your soul shine is an act of courage and authenticity. It is choosing to live in alignment with who you truly are, without apology or fear.

Your light doesn't have to be loud to be powerful. It can radiate through kindness, quiet strength, creativity, compassion, or simply by being present. When you let your soul shine, you inspire others to do the same. You give permission for truth, joy, and freedom to ripple out into the world.

Today, let your light be seen. Speak from your heart. Move from your truth. Offer your energy without shrinking. The world needs the brightness only *you* can bring.

Meditative Prayer

Divine Light Within,
Help me shine with the truth of who I am.
Clear away fear,
And make space for bold love.

When I feel the urge to dim myself,
Remind me that I was created to glow.
When I doubt my worth,
Let Your light rise within me.

May my soul shine in every step I take,
In every word I speak,
In every space I enter.

I was made to shine.
I reflect divine beauty.
And I light the world with my presence.

DAY 155:
Walking with the Confidence of Divine Support

Lesson for the Day

There is a powerful shift that happens when you stop walking through life feeling alone and start moving with the quiet confidence that the Divine walks with you. Divine support is not always loud or visible, but it is constant—woven through every breath, every step, every unfolding moment.

When you walk with this awareness, your posture changes. You no longer move from fear, but from faith. You make choices not from scarcity, but from trust. The weight you once carried alone is now shared with a presence that holds you completely. Confidence doesn't mean you never struggle—it means you know you are never walking alone.

Today, take a step forward knowing you are supported. Speak with the voice of one who is backed by love. Act with the assurance that your path is guided. The Divine is with you—in every thought, every movement, every heartbeat.

Meditative Prayer

Divine Companion,
Thank You for walking beside me.
When I feel unsure,
Strengthen my spirit.
When I feel alone,
Remind me of Your constant presence.

Let me move through this day
With the confidence of one who is supported,
Loved, and led.
Fill me with quiet strength,
And peace that grounds my every step.

May my choices reflect faith,
And my words carry light.
I walk forward,
Held by You,
Confident in Your care.

DAY 156:

The Power of Positive Expectation

Lesson for the Day

There is a quiet force that shapes your day before it even begins. It is your expectations. When you wake up expecting good, you open your heart to receive it. Positive expectation is not wishful thinking—it is a deep trust in the goodness of life, the presence of the Divine, and the unfolding of grace in ordinary moments.

Your energy becomes a magnet for what you believe is possible. When you choose to expect joy, peace, connection, or purpose, your actions and perceptions align with those hopes. Even in difficult seasons, positive expectation keeps your heart open and your spirit lifted, ready to notice blessings that might otherwise be missed.

Today, begin with faith in what can go right. Expect goodness. Expect growth. Expect connection with the Divine and alignment with your highest path. What you expect with hope, you welcome with love.

Meditative Prayer

Loving Presence,
Fill my heart with hope today.
Let me rise with joy,
And walk with positive expectation.

Where I've grown weary,
Renew my belief in what is possible.
Where I've expected the worst,
Shift my gaze toward Your goodness.

Help me trust in blessings unseen,
And move through this day with a heart wide open.
I expect love.
I expect peace.
I expect You.

With faith in my steps
And light in my spirit,
I walk into this day full of hope.

DAY 157:
Rising with New Strength

Lesson for the Day

Every day offers a chance to begin again—not just with a new routine or intention, but with a renewed spirit. Rising with new strength means drawing from the well within you that has not run dry. Even when you've felt weary, uncertain, or stretched thin, there is still power in you waiting to be awakened by grace.

This strength is not forced. It is not the kind that pretends everything is fine. It is quiet, rooted, and honest. It says, *I've been through something, and I'm still here.* It comes from surrendering to the Divine and allowing yourself to be carried, restored, and infused with new energy and purpose.

Today, rise knowing that you are stronger than you were yesterday— not because nothing touched you, but because you've grown through it. Let your strength be soft, sacred, and full of truth. The Divine is lifting you, and your spirit is rising.

Meditative Prayer

Divine Strength,
Thank You for the new strength rising within me.
Even when I've felt empty,
You have filled me again.

Help me rise today with grace,
With courage,
And with faith in what lies ahead.

Renew my heart,
Refresh my soul,
And remind me that I carry power
Rooted in Your love.

I rise—not in striving,
But in surrender.
I rise with purpose.
I rise with You.

DAY 158:
Choosing Hope Every Day

Lesson for the Day

Hope is not a passive feeling—it is an active choice. Each day, you are given the opportunity to choose hope over despair, trust over doubt, light over darkness. Even when life feels uncertain or heavy, hope is the quiet force that says, *Keep going. Something beautiful is still possible.*

Choosing hope doesn't mean ignoring pain or pretending everything is perfect. It means believing that, even in the struggle, there is a path forward. It is the soul's refusal to give up, the heart's whisper that healing is happening, and the spirit's resilience rooted in divine love.

Today, choose hope. Let it color your thoughts, your words, your actions. Let it soften what's hard and brighten what's dim. Hope isn't found—it's created, nurtured, and lived. And the more you choose it, the more it grows.

Meditative Prayer

Divine Light,
Today, I choose hope.
Even when it's hard,
Even when it's quiet,
Let it rise in me like the morning sun.

Help me trust in what I can't yet see,
And believe in what You are making new.
When I feel the weight of the world,
Lift my spirit with gentle grace.

Let my heart stay open,
My eyes lifted,
And my soul anchored in You.

I choose hope over fear,
Light over doubt,
And life over limitation.

DAY 159:

Embracing the Possibilities of a New Season

Lesson for the Day

Each new season brings with it a sacred invitation—an opportunity to shift, to begin again, and to step into something fresh and full of possibility. Whether this season is one of growth, rest, rebuilding, or rising, it carries gifts waiting to be discovered. Embracing a new season means releasing the weight of what was and opening your heart to what could be.

You don't have to have it all figured out to move forward. All that's required is a willingness to trust, to hope, and to show up with openness. The Divine is already present in this new chapter, preparing the way and gently guiding your steps. Your role is simply to say *yes* to what's calling you.

Today, breathe in the energy of renewal. Let go of what belonged to yesterday, and turn your face toward the promise of what's unfolding. This new season holds beauty, purpose, and possibility—and it's meant for you.

Meditative Prayer

Divine Creator of Seasons,
Thank You for this new beginning.
Help me step into it with courage,
And a heart open wide to possibility.

Where I've held on too tightly,
Teach me to release with grace.
Where I've feared change,
Fill me with hope for what's ahead.

Let me see this season as a gift,
Full of promise,
Full of purpose,
Full of You.

I embrace what is new.
I trust what is unfolding.
And I walk forward with joy.

Day 160:

The Sacredness of the Present Moment

Lesson for the Day

So often, the mind drifts to what was or what could be—but the present moment is where life truly happens. It is in the here and now that you breathe, connect, grow, and encounter the Divine. This moment, just as it is, holds sacred potential. When you pause long enough to truly be present, you realize the miracle of simply *being*.

The present doesn't demand perfection—it asks for awareness. It invites you to notice the beauty around you, to feel what you feel, and to listen to the quiet guidance of your soul. In this space, you are not your past or your future. You are whole. You are alive. You are enough.

Today, allow yourself to slow down. Inhale deeply. Look around you with fresh eyes. Feel the ground beneath your feet and the light within your heart. This moment is a gift. And in it, you are already exactly where you need to be.

Meditative Prayer

Divine Presence,

Thank You for this moment.

Help me return to now,

Not to fix it,

But to feel it.

Clear the distractions from my mind,

And let my heart settle into stillness.

Teach me to notice the beauty here,

To honor what is,

And to trust in the grace of this breath.

I release the past.

I release the future.

I dwell fully in the now,

Where You are always waiting.

This moment is sacred.

And so am I.

DAY 161:

Awakening to the Beauty Within You

Lesson for the Day

There is a quiet, radiant beauty within you—one that has always been there, even if you haven't fully seen it. Awakening to your inner beauty means beginning to see yourself as the Divine sees you: worthy, whole, and filled with light. It is a recognition of your soul's brilliance beyond appearances, roles, or achievements.

This beauty is not something you earn. It exists in your truth, your compassion, your resilience, your presence. When you acknowledge the sacred light within you, you begin to carry yourself differently—with gentleness, confidence, and grace. You stop seeking validation from the world and begin reflecting the love you've found within.

Today, take a moment to truly see yourself. Look beyond flaws or failures. Honor your journey, your heart, your spirit. The Divine dwells within you—and that is the most beautiful truth of all.

Meditative Prayer

Divine Mirror of Love,
Help me see the beauty You placed within me.
Clear my eyes of judgment,
And open my heart to truth.

Where I've forgotten my worth,
Remind me.
Where I've hidden my light,
Awaken it.

Let me walk in the fullness of who I am,
Embracing every part of my becoming.
May I reflect love,
Radiate truth,
And shine from within.

I am sacred.
I am beautiful.
I am already whole.

DAY 162:

Stepping Into Your Power

Lesson for the Day

There comes a moment when you are called to remember who you truly are—not who the world told you to be, but who you were divinely created to be. Stepping into your power means reclaiming your voice, your worth, your truth. It means standing in alignment with your soul and knowing that you carry light, wisdom, and strength within you.

Your power is not about control—it's about presence. It's the quiet confidence that comes from being rooted in your spirit, led by love, and supported by the Divine. You don't have to force anything. When you are fully yourself, your energy speaks for you. You move in truth, and truth moves mountains.

Today, rise into your power. Speak with clarity. Act with intention. Trust your gifts and honor your boundaries. The world doesn't need a smaller version of you—it needs the full, empowered light of your presence.

Meditative Prayer

Divine Light Within,
Thank You for the strength You've placed in me.
Help me step fully into my power,
With love, grace, and truth.

Where I've held back,
Let courage rise.
Where I've doubted,
Let clarity guide me.

May I honor my voice,
Stand in my truth,
And move through the world as the soul You created me to be.

I do not shrink.
I do not fear.
I rise in my power,
Rooted in You.

DAY 163:

The Lightness of Letting Go

Lesson for the Day

Letting go is not about loss—it's about freedom. When you release what no longer serves your highest good, you make space for healing, clarity, and peace. You were never meant to carry everything forever. There is a lightness that comes when you choose to lay your burdens down and trust that the Divine will hold what you no longer need to bear.

Letting go doesn't always mean forgetting. Sometimes it means forgiving. Sometimes it means surrendering the need to control, to fix, or to understand. Whatever it is you're being asked to release, know that you are not losing yourself—you are returning to yourself.

Today, breathe deeply and feel the weight begin to lift. Hand over the heaviness to the Divine. Let go with love, and let in the peace that's been waiting for you all along.

Meditative Prayer

Divine Release,
Help me let go of what no longer serves me.
I lay down the weight of the past,
And open my hands to freedom.

Where I've held on too tightly,
Teach me to trust.
Where I've carried what's not mine,
Lift the burden from my heart.

Let Your peace fill the empty spaces,
And Your love surround me as I surrender.
I let go of fear.
I let go of control.
I let go of what I was never meant to keep.

I am lighter.
I am freer.
I am held by grace.

DAY 164:
Walking with an Open Heart

Lesson for the Day

To walk with an open heart is to live in a space of vulnerability, courage, and love. It means choosing to remain soft even when life has tried to harden you. An open heart allows you to connect more deeply—with yourself, with others, and with the Divine. It is a doorway to grace, compassion, and healing.

An open heart does not mean you lack boundaries. It means your spirit remains receptive to joy, forgiveness, and truth. Even after pain or disappointment, you continue to believe in goodness. You trust that love is still worth offering, that kindness still matters, and that each step forward can be taken in light.

Today, open your heart just a little more. Let love in. Let love out. Let your heart be a sacred vessel through which peace flows. The Divine speaks most clearly through a heart that remains open.

Meditative Prayer

Divine Love,
Keep my heart open today.
Even when it's easier to close,
Let me choose softness and trust.

Where I have been hurt,
Bring healing.
Where I feel guarded,
Breathe courage.

Help me meet the world with compassion,
And walk in the fullness of love.
Let my heart be a sanctuary,
Strong, tender, and true.

I walk in love.
I walk in light.
I walk with an open heart.

DAY 165:
The Power of Perspective

Lesson for the Day

Perspective is a sacred lens—it can shift everything without changing anything outside of you. When you choose to see through eyes of faith, gratitude, and love, even challenges become invitations for growth. You begin to notice the Divine at work not just in the miracles, but in the mundane, the messy, and the misunderstood.

You always have a choice in how you see a moment. Will you view it through fear or trust? Through frustration or opportunity? Perspective does not deny reality—it reshapes your relationship with it. It empowers you to respond with wisdom, to find the beauty in the broken, and to uncover meaning even in the waiting.

Today, pause and look again. Where have you seen only problems, ask for vision to see potential. Where you've been discouraged, ask to see the bigger picture. The Divine can reveal great things when you choose to shift your gaze.

Meditative Prayer

Divine Wisdom,
Grant me a new perspective today.
Clear the fog of fear,
And lift my thoughts to see through Your eyes.

Help me to see the blessing in the burden,
The growth in the challenge,
And the light in the shadow.

When I feel overwhelmed,
Remind me that I can shift my view.
Give me eyes to see grace,
And a heart open to possibility.

I choose faith over fear.
I choose clarity over confusion.
And I walk today with renewed perspective.

DAY 166:

Finding the Sacred in the Simple

Lesson for the Day

Sometimes we look for the Divine in grand moments—mountaintop revelations, dramatic change, or spiritual breakthroughs. But more often, the sacred meets us in the simple. It lives in a kind word, a breath of stillness, the warmth of sunlight, or the rhythm of your heartbeat. These ordinary moments are filled with extraordinary presence—if you slow down enough to notice.

The sacred doesn't require perfection or performance. It asks only that you be present. When you tune in with a heart open to wonder, you begin to see holiness woven into your daily life. Every sip of water, every shared smile, every quiet pause becomes a chance to remember that you are connected to something greater.

Today, look for the sacred in the small. Be still for a moment longer. Feel the softness of grace in the simplest things. The Divine is not far away—it is here, now, in the beauty of this breath.

Meditative Prayer

Divine Presence,
Thank You for meeting me in the simple.
Help me slow down,
And open my eyes to the wonder around me.

Let me find You in the quiet moments,
The daily rhythms,
The unnoticed gifts.

May I never overlook the beauty
That fills my life with meaning.
Teach me to see the sacred everywhere,
And to walk in awe through the ordinary.

This moment is holy.
This life is sacred.
And I am awake to it all.

DAY 167:
Embracing Life's Divine Surprises

Lesson for the Day

Life rarely unfolds exactly as planned, and sometimes the most beautiful moments are the ones we never saw coming. Divine surprises come in many forms—a sudden connection, an unexpected answer, a shift that opens a new door. When you open your heart to receive them, you begin to see that the Divine is constantly working behind the scenes, guiding you in ways you couldn't have imagined.

Embracing divine surprises means letting go of rigid expectations and trusting that what arrives—however unexpected—is part of a greater plan. It invites you to be curious instead of controlling, to welcome wonder, and to believe that even detours can lead to sacred destinations.

Today, walk with openness. Make space for the unexpected blessings, the spontaneous joy, and the surprising moments of grace. The Divine loves to work through mystery—and often, what you didn't plan turns out to be exactly what you needed.

Meditative Prayer

Divine Mystery,
Thank You for the surprises You place along my path.
Help me let go of rigid plans,
And open my heart to wonder.

When things don't go as I expected,
Let me trust that You are still guiding me.
When something new appears,
Help me receive it with joy and curiosity.

May I embrace the unexpected,
And find peace in Your perfect timing.
Let Your surprises remind me
That I am loved,
And never alone.

I welcome the unknown.
I trust in Your surprises.
I walk with joy into what comes next.

DAY 168:

Seeing Every Moment as a Gift

Lesson for the Day

Each moment you are given is a sacred offering. Some arrive wrapped in joy, others in challenge—but all are invitations to live fully, to feel deeply, and to grow gently. When you choose to see every moment as a gift, you step into gratitude, presence, and grace. You stop rushing through life and start receiving it.

Not every moment feels easy, but even the hard ones can bring wisdom, compassion, or strength. The gift is not always obvious—it may be hidden in a lesson, a connection, or simply the reminder that you are still here, still breathing, still becoming. When you shift your perspective, life becomes less about what's missing and more about what's being offered.

Today, pause and notice the moment you're in. Take a breath. Feel the light on your skin, the beat of your heart, the quiet presence of the Divine. This moment is a gift—and so are you.

Meditative Prayer

Divine Giver of Life,
Thank You for this moment.
Help me receive it fully,
With open hands and a grateful heart.

Even when life feels ordinary,
Remind me of the beauty in right now.
Even when it's hard,
Show me the hidden blessings.

Teach me to slow down,
To see with wonder,
To honor every breath as sacred.

This day is a gift.
This life is a miracle.
And I choose to live it with love.

Day 169:

A Soul That Rises with the Sun

Lesson for the Day

Each sunrise is a sacred invitation—a reminder that no matter what came before, you have another chance to begin again. A soul that rises with the sun is one that embraces renewal, welcomes hope, and chooses to show up with courage, even after difficulty or doubt. It means aligning your heart with the rhythm of the day and opening yourself to its unfolding gifts.

There is strength in beginning again, in letting the light of a new day warm your spirit and call you into presence. When you rise with intention, you allow grace to meet you in the morning stillness. You declare to the world—and to yourself—that you are ready to live, love, and grow again.

Today, rise with the sun in your soul. Let its light awaken your joy, your purpose, and your trust. No matter how yesterday felt, today is new. And you are rising with it—strong, radiant, and whole.

Meditative Prayer

Divine Light of the Morning,
Thank You for this new beginning.
As the sun rises,
So does my soul.

Fill me with warmth and renewal.
Let this day be touched by Your grace.
Where I felt heavy, bring light.
Where I felt lost, bring direction.

Help me meet this day with open arms,
A peaceful heart,
And the courage to begin again.

I rise in hope.
I rise in love.
I rise with the sun.

DAY 170:
The Peace That Comes from Trusting the Divine

Lesson for the Day

There is a deep and lasting peace that flows not from perfect circumstances, but from perfect trust. When you place your heart in the care of the Divine—when you choose to believe that you are being guided, protected, and loved—something within you settles. The noise quiets. The worry fades. You remember that you are not walking alone.

Trusting the Divine does not mean life will be without hardship. It means you carry peace through the hardship. It means knowing that even when you don't understand the "why," you can trust in the "who"—the presence that holds all things together and gently leads you forward.

Today, release the need to figure everything out. Let your soul lean into the arms of Divine love. Trust that you are exactly where you need to be, and that all is unfolding in perfect time. Peace comes not from control, but from surrender.

Meditative Prayer

Divine Source of Peace,
I place my trust in You today.
When my mind races,
Still my thoughts.
When fear rises,
Fill me with calm.

I surrender my plans,
My worries,
And my need to control.
Let Your presence be my anchor,
And Your love be my guide.

In You, I find rest.
In You, I find peace.
I trust the journey,
Because I trust in You.

DAY 171:
Letting Hope Guide You Forward

Lesson for the Day

Hope is not just a feeling—it's a compass. It points you forward when the road is unclear and shines light when all you can see are shadows. Letting hope guide you means choosing to believe that something good is still ahead, even if you don't know how or when it will arrive. It's trusting in the possibility of beauty rising from the broken and peace following the storm.

When you let hope lead, you walk with your heart open. You stay soft in a world that often asks you to be hardened. You continue to dream, to trust, and to love, even when life has tried to dim your spirit. The Divine walks closely with those who dare to hope—because hope is the language of faith in action.

Today, let hope be your guide. Let it color your thoughts, influence your choices, and steady your steps. You don't have to know what's coming—just believe that something beautiful is possible.

Meditative Prayer

Divine Light of Hope,
Lead me forward today.
When I feel uncertain,
Let hope be my compass.

When fear speaks loudly,
Let hope speak louder.
When the way is hidden,
Shine Your promise on my path.

Help me believe in what I can't yet see,
And trust that You are guiding me with love.
Let my heart rise again with courage,
And my soul walk in hope's direction.

I am led by faith.
I am carried by hope.
I am moving forward in grace.

Day 172:

The Joy of Rebirth

Lesson for the Day

Rebirth is the sacred process of returning to life after a season of stillness, shedding, or loss. It is the quiet miracle of discovering that something new is growing where something old once ended. The joy of rebirth comes not just from what is emerging—but from who you've become in the becoming.

In every rebirth, there is joy. Not always loud or celebrated, but deep and true—a joy that rises from knowing you've made it through, that light has found its way back in, and that your spirit is more alive than before. This joy is rooted in resilience, trust, and grace.

Today, celebrate your own rebirths—big or small. Honor the ways you've come back to yourself, the moments you chose healing, the pieces of your soul that began again. New life is rising in you. Let joy greet it with open arms.

Meditative Prayer

Divine Source of Renewal,
Thank You for the beauty of new beginnings.
Thank You for the life
That rises in me again and again.

Where I once felt lost,
You led me home.
Where I was weary,
You breathed new strength.

Let me embrace this sacred season of rebirth,
With joy in my heart
And trust in my step.
May I bloom freely,
Knowing I am guided by grace.

I am renewed.
I am alive.
I rejoice in this new beginning.

DAY 173:

Awakening to the Magic of Life

Lesson for the Day

There is magic all around you—woven into the quiet moments, the everyday miracles, the way the light hits the trees, or how your breath moves through your body. Awakening to the magic of life doesn't require a perfect day or grand event. It simply asks you to pay attention with wonder, to see with your soul, and to feel with an open heart.

The Divine speaks through this magic—reminding you that life is not ordinary, even in its simplicity. When you slow down and begin to truly notice, you find beauty where you once saw routine, connection where you once felt alone, and grace where you once expected resistance.

Today, look around with awakened eyes. Let the smallest moments stir your spirit. The magic of life is not somewhere far off—it is here, now, waiting for you to see it.

Meditative Prayer

Divine Enchantment,
Awaken me to the beauty of this life.
Help me see through eyes of wonder,
And feel with a heart open to joy.

Let me notice the sacred in the simple,
The divine in the daily,
And the miracles in the mundane.

When I grow numb to the world around me,
Remind me that magic is still alive.
Let each breath be a blessing,
Each step a prayer.

I am awake.
I am alive.
And I delight in the wonder of this life.

Day 174:

Choosing to Walk in Faith and Joy

Lesson for the Day

Every day presents a choice To walk in fear or to walk in faith. To carry heaviness or to welcome joy. Faith and joy are not reserved for the easy days—they are sacred choices you can make in the midst of uncertainty, challenge, and change. They are your spiritual anchors, lifting your heart and guiding your steps.

Walking in faith means trusting the unseen, believing in the goodness of what's ahead, and knowing that the Divine walks with you. Walking in joy means finding light in the present moment, even when things feel incomplete. When you choose both, you align your spirit with hope, strength, and the rhythm of grace.

Today, choose your path with intention. Let your steps be guided by trust and your heart be lifted by joy. No matter what comes your way, you are walking in truth, in light, and in the fullness of the Divine's love.

Meditative Prayer

Divine Companion,
Today I choose to walk in faith and joy.
Not because everything is perfect,
But because You are with me.

When doubt whispers,
Let faith rise louder.
When heaviness lingers,
Fill me with lightness and laughter.

Let my steps reflect trust,
And my spirit overflow with joy.
I walk with purpose,
With peace,
And with praise.

Faith is my compass.
Joy is my strength.
And You are my guide.

DAY 175:
The Gift of a New Beginning Every Day

Lesson for the Day

No matter what yesterday held—joy or sorrow, success or struggle—today is a new beginning. The Divine gifts you with the sacred reset of a fresh start each morning, inviting you to begin again with grace, courage, and an open heart. Every sunrise carries the quiet promise. *You are not bound by your past. You are free to grow forward.*

A new beginning doesn't require a dramatic change. It starts in your thoughts, your breath, your intention. It's the choice to try again, to show up with love, and to believe that healing and transformation are always possible. Each day is a blank page, waiting to be written with hope.

Today, receive this gift fully. Lay down yesterday's weight, and walk into today with the lightness of renewal. The Divine delights in your becoming—and each new beginning is proof that you are not alone on the journey.

Meditative Prayer

Divine Creator of Dawn,
Thank You for this new beginning.
With this breath,
I release what no longer serves me.

Renew my heart,
Restore my hope,
And awaken me to what is possible today.

Let me move forward without fear,
And meet this day with fresh eyes and a willing spirit.
May I live with intention,
Speak with kindness,
And walk in grace.

Each day is a gift.
Each moment a miracle.
And I begin again with You.

DAY 176:

Standing in the Light of Your Truth

Lesson for the Day

There is power in knowing who you are—and even greater power in choosing to live from that truth. Your inner truth is not shaped by others' opinions or expectations. It is the sacred knowing that lives within your soul, calling you to be authentic, to speak honestly, and to live boldly aligned with your heart.

Standing in your truth may feel vulnerable at times, but it is also deeply freeing. When you honor your inner voice, you stop seeking validation outside of yourself. You remember that your worth is inherent, your voice is valuable, and your truth is a light the world needs. The Divine supports you when you live in alignment with who you truly are.

Today, stand tall in your truth. Let your words and actions reflect what matters most to your spirit. You are not here to dim your light—you are here to shine with honesty, love, and divine confidence.

Meditative Prayer

Divine Light Within,
Help me stand in the truth of who I am.
Let my heart be steady,
And my voice be strong.

Where I've hidden parts of myself,
Bring them into the light.
Where I've feared judgment,
Fill me with courage.

May I walk in alignment,
Speak with clarity,
And live from a place of deep knowing.

I am rooted in truth.
I am guided by love.
And I am free to be fully me.

DAY 177:
The Healing Power of Hope

Lesson for the Day

Hope has a quiet strength—it doesn't always remove the pain, but it brings light into the darkness. It reminds you that healing is possible, that tomorrow can be brighter, and that even in your deepest wounds, something new can grow. Hope doesn't erase the past—it helps you carry it with more grace, and look forward with gentleness and trust.

When you choose hope, you invite healing into your story. You begin to shift from survival to restoration, from despair to possibility. The Divine works through hope—gently, patiently, always moving you toward wholeness. Even the smallest flicker of hope can guide you through the longest night.

Today, allow hope to be part of your healing. Let it enter the places that feel tired, broken, or afraid. Trust that hope is not just an emotion—it's a sacred medicine, flowing from the heart of the Divine, and ready to restore yours.

Meditative Prayer

Divine Healer,
Thank You for the gift of hope.
Even when I feel worn,
Let hope rise within me.

Where my heart feels heavy,
Let hope bring light.
Where I've grown tired of waiting,
Let hope bring patience.

Heal me gently through hope,
And remind me that I am never too far from joy.
I open to the light,
I open to the new,
And I welcome the peace that hope brings.

DAY 178:
Trusting That Life is Unfolding for Your Highest Good

Lesson for the Day

There are times when life feels uncertain—when outcomes shift, plans fall apart, or the road ahead is unclear. But even in those moments, there is a sacred truth at work. Life is always unfolding for your highest good. You may not always understand the *how* or *why*, but the Divine sees the whole picture, and you are being guided with love and purpose.

Trusting in this truth means choosing faith over fear, even when the path doesn't make sense. It means letting go of the need to control and leaning into the belief that every delay, every detour, and every challenge is shaping you for something greater. The journey may not always be easy, but it is always leading you somewhere meaningful.

Today, let your heart rest in trust. Breathe deeply and surrender the urge to rush or resist. Know that the Divine is orchestrating something beautiful behind the scenes, and you are being gently moved into alignment with your highest path.

Meditative Prayer

Divine Planner,
Thank You for guiding my life with love.
When I cannot see the full picture,
Help me trust that You are still working for my good.

Let me release the need to control,
And rest in the peace of Your timing.
Even in uncertainty,
Anchor me in faith.

Shape me through the journey,
Strengthen me through the waiting,
And lead me into the fullness of Your promise.

I trust the process.
I trust the path.
And I trust that all is unfolding for my highest good.

DAY 179:

A Heart That Rests in Divine Love

Lesson for the Day

There is no safer place than the presence of Divine love. It asks nothing of you but to be as you are—whole, broken, growing, or healing. A heart that rests in Divine love no longer seeks approval, worthiness, or direction from the outside world. It knows it is already held, already enough, already home.

Resting in Divine love means choosing to believe that you are fully accepted and deeply cherished. It is allowing yourself to exhale, to soften, to let go of the striving and simply *be*. This love doesn't waver with your moods or change with your choices—it is steady, eternal, and always here.

Today, let your heart rest. Return to that inner sanctuary where Divine love surrounds and sustains you. You don't have to do anything to earn it. Just receive. Let it fill you with peace, renew your spirit, and remind you that you are never alone.

Meditative Prayer

Divine Beloved,
Wrap me in the safety of Your love today.
Let my heart rest,
Not in worry or effort,
But in the calm of Your presence.

When I feel unworthy,
Remind me I am already enough.
When I feel alone,
Show me I have never been without You.

Let Your love fill every empty space,
Heal every weary place,
And hold me in quiet peace.

I rest in You.
I am loved by You.
And in that love, I am whole.

DAY 180:

Embracing the Journey with Open Arms

Lesson for the Day

Life is not a straight path—it is a winding, sacred journey filled with twists, turns, pauses, and revelations. Embracing the journey with open arms means letting go of rigid expectations and choosing to welcome each step as a teacher. It is the act of opening your heart to what *is*, rather than resisting what *isn't*.

When you live this way, every moment becomes meaningful. Even the challenges begin to shape you in beautiful ways. You stop waiting for life to "begin" and start realizing it's happening right here, in every breath, every choice, every moment of becoming. The Divine walks with you—not only at the destination but through the entire journey.

Today, take a breath and open your arms to this life—messy, beautiful, unpredictable, and holy. Trust that you are right where you need to be. Each step, no matter how small, is a part of your sacred unfolding.

Meditative Prayer

Divine Traveler,
Walk with me on this journey.
Help me embrace the road ahead
With trust, with hope, with peace.

Where I feel uncertain,
Anchor me in Your love.
Where I resist the unknown,
Open my heart with grace.

Let me receive each moment,
Each lesson, each blessing,
With open arms and a willing spirit.

I do not walk alone.
I do not walk in fear.
I embrace this sacred path with You.

Day 181:

The Fire Within You

Lesson for the Day

There is a sacred fire within you—a light that cannot be extinguished, even in your darkest moments. It is the fire of purpose, passion, resilience, and Divine spark. This fire is not loud or reckless, it is steady, powerful, and deeply rooted in who you are. It reminds you that no matter what life brings, you have the strength to rise, the courage to keep going, and the wisdom to burn brightly from within.

You were never meant to live dimmed. When you honor the fire within you, you align with your truth, your creativity, and your soul's deepest calling. This inner flame doesn't need permission—it needs space. Trust it. Feed it. Let it illuminate your path and the paths of those around you.

Today, reconnect with your fire. Ask yourself, *What sets my soul alight?* Then move in that direction, even if it's only a small step. The Divine placed this fire in you for a reason. Let it burn with purpose and love.

Meditative Prayer

Divine Flame Within,
Ignite the fire of my spirit today.
Let it burn away doubt,
And awaken my deepest truth.

Fan the flames of passion,
Of purpose,
Of joy.
Let me walk boldly,
Lit from the inside out.

When the world tries to dim my light,
Remind me who I am.
When I feel weary,
Stoke the embers of courage.

I carry Your fire.
I burn with love.
And I shine with holy light.

DAY 182:

Stepping Into Your Power

Lesson for the Day

True power is not about control, dominance, or force—it is about authenticity, alignment, and the sacred courage to be who you are. Stepping into your power means standing tall in your truth, honoring your voice, and choosing to live in alignment with your soul's purpose. It's about recognizing that you are not separate from Divine strength—you are a vessel for it.

Your power is found in the moments you trust your intuition, speak your truth with love, and say yes to the life that calls to you. It's in the quiet confidence that you are enough—not because of what you've done, but because of who you are. The Divine didn't create you to stay small. You were made to rise.

Today, step fully into your power. Let go of the fear that you are too much or not enough. Walk forward with intention, with clarity, and with grace. Your light is needed. Your presence matters. You were born to embody your power.

Meditative Prayer

Divine Source of Strength,
Awaken the power within me.
Let me stand in my truth,
With courage and compassion.

Where I have doubted myself,
Plant seeds of confidence.
Where I have held back,
Unleash the fullness of who I am.

Help me walk in alignment,
Live with purpose,
And move with the strength of Your spirit.

I am powerful.
I am worthy.
I am guided by Divine truth.

DAY 183:

A Soul That Stands Tall

Lesson for the Day

There is a quiet dignity in a soul that stands tall—not in pride or arrogance, but in grace and truth. A soul that stands tall knows its worth, even when the world tries to make it small. It honors its journey, holds space for its healing, and walks forward with humility, resilience, and strength rooted in the Divine.

To stand tall is to be grounded in who you are and who you are becoming. It is choosing not to shrink to fit in or stay silent to be accepted. It's allowing your soul to take up space in the world with authenticity, gentleness, and courage. You don't need to shout to be powerful—your grounded presence speaks volumes.

Today, rise in your soul. Let your posture reflect the truth that you are worthy, seen, and supported by the Divine. Breathe deeply. Hold your head high. Walk in the fullness of your light. You are not here to hide—you are here to shine.

Meditative Prayer

Divine Ground of My Being,
Help me stand tall today.
Not above others,
But fully in my truth.

When I feel small,
Remind me of who I am.
When I feel unseen,
Shine Your light through me.

Let my soul rise in quiet strength,
Anchored in grace,
Rooted in love.
May I walk tall in spirit,
And move with peaceful power.

I am enough.
I am grounded.
I stand tall in You.

DAY 184:

Walking Boldly in Your Truth

Lesson for the Day

There is a sacred boldness that awakens when you choose to walk in your truth. It doesn't mean you have all the answers or never feel fear—it means you're willing to be honest with yourself and others about who you are, what you value, and what your soul knows to be real. Your truth is a light, and when you walk in it, you shine.

Boldness in truth doesn't need to be loud or confrontational. It can be quiet, steady, and rooted. It is found in living with integrity, setting boundaries with love, and expressing your authentic self without apology. When you walk in your truth, you align with the Divine, and life flows more freely.

Today, let your steps be guided by truth. Speak with sincerity, act with purpose, and live from your inner knowing. You don't need permission to be real. The world needs your truth more than your perfection. Walk boldly—you are being divinely supported every step of the way.

Meditative Prayer

Divine Voice of Truth,
Help me walk boldly in who I am.
Clear away the fear of being misunderstood,
And replace it with the peace of being real.

Where I've hidden my truth,
Give me the courage to speak.
Where I've softened my light,
Let me shine in full color.

May I walk with integrity,
Live with authenticity,
And honor the voice within.

I am not afraid to be true.
I am not afraid to be me.
I walk boldly in Your light.

DAY 185:
The Strength to Keep Going

Lesson for the Day

Some days, strength doesn't look like charging ahead—it looks like taking one steady breath, one small step, one quiet choice to not give up. The strength to keep going is sacred. It's not about never feeling tired or lost, it's about showing up anyway, trusting that even in your weariness, you are not alone.

The Divine meets you in those moments when you feel like you have nothing left and gently reminds you that there is more within you than you realize. You've made it through hard things before. You are not weak for needing rest. You are strong because you keep choosing to rise.

Today, honor your resilience. Even if the path feels slow or heavy, know that each step you take matters. Let the Divine refill your spirit and renew your courage. You have what it takes to continue—because you carry Divine strength within you.

Meditative Prayer

Divine Sustainer,
When I feel tired,
Be my rest.
When I feel weak,
Be my strength.

Help me keep going,
Even when the road feels long.
Remind me that I don't walk alone,
And that every step forward is enough.

Lift my spirit with Your presence,
And refill my heart with courage.
I may bend,
But I will not break.
I trust in Your strength within me.

Day 186:

Embracing Courage in Uncertainty

Lesson for the Day

Uncertainty is often the place where faith is stretched and courage is born. It's natural to want clarity, predictability, and control—but life asks us to grow through the unknown. Embracing courage in uncertainty means choosing to trust the journey, even when the next step is not yet revealed.

Courage doesn't mean you have no fear—it means you keep moving despite it. It's the quiet strength to show up, to stay open, and to believe that something meaningful is unfolding, even when the path ahead is blurry. In the space of uncertainty, the Divine is closer than ever, guiding each moment with care.

Today, choose courage. Take a breath and lean into trust. Let your heart be brave enough to remain soft, your soul bold enough to keep going, and your spirit strong enough to say, *I don't know what's next, but I know I'm held.*

Meditative Prayer

Divine Steadiness,
In the midst of uncertainty,
Anchor me in Your peace.
When I cannot see the way,
Give me the courage to trust.

Let fear fall away,
And let bold faith rise within me.
Help me embrace the unknown,
Knowing You are already there.

May I walk with a brave heart,
An open mind,
And a soul ready to grow.
I choose courage over fear,
And trust over control.

DAY 187:

Taking Inspired Action

Lesson for the Day

There are moments when your spirit nudges you—soft whispers from the Divine calling you to move, to create, to speak, or to begin. Taking inspired action means listening to those inner stirrings and allowing your steps to be led by purpose, not pressure. It's not about doing more—it's about doing what matters, what aligns, what awakens your soul.

Inspired action comes from a place of connection, not urgency. It is grounded in faith and guided by love. When you act from inspiration, you move in harmony with the Divine plan. Your efforts carry deeper meaning, and even small steps create sacred ripples.

Today, tune into the voice of your soul. What is calling you forward? What feels aligned, true, and lit with purpose? Then take one inspired step, no matter how small. You don't have to have it all figured out—you just have to begin.

Meditative Prayer

Divine Inspirer,
Awaken my heart to Your guidance.
Help me hear the quiet call,
And respond with courage and clarity.

Let my actions come from alignment,
Not from fear or force.
May every step I take
Be filled with purpose and peace.

Where I hesitate,
Give me confidence.
Where I feel unclear,
Shine light on the path ahead.

I am ready to move with You,
Led by love,
And rooted in truth.

DAY 188:

Trusting Your Inner Wisdom

Lesson for the Day

Within you is a deep well of wisdom—sacred knowing that comes not from books or voices around you, but from the Divine light that lives inside your soul. Trusting your inner wisdom means honoring your intuition, listening to your inner voice, and believing that the guidance you receive is worthy and true.

You are not separate from Divine truth—you are connected to it. That quiet nudge, that deep sense of knowing, the calm in your belly or the warmth in your chest—these are all ways your spirit speaks. When you slow down and listen, clarity comes not from outside noise, but from the quiet truth within.

Today, make space to hear yourself. Ask for Divine confirmation, then trust the guidance that flows from your center. You are wiser than you realize. When you honor that wisdom, you walk in alignment with your soul and the Divine.

Meditative Prayer

Divine Voice Within,
Help me trust the wisdom You've placed inside me.
Quiet the noise around me,
So I may hear the truth in my heart.

When I doubt myself,
Remind me that I am connected to You.
When I feel unsure,
Let Your peace confirm my direction.

Guide my thoughts,
Align my steps,
And strengthen my trust in what I know to be true.

I am wise.
I am led.
And I trust the sacred wisdom within me.

DAY 189:
The Power of Determination

Lesson for the Day

Determination is the quiet, steady fire that keeps you moving forward when things feel difficult. It's the sacred commitment to keep going—not because the path is easy, but because your heart knows it's worth it. Determination doesn't always roar, sometimes it whispers, *just one more step,* and that is enough to carry you through.

There is Divine strength behind your persistence. Each time you rise after a setback, keep showing up for your dreams, or stay faithful to your healing, you are honoring the power within you. Determination transforms small efforts into big breakthroughs over time. Trust that even when progress feels slow, it is still progress.

Today, reconnect with your why. Let your inner fire burn a little brighter. You were not given your dreams by accident—you were given the strength to follow through. Keep going. The Divine walks beside you with every determined step.

Meditative Prayer

Divine Strength,
Fuel my spirit with determination today.
When the path feels long,
Remind me why I began.

Help me rise with resolve,
And move with unwavering faith.
Let my heart stay strong,
Even when my body feels tired.

One step at a time,
One breath at a time,
I move forward with You.

My dreams are sacred.
My effort is enough.
And I am stronger than I know.

Day 190:
Bold Steps Toward Your Dreams

Lesson for the Day

Your dreams were planted in your heart for a reason. They are not random or unreachable—they are sacred invitations to step into the fullness of who you are. Taking bold steps toward your dreams means choosing courage over comfort and believing that the Divine is partnering with you in every moment of your becoming.

Boldness doesn't mean having all the answers. It means trusting enough to begin. It means moving forward even when the path is unclear, even when fear whispers you're not ready. Every bold step, no matter how small, sends a message to the universe. *I believe in what's possible.* That belief activates doors, connections, and divine support.

Today, take one bold step. Say yes to something that aligns with your soul. Speak your vision aloud. Share your light. The Divine is not asking you to be fearless—only to be faithful to what's calling you forward.

Meditative Prayer

Divine Dream-Giver,
Thank You for the visions You've placed in my heart.
Give me the courage to take bold steps,
Even when the way is unclear.

Quiet the voice of fear,
And strengthen the voice of trust.
Let me move in faith,
With joy, purpose, and divine support.

Guide my feet,
Inspire my spirit,
And remind me that I do not dream alone.

I walk boldly.
I move with intention.
And I rise into the life You've called me to live.

DAY 191:

Embracing the Warrior Spirit

Lesson for the Day

There is a warrior spirit within you—fierce, resilient, and deeply rooted in love. It is the part of you that rises after falling, speaks truth in the face of fear, and fights not with force, but with unwavering faith. Embracing the warrior spirit doesn't mean you're never afraid—it means you move forward anyway, anchored in divine strength.

The warrior spirit is not about aggression. It's about devotion to your soul's path, your healing, and your purpose. It's the strength to protect your peace, stand for what's right, and persevere through storms with grace. This spirit within you is sacred—it is the fire of your ancestors, the courage of your higher self, and the light of the Divine.

Today, call upon your inner warrior. Let it remind you of your strength, your power, and your ability to overcome. You were not made to live small—you were born to rise with honor, truth, and divine fire.

Meditative Prayer

Divine Warrior,
Awaken the strength within me.
Help me stand tall in truth,
And move with unwavering courage.

When I feel weak,
Be my shield.
When I face fear,
Be my fire.

Let my spirit fight with love,
Lead with light,
And rise with purpose.
I am not alone.
Your power flows through me.

I am strong.
I am fierce.
I walk with the heart of a warrior.

DAY 192:
The Sacred Balance of Strength and Surrender

Lesson for the Day

True power lies not in choosing only strength or only surrender—but in knowing when to hold on and when to let go. Strength is what keeps you grounded, showing up, and moving forward. Surrender is what allows grace to flow, wisdom to emerge, and divine timing to take root. Both are sacred. Both are necessary.

This balance is a dance between action and trust, between effort and rest. When you try to control everything, you miss the beauty of what is unfolding. When you give up too soon, you miss the opportunity to rise. But when you align both—when you bring your strength and then release the outcome to the Divine—miracles unfold.

Today, ask yourself, *Is this a moment to act, or a moment to let go?* Let your inner knowing guide you. In this balance, you find peace. In this balance, you become unstoppable in grace.

Meditative Prayer

Divine Balance,
Teach me when to be strong,
And when to surrender.

When I need to act,
Let me move with courage.
When I need to rest,
Let me release with trust.

Help me hold space for both,
For power and softness,
For direction and stillness.
Let me walk in harmony,
With You beside me always.

I do not walk alone.
I move in balance.
And I am held in sacred rhythm.

DAY 193:
Walking the Path of Purpose

Lesson for the Day

Your life is not an accident—there is purpose woven through every breath, every step, every moment of becoming. Walking the path of purpose means choosing to live with intention, to align your actions with your values, and to follow the call that stirs your soul, even when the way forward feels uncertain.

Purpose isn't always loud or grand. Sometimes it's found in quiet consistency, in loving those around you, in showing up fully where you are. Your purpose doesn't need to be proven—it needs to be lived. And the more you say yes to your truth, the more the Divine opens the road before you.

Today, walk forward with purpose in your heart. Ask yourself, *What lights me up? What feels aligned?* Then take one step in that direction. Trust that your path is unfolding as it should—and every step, no matter how small, is sacred.

Meditative Prayer

Divine Guide,

Thank You for the purpose You've placed within me.

Help me walk in alignment with that calling.

Let my steps be steady,

And my heart be clear.

When I feel lost,

Remind me that I am on holy ground.

When I doubt my path,

Shine light on what is true.

Let me live with intention,

Act with love,

And follow the quiet voice that leads me home.

I walk in purpose.

I walk in trust.

And I walk with You.

Day 194:
The Energy of Forward Motion

Lesson for the Day

There is sacred momentum in choosing to move forward—no matter how slowly, no matter how uncertain the path. The energy of forward motion doesn't require that you know the destination. It only asks that you trust the direction. Even one small step taken in faith can shift everything.

When you begin moving—emotionally, spiritually, or physically—you align yourself with transformation. Stagnation begins to break apart. Clarity begins to rise. The Divine meets you in motion, guiding and adjusting your course as you go. What matters is not how fast you move, but that you keep going with intention and grace.

Today, invite motion into your life. Shake off the weight of fear or perfectionism. Take one bold, honest step toward what feels right. The energy of forward motion is already within you, waiting to be awakened. Trust it. Follow it. Let it carry you forward.

Meditative Prayer

Divine Mover of My Soul,
Thank You for the momentum rising within me.
Guide my steps,
And give me the courage to move.

Even when the way is unclear,
Let me walk with faith.
Even when progress feels slow,
Let me trust the journey.

Break apart what keeps me stuck,
And awaken the flow of forward motion.
I don't need to know it all.
I just need to take the next step.

With You, I am moving.
With You, I am becoming.
With You, I am free.

DAY 195:
The Fire of Divine Passion

Lesson for the Day

Divine passion is the sacred flame that burns within your soul—the part of you that lights up when you're doing what you love, when you're aligned with your purpose, and when you're living fully from your spirit. This fire is not fueled by ego or ambition, but by a deep connection to the Divine and a desire to create, serve, and live with meaning.

When you honor your divine passion, you awaken something powerful within. Life begins to feel more vibrant, more purposeful. You stop just existing and start truly living. The fire of passion energizes you, draws others to your light, and inspires transformation not just in you—but around you.

Today, reconnect with your inner fire. What stirs your soul? What excites your heart? Give it space to burn bright. The Divine placed this fire within you for a reason—let it guide your steps, fuel your voice, and shape the life you are meant to live.

Meditative Prayer

Divine Flame,
Ignite the passion within me.
Let it burn with purpose,
With joy,
With sacred energy.

Where I've gone numb,
Wake me up.
Where I've lost connection,
Bring me home to what matters.

Help me live boldly,
Love deeply,
And create with Your fire in my soul.

This passion is holy.
This fire is mine to tend.
And I will burn bright for You.

DAY 196:

Owning Your Authentic Voice

Lesson for the Day

Your voice is sacred. It carries the truth of who you are, the wisdom you've lived, and the light you are here to share. Owning your authentic voice means speaking from the heart, not from fear. It means honoring your experience, trusting your intuition, and knowing that what you have to say matters.

There is power in vulnerability and strength in sincerity. When you speak from your soul, you inspire others to do the same. Your voice doesn't need to be loud to be impactful—it only needs to be true. The Divine speaks through you when you allow your voice to rise from a place of alignment and love.

Today, choose to express yourself clearly and boldly. Whether in a quiet conversation or a creative expression, let your voice reflect your truth. You don't need permission to be real—you were born to speak with purpose and presence.

Meditative Prayer

Divine Expression,
Awaken my voice today.
Let me speak with honesty,
With clarity,
With courage.

Where I've been silent,
Give me strength.
Where I've hidden my truth,
Bring it gently into the light.

Let my words carry wisdom,
And my voice reflect my soul.
I will not shrink.
I will not pretend.
I speak from love,
And I speak with You.

DAY 197:
Strength in Every Challenge

Lesson for the Day

Every challenge you face carries within it the opportunity to uncover your strength. While it may not feel like it in the moment, each trial is an invitation to rise, to grow, and to become more grounded in your truth. Strength isn't the absence of struggle—it is the grace with which you move through it.

You have already overcome so much. The strength that got you here will carry you forward. Challenges do not define your worth—they reveal your resilience. And through every difficulty, the Divine is not testing you, but walking with you, whispering, *You are stronger than you know.*

Today, stand in the quiet confidence that you are equipped for whatever comes your way. You don't have to face it alone. Your strength is sacred, supported by the Divine, and forged in love.

Meditative Prayer

Divine Strength,
Be with me in every challenge.
Remind me that I am never alone,
Even when the road is hard.

Let my heart stay steady,
And my soul stay strong.
Where I feel overwhelmed,
Breathe peace into my spirit.

Thank You for the strength within me.
Not born from force,
But from faith.
I rise with courage.
I move with grace.
And I walk through every challenge
Held in Your hands.

DAY 198:
Choosing Action Over Fear

Lesson for the Day

Fear often shows up when you're on the edge of something meaningful. It whispers doubts, fuels hesitation, and tries to convince you to stay small. But you have another choice—a more powerful one, action. Every time you take a step forward, no matter how small, you reclaim your power from fear.

Action doesn't require the absence of fear—it simply asks for willingness. When you move forward in faith, you tell the fear it doesn't get to lead your life. Each act of courage builds momentum, clarity, and trust. The Divine doesn't ask you to be fearless, only faithful.

Today, choose one action that moves you closer to what matters. It might be a bold leap or a gentle nudge forward—but let it be yours. Let action be your prayer, your courage, and your response to fear.

Meditative Prayer

Divine Courage,
Thank You for the strength to act,
Even when fear is present.
Help me choose movement,
Over hesitation.

Let each step I take
Be rooted in trust,
Not fear.
Where I feel stuck,
Set me free with clarity and peace.

Let my actions align with truth,
And reflect the light within me.
I move with purpose.
I rise in courage.
And I am not led by fear.

DAY 199:
Finding Strength in Your Struggles

Lesson for the Day

Struggles are not signs of weakness—they are places where your strength is being refined, deepened, and revealed. Every challenge you face holds within it a lesson, a breakthrough, and an opportunity to rise stronger than before. The pain you endure is not in vain. It becomes the soil where resilience and wisdom take root.

You may not always understand why a struggle appears, but you can trust that the Divine is present within it, walking beside you. Strength is not about always holding it together—it's about allowing yourself to grow through the discomfort, to feel fully, and to continue forward with grace.

Today, instead of resenting your struggles, honor them. Look for the strength they've awakened in you. You are not being broken—you are being shaped, empowered, and prepared for what's next. Trust in your becoming.

Meditative Prayer

Divine Presence in My Pain,
Thank You for being with me in every struggle.
Help me see the strength growing within me,
Even when the way is hard.

When I feel weary,
Renew my spirit.
When I feel lost,
Guide me with love.

Let my challenges become my teachers,
And my pain become my power.
I trust that nothing is wasted,
And everything is being transformed for good.

I am growing.
I am rising.
And I am stronger than I've ever been.

DAY 200:

Moving with Intention

Lesson for the Day

Living with intention means moving through life with awareness, clarity, and purpose. Instead of rushing, reacting, or running on autopilot, you choose to align your actions with your values. Each step becomes a reflection of your inner truth. Every decision becomes a conscious offering to your highest self and the Divine.

Intentional movement is powerful. It doesn't always mean doing more—it means doing what matters. It invites you to pause, reflect, and act from a place of centered wisdom. When you move with intention, life becomes more meaningful, your energy becomes more focused, and your path becomes more aligned.

Today, choose to move with purpose. Whether it's in your words, your work, or your rest, let your actions reflect what truly matters to you. The Divine meets you in these sacred, mindful moments— where intention and grace become one.

Meditative Prayer

Divine Guide,
Help me move with intention today.
Let my steps be mindful,
And my choices aligned with truth.

Clear the noise that distracts me,
And awaken my awareness
To what matters most.

May my actions reflect my soul,
And my energy flow with purpose.
I walk not to chase,
But to create,
To honor,
To become.

With You, I move with meaning.
With You, I live with light.

Day 201:

Rising with Unshakable Faith

Lesson for the Day

There will be times when the ground beneath you feels unsteady—when answers are unclear and the future feels uncertain. But even then, you can rise. Not by your own strength alone, but through unshakable faith—the deep, unwavering trust that the Divine is holding you, guiding you, and carrying you forward through it all.

Unshakable faith doesn't mean you never doubt or feel fear. It means you choose to believe anyway. It means your roots go deep into the soil of truth, where storms may bend you but never break you. This faith is your anchor, your compass, your flame that keeps burning through the night.

Today, rise with that kind of faith. Let it lift your head, steady your step, and remind you that no matter what you face, you are never alone. You are upheld by something greater—and nothing can shake what is grounded in the Divine.

Meditative Prayer

Divine Anchor,
When the winds of life blow strong,
Let me rise with unshakable faith.
When I cannot see the way,
Let me trust in Your presence.

Root me in Your truth,
Steady me in Your love,
And lift me with Your strength.

Even when I feel afraid,
Let my spirit believe.
Even when I don't understand,
Let my soul remain sure.

I rise in faith.
I walk in trust.
And I stand unshaken,
Held by You.

DAY 202:

A Heart on Fire with Purpose

Lesson for the Day

There is nothing more powerful than a heart lit by purpose—a deep inner knowing that you are here for a reason and that your life is meant to make a difference. When you awaken to your purpose, you move through life with clarity, courage, and conviction. This fire within doesn't burn you out—it fuels you. It energizes your spirit and aligns you with the Divine.

A purposeful heart doesn't need to be loud or flashy. It's found in the quiet commitment to live with meaning, to love with intention, and to show up fully. Your purpose may evolve, but the fire stays lit when you nurture it with trust, faith, and love. You are not aimless—you are being led.

Today, reconnect with what sets your soul ablaze. What brings you alive? What feels sacred and true? Let your purpose guide your words, your steps, and your energy. You were made to burn bright—for yourself and for the world.

Meditative Prayer

Divine Flame of Purpose,
Light my heart again today.
Let passion rise where fear once lived,
And clarity replace confusion.

Show me what matters most,
And guide me to live it fully.
Keep my spirit aligned with Your will,
And my actions rooted in meaning.

Let this fire within me burn with love,
With faith,
With sacred direction.

I am here on purpose.
I live with intention.
And I shine with Your divine light.

DAY 203:
Facing Obstacles with Confidence

Lesson for the Day

Obstacles are not signs that you're on the wrong path—they're often the very things that shape you into who you're becoming. Facing obstacles with confidence doesn't mean you never struggle or question—it means you trust yourself and the Divine enough to know you can overcome whatever stands before you.

Confidence isn't about having all the answers. It's about carrying a calm inner knowing that you are equipped, supported, and not alone. When you meet challenges with faith and presence, you begin to see them as stepping stones rather than roadblocks. Every obstacle is an opportunity to grow stronger, deeper, and more aligned.

Today, face what's in front of you with courage. You have overcome before—and you will again. Let confidence rise from within, not from your circumstances, but from your connection to Divine strength. You've got this. And even more, you're guided through it.

Meditative Prayer

Divine Strength Within Me,
Help me face today's challenges with courage.
Let confidence rise like a river in my soul.
Not from pride,
But from deep trust in You.

Where I feel uncertain,
Remind me I am capable.
Where the road feels blocked,
Show me the way through.

Thank You for the wisdom hidden in every challenge,
And the strength You've placed in me to rise.
With You, no obstacle is greater than my purpose.

I walk forward.
I stand strong.
And I meet this moment with faith.

Day 204:

Turning Pain into Power

Lesson for the Day

Pain is a sacred teacher—it softens, shapes, and strengthens you in ways nothing else can. While you may not choose your pain, you can choose what you do with it. Turning pain into power is not about pretending it didn't hurt. It's about transforming it into wisdom, compassion, and courage that you carry forward with grace.

Within every wound lies an opportunity for awakening. The Divine doesn't waste your sorrow—it becomes the soil in which resilience grows. The tears you've cried water the seeds of deeper purpose. And slowly, the very thing that once broke you becomes the source of your becoming.

Today, honor your pain. Don't run from it—listen to what it's taught you. Then rise. Let your story be one of healing, strength, and transformation. You are not defined by what hurt you—you are empowered by how you've risen from it.

Meditative Prayer

Divine Healer,
Thank You for being with me in my pain.
Help me transform what hurt me
Into something holy and strong.

Let the lessons I've learned
Become light for my path.
Let the wounds I've carried
Become wisdom in my soul.

I release bitterness,
And I choose healing.
I release despair,
And I choose power.

With You,
My pain becomes purpose,
And my story becomes strength.

DAY 205:

Strengthen the Spirit Within

Lesson for the Day

Your outer world may shift and shake, but your inner spirit can remain grounded, steady, and strong. Strengthening the spirit within means returning to the practices, truths, and presence that anchor you no matter what life brings. It's about building resilience from the inside out—layer by layer, breath by breath, prayer by prayer.

When your spirit is strong, you respond to life with grace instead of reactivity. You walk through uncertainty with trust, and you hold peace in the midst of pressure. Strengthening your spirit isn't about being unaffected—it's about being deeply rooted in the Divine, so you are never easily moved.

Today, take time to nourish your spirit. Breathe, reflect, pray, and reconnect to your soul. The more you tend to your inner strength, the more powerfully you can move through the world. You are not just surviving—you are becoming unshakable.

Meditative Prayer

Divine Strength,
Build me from the inside out.
Let my spirit grow strong and steady,
Rooted in truth,
Anchored in love.

Where I feel fragile,
Pour in Your peace.
Where I feel empty,
Fill me with Your presence.

Help me rise with quiet power,
Face life with grace,
And move with unbreakable faith.

My strength is not just mine,
It is Yours within me.
I stand firm,
I stand whole,
I stand held.

DAY 206:

Becoming a Beacon of Light

Lesson for the Day

You were not made to hide your light—you were created to shine. Becoming a beacon of light means allowing your life to radiate love, truth, and peace. It's not about being perfect or always having it all together. It's about choosing to live with openness, compassion, and integrity so that others feel safe, seen, and inspired in your presence.

Your light can guide others without even trying—simply by being who you are. Every time you lead with kindness, speak with truth, and show up with grace, you become a reflection of the Divine. The world doesn't need more noise—it needs more light. And your light has the power to illuminate dark places, both within and around you.

Today, let your light shine without fear. Be a presence of hope, a voice of encouragement, a reminder of love. The brighter you shine, the more you help others find their own light too.

Meditative Prayer

Divine Light,
Shine through me today.
Let my words carry hope,
And my actions reflect Your love.

Where there is darkness,
Let me bring clarity.
Where there is heaviness,
Let me offer peace.

Help me to live openly,
To love boldly,
And to be a light in this world.

I am not afraid to shine.
I am not afraid to lead with love.
Make me a beacon of Your presence,
Wherever I go.

DAY 207:

Walking with the Energy of the Sun

Lesson for the Day

The sun rises each day without hesitation—radiating warmth, light, and life. To walk with the energy of the sun is to move through life with confidence, clarity, and purpose. It means carrying light within you, even when clouds gather, and shining your truth no matter the circumstances around you.

This energy isn't about constant brightness—it's about being steady, present, and strong. It's the joy that radiates from a grateful heart, the fire that fuels your passion, and the glow that comes from walking in alignment with your soul. The sun does not ask permission to shine, and neither should you.

Today, embody the sun's energy. Rise with hope. Move with warmth. Speak with clarity. Let your light illuminate your path and the paths of others. The Divine has placed this radiant power within you—let it shine through everything you do.

Meditative Prayer

Radiant Creator,
Fill me with the energy of the sun today.
Let me rise with confidence,
And shine with purpose.

Where there is doubt,
Bring clarity.
Where there is fear,
Bring light.

Help me move with joy,
Speak with love,
And live with radiant truth.

I am a reflection of Your brilliance.
I am warmth.
I am light.
I am here to shine.

DAY 208:

Trusting the Power Within You

Lesson for the Day

There is a deep, sacred power that lives within you—a quiet strength that comes from your connection to the Divine. Trusting the power within doesn't mean you always feel certain or fearless, it means you choose to believe in your inner wisdom, resilience, and ability to rise, even when the path feels unclear.

You were created with purpose. The same energy that moves the stars flows through your soul. When you trust the power within, you stop looking outside yourself for validation and begin moving in alignment with the truth already planted in your heart. You begin to live from the inside out.

Today, trust that what you need is already inside you. Breathe deeply, listen inwardly, and step forward boldly. The Divine lives in you—not just around you—and that is where your greatest strength begins.

Meditative Prayer

Divine Source Within Me,
Help me trust the power You've placed in my soul.
When I doubt,
Remind me of who I am.

Let me move with confidence,
Not from ego,
But from sacred truth.

Awaken my gifts,
Strengthen my spirit,
And guide me from within.

I trust my voice.
I trust my knowing.
I trust the light that lives inside of me.

DAY 209:
The Sacred Power of Commitment

Lesson for the Day

Commitment is more than discipline—it is a sacred devotion to something greater than convenience. Whether it's your healing, your growth, your purpose, or your relationship with the Divine, commitment holds the power to transform your life. It anchors you when the path feels long and fuels your journey when motivation fades.

The sacred power of commitment doesn't come from striving—it comes from love. When you commit to what matters most, you align your heart with your actions. You choose to show up again and again, even when it's hard. That consistency becomes a spiritual practice, a devotion, and a declaration of faith in yourself and your calling.

Today, recommit to what your soul knows is true. Even if your steps have wavered, you can begin again. Commitment isn't perfection—it's presence, devotion, and the choice to keep saying yes to what matters.

Meditative Prayer

Divine Keeper of Promises,
Strengthen my spirit today
As I commit to the path before me.
Let my heart be steady,
My focus be clear,
And my steps be true.

Where I've wavered,
Lead me back.
Where I've grown weary,
Renew my devotion.

Help me stay faithful to my growth,
To my calling,
And to You.

I commit not out of pressure,
But from love.
And in that love,
I find power.

DAY 210:

Embracing the Fullness of Life

Lesson for the Day

Life is not meant to be experienced halfway. To embrace the fullness of life is to open your heart wide to all of it—the joy and the sorrow, the beauty and the mess, the stillness and the movement. Every moment carries a lesson, every breath a chance to begin again, and every experience an invitation to awaken more deeply to your soul's journey.

You don't need to wait for things to be perfect to live fully. You only need to be present, willing, and open. The Divine meets you in the rawness of real life—not just in your best moments, but in all moments. When you choose to engage life fully, you step into a sacred partnership with the world around you and the spirit within you.

Today, let yourself feel it all. Laugh. Cry. Reflect. Rejoice. Be fully here. The richness of life is not in escaping the hard parts but in embracing the truth that *all of it* belongs. You are here to live deeply, not just exist.

Meditative Prayer

Divine Life-Giver,
Thank You for the fullness of this life.
Help me receive it all,
The beauty, the lessons, the mystery.

Open my heart to this moment,
And let me be fully alive within it.
Where I hold back,
Let me lean in.

Let me dance in joy,
Stand in truth,
And feel every sacred breath.

I embrace this life,
Unfiltered, whole, and holy.
And I give thanks for every part of it.

DAY 211:

The Glow of a Joyful Heart

Lesson for the Day

Joy is more than a fleeting emotion—it is a radiant energy that flows from a heart aligned with love, gratitude, and presence. A joyful heart doesn't mean you're always smiling or untouched by hardship. It means you've chosen to let light live within you, regardless of what's happening around you.

The glow of a joyful heart is magnetic. It uplifts others, softens heavy moments, and reminds the world that beauty and hope still exist. Joy is sacred—it is a reflection of the Divine within you. When you nurture it, you not only heal yourself, you bless those around you.

Today, make room for joy. Let yourself laugh, play, breathe deeply, and savor the little things. Joy doesn't need a reason—it only needs your permission. And when your heart glows with joy, the world shines a little brighter too.

Meditative Prayer

Divine Joy,
Fill my heart with Your radiant light.
Let joy rise in me today,
Not because everything is perfect,
But because You are present.

Help me see beauty in the simple,
Wonder in the ordinary,
And delight in the now.

Where heaviness lingers,
Bring lightness.
Where sorrow lives,
Let joy grow gently beside it.

I welcome joy.
I share joy.
And I glow from the inside out.

DAY 212:

Becoming a Light in the World

Lesson for the Day

You were created to shine—not just for yourself, but for others walking through the dark. Becoming a light in the world means showing up with love, compassion, and truth in a way that uplifts, encourages, and inspires. It's not about being perfect—it's about being present, honest, and rooted in Divine love.

Your light might be the comfort someone else needs, the kindness that changes a heart, or the quiet presence that brings peace. Never underestimate the impact of simply being who you are when you lead with love. Light doesn't demand attention—it simply reveals what's true and possible.

Today, choose to be a light. Speak with kindness. Listen with care. Serve with joy. Whether you touch one person or many, know that the Divine shines through you. The world needs your light—and it grows brighter each time you choose to share it.

Meditative Prayer

Divine Light of the World,
Shine through me today.
Let my words bring comfort,
And my presence carry peace.

Where there is darkness,
Let me bring hope.
Where there is pain,
Let me carry compassion.

I offer my heart to You,
As a vessel of love,
A source of light,
And a reflection of Your grace.

I am not here by accident.
I am here to shine.
And I choose to be a light in this world.

DAY 213:

The Power of a Grateful Spirit

Lesson for the Day

Gratitude is one of the most powerful energies you can embody. A grateful spirit shifts your perspective, softens your heart, and opens you to the beauty of the present moment. It doesn't erase pain or difficulty, but it transforms how you carry them—turning burdens into blessings and moments into miracles.

When you lead with gratitude, you begin to see life not through lack, but through abundance. You recognize the gifts woven into the ordinary and the Divine presence in all things. Gratitude is not just a response to goodness—it's a way of creating more of it.

Today, choose to walk with a grateful spirit. Give thanks for what is, even as you hope for what's to come. Let gratitude be your grounding and your guide. It has the power to change your heart—and through you, the world.

Meditative Prayer

Divine Giver of All,
Thank You for this day,
For breath, for beauty,
For every quiet blessing.

Let my heart stay open
To the gifts all around me.
Teach me to see with eyes of wonder,
And to love with a grateful spirit.

Where I have focused on what's missing,
Help me see what is abundant.
Where I have felt empty,
Fill me with appreciation.

May gratitude rise in me like sunlight,
Warming every part of my life.
I receive this day with joy.

DAY 214:

Radiating Love Wherever You Go

Lesson for the Day

Love is your most powerful gift—and your greatest purpose. When you choose to radiate love wherever you go, you become a walking blessing. Your presence brings peace, your words offer comfort, and your energy creates a ripple of kindness that reaches farther than you may ever know.

Radiating love doesn't mean you never feel tired or frustrated. It means you return to love again and again, letting it guide your choices, your actions, and your perspective. Love is not just a feeling—it's a force. One that can soften hearts, heal wounds, and transform the spaces you enter.

Today, let love flow from you effortlessly and sincerely. Smile at a stranger, speak gently, extend compassion, and forgive freely. You are here to love—and the world is brighter when you do.

Meditative Prayer

Divine Source of Love,
Fill me so fully with Your presence
That love overflows from my heart.

Let every word I speak
Be rooted in compassion.
Let every step I take
Be guided by kindness.

Where there is tension,
Let me bring peace.
Where there is hurt,
Let me offer healing.

I choose to be a vessel of Your love,
To radiate warmth, truth, and grace
Wherever I go.

Let my presence be a blessing today.

DAY 215:
Seeing the Beauty in Every Moment

Lesson for the Day

Life is made up of countless moments, and each one holds a quiet kind of beauty. It might be the way the light filters through the window, the sound of a loved one's laughter, or the stillness that comes just before you fall asleep. When you slow down and look with your heart, you begin to see that beauty is not rare—it is everywhere.

Seeing the beauty in every moment doesn't mean life is always easy or pain-free. It means choosing to be present, to notice, and to appreciate the sacred hidden in the ordinary. It's a practice of the soul—one that softens your spirit, opens your heart, and connects you to the Divine in all things.

Today, pause and look around you. Take a breath. Find beauty in the simple, in the silent, in the in-between. When you open your eyes to it, you realize it was never far—it was always right here, waiting to be seen.

Meditative Prayer

Divine Artist,

Help me see the beauty You've placed all around me.

Open my eyes to wonder,

And my heart to appreciation.

Let me not rush past the sacred,

Or miss the miracles in the mundane.

Slow me down,

And wake me up to this moment.

May I find You in the quiet details,

In the light, in the laughter,

In the breath of now.

I choose to see beauty.

I choose to honor it.

And I give thanks for the gift of every moment.

Day 216:

Choosing Joy Daily

Lesson for the Day

Joy is not something you wait for—it's something you choose, nurture, and return to again and again. It lives in your heart, not your circumstances. Choosing joy daily is a spiritual decision to embrace what is good, to celebrate what is simple, and to let the light within you rise regardless of what life looks like on the outside.

Joy doesn't ignore pain—it coexists with it. It is the gentle reminder that even in hardship, beauty can still be found. The Divine delights in your joy, and when you choose it intentionally, you align with the very essence of creation. That is light, love, and life.

Today, choose joy—not because everything is perfect, but because your soul deserves light. Laugh freely, notice the blessings, and let gratitude open the door to joy again. It is your birthright, your gift, and your power.

Meditative Prayer

Joyful Creator,
Help me choose joy today.
Let it rise within me like the sun,
Warming every part of my soul.

Even when life feels heavy,
Let joy be my strength.
Even when things are unclear,
Let joy be my compass.

May I smile easily,
Laugh often,
And celebrate the simple gifts.

Thank You for the joy that lives within me.
I choose to feel it,
Share it,
And live in it,
Today and always.

DAY 217:
The Lightness of an Open Heart

Lesson for the Day

An open heart carries a sacred kind of lightness—a freedom born from trust, compassion, and the willingness to feel deeply. When your heart is open, you allow life to move through you rather than weigh you down. You stop guarding yourself against love and begin receiving the fullness of what the Divine has to offer.

Opening your heart doesn't mean letting in everything without boundaries. It means choosing to remain soft in a world that often asks you to harden. It means staying available to joy, to connection, to growth—even when you've been hurt. That kind of openness is brave. That kind of openness is healing.

Today, breathe into your heart. Let go of what you've been clinging to in fear. Trust that it's safe to open, safe to feel, and safe to love. There is a lightness waiting on the other side of release—a Divine ease that fills you when your heart is wide and free.

Meditative Prayer

Divine Heart of Love,
Help me open my heart today.
Where I've built walls,
Let Your grace gently dissolve them.

Teach me to remain soft,
Even in moments of pain.
Teach me to trust love,
Even when it feels vulnerable.

Fill me with lightness,
With ease,
With the sacred freedom of openness.

Let me live with a heart unburdened,
A spirit unguarded,
And a soul that says yes to love.

DAY 218:

Living in the Spirit of Gratitude

Lesson for the Day

Gratitude is more than a moment of thanks—it's a way of life. Living in the spirit of gratitude means choosing to see each day as a gift, each breath as sacred, and each experience as part of your growth. It's an active awareness that reminds your soul, *there is always something to be thankful for.*

When you embody gratitude, your perspective shifts. You stop focusing on what's missing and start recognizing the abundance already present. Even in difficulty, gratitude grounds you in the truth that you are supported, seen, and never alone. It keeps your heart open and your spirit aligned with the Divine.

Today, let gratitude guide your words, shape your thoughts, and soften your actions. Speak thanks aloud. Notice the small blessings. Write them down. Feel them deeply. Gratitude is a quiet miracle— and when you live in it, you become one too.

Meditative Prayer

Divine Giver of Every Good Thing,
Let me live in the spirit of gratitude today.
Open my eyes to what is beautiful,
And my heart to what is true.

Help me give thanks,
Not just in moments of joy,
But also in seasons of challenge.

Let my gratitude be a prayer,
A way of walking,
A way of being.

Thank You for the breath I breathe,
The lessons I learn,
And the love that surrounds me.

I live in appreciation,
I speak with praise,
And I walk with a grateful heart.

Day 219:
The Energy of Pure Love

Lesson for the Day

Pure love is the highest vibration in the universe. It is healing, unifying, and limitless. It doesn't judge, possess, or expect—it simply *is*. When you connect to the energy of pure love, you align yourself with the Divine essence that flows through all things. You become a vessel of peace, kindness, and grace.

This love begins within. It starts with accepting yourself fully—your light and your shadows—and then extending that same compassion to others. Pure love isn't about perfection. It's about presence. It's the energy that holds space, softens pain, and says, *you are worthy just as you are.*

Today, breathe into the energy of pure love. Feel it radiate through your heart, your words, your actions. Let it touch everything you do. You are made of love, held in love, and here to share love. Let that truth guide you.

Meditative Prayer

Divine Love,
Let me embody Your pure and endless grace.
Wash away judgment,
And fill me with compassion.

Help me love myself as I am,
And love others without condition.
Let every thought be rooted in kindness,
Every word carry peace.

May I see through eyes of love,
Speak with the voice of love,
And move with the heart of love.

I am made of love.
I return to love.
And I offer love freely to the world.

DAY 220:
The Abundance Found in Thankfulness

Lesson for the Day

True abundance is not measured by what you possess, but by how deeply you appreciate what you already have. Thankfulness opens the door to that abundance. When you live with a grateful heart, you begin to see blessings where you once saw lack, and miracles in places you might have overlooked.

Gratitude is a magnet for more beauty, more joy, and more clarity. It shifts your focus from scarcity to sufficiency, reminding you that *this moment* holds more than enough. The more you give thanks, the more the Divine flows into your life—not because you are earning it, but because your heart is open to receive.

Today, lean into thankfulness. Let it overflow in your words and ripple through your actions. The more you say *thank you,* the more you realize how rich your life already is. Gratitude is not the end of abundance—it is the beginning.

Meditative Prayer

Generous Creator,
Thank You for all that I have,
And all that I am becoming.

Let my heart overflow with gratitude,
So I may see the richness in every breath.
Help me release thoughts of lack,
And embrace the fullness of this life.

With each *thank you,*
Open my heart a little wider.
With each act of appreciation,
Draw me closer to Your abundant grace.

I am surrounded by blessings.
I am filled with joy.
And I live in the abundance of thankfulness.

DAY 221:

Your Heart as a Reflection of the Divine

Lesson for the Day

Your heart is more than the center of your emotions—it is a sacred vessel, a mirror of the Divine within you. When you live from your heart, you reflect love, compassion, wisdom, and grace into the world. You become a living expression of the Divine's presence— offering light in the way you speak, give, and simply exist.

The more you soften into your heart space, the more you realize that you are not separate from the Divine—you are a part of it. Your heart carries its essence. It knows how to love unconditionally, how to forgive deeply, and how to guide you with clarity and truth.

Today, turn inward and honor your heart. Let it lead. Let it speak. Let it remind you of who you truly are: a radiant reflection of something holy, beautiful, and endlessly loving.

Meditative Prayer

Sacred Heart of the Divine,
Let my heart be a reflection of You.
Fill it with Your love,
Your wisdom,
Your peace.

Teach me to lead with compassion,
To speak with kindness,
And to live with sincerity.

When I forget my sacred nature,
Call me back to my heart.
When I feel lost,
Let love guide me home.

I am a mirror of Your light.
I am a vessel of Your grace.
And I choose to live from my heart today.

Day 222:

Living with Overflowing Gratitude

Lesson for the Day

Gratitude isn't just a moment of thanks—it's a way of being, a way of seeing, a way of living. When gratitude overflows from your heart, it touches everything around you. You begin to move through life with wonder, reverence, and joy. Even ordinary moments become sacred when you meet them with appreciation.

Living with overflowing gratitude means allowing thankfulness to pour into your relationships, your work, your words, and your choices. It changes the energy you carry and the energy you give. The more you thank life, the more life opens its arms to you.

Today, don't just count your blessings—*become one*. Let your gratitude move beyond thought and into action. Give, share, serve, speak love, and honor the Divine by appreciating the fullness of what already is.

Meditative Prayer

Divine Giver of Every Blessing,
Let my heart overflow with gratitude today.
Not just for what I have,
But for who I am,
And who I am becoming.

Let every breath be a thank you.
Let every word carry appreciation.
Let my life become a prayer of praise.

Help me live in awareness of Your gifts,
And share my abundance freely.
I am grateful for this life,
This love,
This sacred moment.

Thank You,
Thank You,
Thank You.

DAY 223:
The Light That Shines From Within

Lesson for the Day

There is a light within you that is eternal, unshakable, and divinely inspired. It is not dependent on circumstances or the approval of others. It is the essence of who you are—pure, radiant, and connected to the heart of the Divine. This light is your truth, your joy, your sacred fire.

When you live from that inner light, you become a source of hope, peace, and clarity for yourself and those around you. Even when the world feels heavy, your light remains. It doesn't have to be loud or dazzling to be powerful—it simply needs to be *true*.

Today, return to the light within. Nourish it with quiet, kindness, prayer, and presence. Trust that your light is enough. Let it guide you, heal you, and gently illuminate the path for others.

Meditative Prayer

Divine Light Within Me,
Help me remember the glow I carry inside.
When the world feels dim,
Let my soul shine brighter.

Clear away doubt,
And fan the flame of truth and peace.
Let my inner light be steady,
Even when all around me shifts.

May I walk as a light-bearer today,
Radiating love,
Kindness,
And clarity.

I am filled with light.
I am guided by light.
And I am here to shine.

DAY 224:
Embracing the Gift of the Present

Lesson for the Day

The present moment is a sacred gift—soft, fleeting, and full of quiet miracles. When you are truly present, you begin to experience life as it is, not as it was or might be. You stop rushing toward the future or dwelling in the past and instead discover the beauty and depth of *now*.

To embrace the present is to breathe deeply, notice the details, and allow yourself to fully be. This is where peace lives. This is where the Divine meets you. In this still point, where nothing else is required, you are enough, and life is already full.

Today, release the need to be anywhere else. Come home to this moment. Let it nourish you, ground you, and awaken you to the wonder that's been here all along.

Meditative Prayer

Divine Presence,
Thank You for the gift of this moment.
Help me slow down,
And be fully here.

Quiet my thoughts of yesterday,
Calm my worries for tomorrow,
And center me in the peace of now.

Let me feel the breath in my body,
The love that surrounds me,
And the light that lives within me.

This moment is enough.
I am enough.
And I meet You here,
In the sacred now.

Day 225:
The Healing Power of Joy

Lesson for the Day

Joy is more than happiness—it's a deep, soul-level energy that brings lightness, hope, and healing. It doesn't deny pain or ignore sorrow, it exists alongside them, offering balance and reminding you that beauty still lives here. Joy lifts the spirit, opens the heart, and invites healing where heaviness has lingered.

When you welcome joy, even in small doses, you create space for your spirit to breathe. A laugh, a smile, a song, a moment of delight—these are not distractions from your healing journey, they *are* part of the healing. Joy reminds you of your aliveness, your wholeness, and your connection to the Divine.

Today, let joy in. Let it be your medicine, your warmth, your sacred yes to life. Healing doesn't always look like rest or tears—sometimes, it looks like dancing, laughter, and feeling the sun on your skin. Let joy heal you from the inside out.

Meditative Prayer

Divine Joy,
Thank You for the healing power of laughter and light.
Let joy rise within me today,
Soft and bright like morning sun.

Heal the weary places in me
With gentle moments of delight.
Let me laugh freely,
Smile easily,
And receive joy without guilt or fear.

May my joy be holy.
May it renew my spirit.
And may I remember
That joy is not a luxury,
It is a gift of healing and grace.

DAY 226:

Choosing Love in Every Circumstance

Lesson for the Day

Love is the highest choice you can make—and the most powerful. To choose love in every circumstance doesn't mean ignoring boundaries or avoiding hard truths. It means leading with compassion, responding with grace, and holding space for peace even in moments of tension or pain. Love is not weakness—it is strength in its purest form.

Every moment gives you an opportunity to respond from fear or from love. When you choose love, you elevate the energy in the room, shift your own heart, and invite healing where hurt might otherwise grow. The Divine is love—and when you choose it, you align yourself with that sacred energy.

Today, no matter what you face, ask yourself, *What would love do here?* Let that answer guide your words, your thoughts, and your presence. Love is always an option—and it is always enough.

Meditative Prayer

Divine Love,
Help me choose love today.
In my words,
In my actions,
In every silent thought.

When I am tempted to judge,
Let me choose grace.
When I feel hurt,
Let me respond with peace.

Let love be my compass,
My strength,
My offering.
May every circumstance
Be touched by the light of love
Flowing through me.

I choose love.
Again and again.

DAY 227:
Finding Happiness in Simplicity

Lesson for the Day

True happiness often lives in the simplest moments—the quiet cup of tea, the sound of birdsong, the laughter shared between loved ones, the warmth of sunlight on your skin. In a world that constantly calls you to do more, be more, and have more, simplicity offers a return to what truly matters.

When you choose simplicity, you make space for peace. You begin to notice the richness in the present, the beauty in the small, and the joy that doesn't need to be chased. Happiness rooted in simplicity is sustainable, grounding, and deeply nourishing for the soul.

Today, slow down. Let go of the need to impress or accumulate. Instead, appreciate what is already around and within you. In that stillness, you'll find that happiness was never far—it was quietly waiting for your attention.

Meditative Prayer

Divine Simplicity,
Help me find joy in the small and sacred.
Clear the clutter in my mind and heart,
So I may see the beauty already here.

Let me rest in the quiet,
Appreciate the ordinary,
And celebrate the little gifts that fill my day.

Where I seek more,
Remind me I have enough.
Where I rush,
Teach me to pause.

Thank You for the happiness
That lives in simplicity.
I receive it with gratitude,
And I carry it gently.

DAY 228:

Gratitude as a Path to Peace

Lesson for the Day

Gratitude is more than a moment—it's a practice, a perspective, and a sacred path that leads you gently back to peace. When you focus on what you're thankful for, your spirit softens, your mind quiets, and your heart opens. In gratitude, you stop resisting life and begin receiving it.

Peace isn't found in having everything figured out—it's found in appreciating what is, right here, right now. Gratitude grounds you. It reminds you that even in uncertainty, there is still goodness. Even in sorrow, there is still light. And even in waiting, there is still wonder.

Today, let gratitude guide you to peace. Take a breath. Say *thank you* for something simple, something sacred. Let that thankfulness fill your spirit and clear the noise. In that space, peace will find you.

Meditative Prayer

Divine Source of Peace,
Thank You for this breath,
This moment,
This life.

Let my heart open wide in gratitude,
So peace may fill the empty places.
Teach me to notice the blessings,
Even when they're quiet.

Where there is chaos,
Let thankfulness steady me.
Where there is doubt,
Let gratitude ground me.

I choose to walk the path of peace,
One grateful step at a time.

Day 229:
The Power of a Thankful Heart

Lesson for the Day

A thankful heart is a powerful force—it shifts your focus, renews your spirit, and transforms even the most ordinary moments into something sacred. When your heart is filled with gratitude, you carry a lightness that no challenge can dim and a clarity that lifts you above fear and doubt.

Gratitude doesn't mean you ignore what's hard. It means you choose to honor what is good, even in the midst of what's difficult. A thankful heart becomes a sanctuary of peace, resilience, and love. It makes room for miracles, attracts abundance, and opens your life to grace.

Today, nurture the power of thankfulness. Let it be your prayer, your posture, and your presence. Speak it. Write it. Live it. A heart that gives thanks is a heart that changes the world—quietly, lovingly, and powerfully.

Meditative Prayer

Divine Giver of All Good Things,
Fill my heart with thankfulness.
Let gratitude rise in me
Like the morning sun.

When I feel weary,
Remind me of my blessings.
When I feel lost,
Anchor me in what is already good.

Let thankfulness be my strength,
My guide,
And my song.

I receive this day with open hands,
And I give thanks with an open heart.
Let my gratitude shine brightly today.

DAY 230:
Illuminating the World with Kindness

Lesson for the Day

Kindness is a light that reaches beyond words. It has the power to heal wounds, restore hope, and connect hearts. Even the smallest act of kindness—offering a smile, listening with care, holding a door—sends ripples of light into the world. You may never know the full impact of your kindness, but its energy is never lost.

In a world that often moves too fast and speaks too loud, kindness slows us down and softens the edges. It reminds us of our shared humanity and our divine connection. Each time you choose kindness, you mirror the heart of the Divine and become a beacon of light to someone who may need it more than you know.

Today, let kindness be your offering. Let it be intentional, sincere, and freely given. The world doesn't need more noise—it needs more light, and that light begins with you.

Meditative Prayer

Divine Light of Love,
Let kindness flow through me today.
Let it shine in my words,
My thoughts,
My presence.

Where there is hurt,
Let me bring comfort.
Where there is need,
Let me offer care.

Make me a vessel of compassion,
A source of gentle strength,
A light in someone's darkness.

I choose kindness,
Again and again,
To illuminate the world with love.

DAY 231:

Living in Harmony with Yourself

Lesson for the Day

Living in harmony with yourself means honoring all that you are—your light and your shadows, your strength and your softness, your past and your becoming. It is a gentle, ongoing practice of self-acceptance and self-trust. When you live in harmony within, you create peace that naturally flows into every area of your life.

This inner harmony is not about perfection, it's about balance. It's choosing to speak to yourself with kindness, to listen to your needs, and to show up for yourself with the same love and care you offer to others. When your inner world is at peace, the outer world feels less chaotic.

Today, give yourself the gift of understanding. Pause, breathe, and listen to what your soul needs. Let your thoughts, emotions, and actions find alignment. You are your own sanctuary—and the more harmony you cultivate within, the more grace you will carry into the world.

Meditative Prayer

Divine Presence Within,
Help me live in harmony with who I am.
Let peace flow through my thoughts,
And compassion guide my heart.

Teach me to listen without judgment,
To speak to myself with love,
And to honor the rhythm of my soul.

Where I am out of balance,
Restore me.
Where I am hard on myself,
Soften me.

May I walk in alignment,
Rooted in grace,
Living in harmony from the inside out.

DAY 232:

Seeing Every Moment as Sacred

Lesson for the Day

Every moment carries the presence of the Divine—each breath, each step, each pause holds the potential to connect you to something greater. Seeing every moment as sacred is not about grand gestures or perfect circumstances—it's about presence. It's about recognizing that holiness lives in the ordinary when you choose to look with reverence.

When you honor the sacredness of now, your life becomes a living prayer. Washing the dishes, walking through nature, sharing a quiet conversation—these become gateways to grace when done with awareness. You begin to realize that you are never far from Spirit, because Spirit is woven into every part of your day.

Today, slow down and invite the sacred into your awareness. Whisper *thank you* for the small things. Bless the moment you're in. Let your life be transformed by the quiet truth that every moment is holy when your heart is open.

Meditative Prayer

Divine Presence,
Open my eyes to the sacred all around me.
Let me see You
In the ordinary,
In the stillness,
In the now.

Teach me to honor each breath,
Each task,
Each connection.
Let my life become a living prayer,
Rooted in awareness and awe.

Where I rush,
Slow me.
Where I forget,
Remind me.

Every moment is a gift.
Every moment is sacred.
And I receive this one fully.

DAY 233:
Embracing the Light of the Sun

Lesson for the Day

The sun rises each day without fail—offering warmth, clarity, and life. It is a symbol of renewal, resilience, and divine constancy. To embrace the light of the sun is to welcome a new beginning, to allow light to touch the dark places within you, and to trust in the steady rhythm of grace.

Let the sun remind you of what is always available. which is hope, healing, and illumination. Just as the sun does not ask the world for permission to shine, neither should you hold back your own light. You were made to reflect the same brilliance, the same unwavering strength, the same invitation to begin again.

Today, turn your face to the sun—physically or spiritually—and breathe in its light. Let it awaken joy in you. Let it clear what no longer serves. Let it fill you with radiant truth. The light is not only around you—it is within you.

Meditative Prayer

Radiant Creator,
Let me embrace the light of the sun today.
Warm my heart,
Clear my mind,
And awaken my soul.

Shine through the shadows within me,
Bringing healing and truth.
Help me to rise with each new dawn,
With hope,
With clarity,
With joy.

May I reflect Your light in all I do.
Let me shine boldly,
Like the sun,
Steady and full of grace.

DAY 234:

A Heart That Sees Blessings Everywhere

Lesson for the Day

To have a heart that sees blessings everywhere is to live with spiritual eyes—eyes that look beyond circumstances and into the deeper truths of love, grace, and abundance. It's not that blessings suddenly appear when life is easy, it's that your heart becomes more open to recognizing them, even in unlikely places.

This kind of heart lives in a posture of wonder. It sees beauty in a smile, hope in a challenge, and grace in the quiet moments between. It chooses to focus on what's good—not in denial of pain, but in devotion to gratitude. The more you train your heart to see blessings, the more blessings seem to multiply.

Today, open your heart wide. Look for the blessings—big or small, obvious or hidden. They are always there, waiting to be seen and received. The more you recognize them, the more your spirit is filled with joy.

Meditative Prayer

Divine Giver of All Good,
Teach me to see with a grateful heart.
Open my spirit to the blessings
That surround me in every moment.

Let me find beauty in simplicity,
Grace in the waiting,
And light in the unexpected.

When my heart feels heavy,
Lift it with reminders of Your goodness.
When I feel lost,
Let the blessings guide me home.

I choose to live in wonder.
I choose to live in thanks.
I see Your blessings everywhere.

DAY 235:
The Energy of Celebration

Lesson for the Day

Celebration is a sacred expression of gratitude and joy. It is the soul's way of saying, *I recognize the beauty of this moment.* The energy of celebration lifts your spirit, opens your heart, and honors not just milestones, but the everyday victories—those small, often unnoticed triumphs that carry deep meaning.

You don't need a special occasion to celebrate. You can celebrate growth, presence, healing, and even the courage to keep going. When you live with the energy of celebration, you affirm that life is worthy of joy, and that every step forward—no matter how small—is worth honoring.

Today, find something to celebrate. Your breath. Your resilience. A moment of peace. Let your celebration be a sacred act of appreciation, a spark of joy that lights the way for others. Celebration is not an ending—it is a beginning filled with intention and light.

Meditative Prayer

Joyful Spirit,
Fill me with the energy of celebration.
Let my heart rejoice in the now,
And my soul dance in gratitude.

Help me celebrate not just outcomes,
But the journey itself.
Let me honor growth,
Moments of clarity,
And the grace that carries me.

May I never miss a chance
To smile,
To laugh,
To give thanks.

I choose celebration
As a way to praise,
To remember,
And to live fully.

DAY 236:
Dancing in the Radiance of Life

Lesson for the Day

There are moments when life invites you to let go—of fear, of heaviness, of expectation—and simply dance in its radiance. To dance in the radiance of life is to celebrate your aliveness, to say yes to joy, and to move with the rhythm of your soul, fully present and fully free.

This radiance is not reserved for perfect days. It shines in the messy, the beautiful, and everything in between. It's the Divine pulse that beats within all creation, calling you back to your essence of light, joy, movement, and truth. When you dance in it—literally or metaphorically—you reconnect to the sacred flow of life.

Today, let yourself move freely. Breathe deeply. Smile without reason. Whether you dance with your body or your spirit, let joy move through you. Life is radiant—and so are you. Let yourself feel it, and let it shine through you.

Meditative Prayer

Divine Light,
Let me dance in the radiance of this life.
Let joy move through my body,
And love flow through my spirit.

Where I've felt heavy,
Lift me.
Where I've been still too long,
Awaken movement.

Help me embrace the light,
The music,
The miracle of now.

May I celebrate the sacred rhythm
Of being fully alive.
And may I never forget,
I was made to shine.

DAY 237:
The Joy That Comes from Within

Lesson for the Day

True joy is not something you chase—it is something you uncover. It doesn't rely on external success, perfect conditions, or the approval of others. The joy that comes from within is rooted in your connection to the Divine, in your acceptance of who you are, and in your willingness to find light even in the shadows.

This kind of joy is quiet yet powerful. It's the peaceful smile that arises from gratitude, the warmth in your chest when you feel aligned, the gentle laughter that bubbles up for no reason other than being alive. It is steady. It is sacred. It is yours.

Today, turn inward and listen for the joy already living inside you. Give it space to rise. Nourish it with stillness, with breath, with love. No matter what today holds, this joy is a gift you carry—and you can return to it at any time.

Meditative Prayer

Divine Source of Joy,
Awaken the joy within me today.
Not joy from circumstance,
But joy that flows from my soul.

Let it rise like morning light,
Soft and steady,
Filling every corner of my being.

When I feel disconnected,
Bring me back to this truth:
Joy lives within me.
Joy is part of me.

Thank You for this sacred gift,
Always available,
Always enough.

I choose to live from that joy today.

DAY 238:

Living with Overflowing Love

Lesson for the Day

Love is your true nature—it is the Divine essence within you, and when you live from that space, your life becomes a blessing to others. Living with overflowing love means allowing that love to move freely through you, without fear, condition, or hesitation. It's the kind of love that heals, uplifts, and gently transforms everything it touches.

Overflowing love is not about perfection or always getting it right. It's about choosing compassion, showing grace, and leading with your heart—even when it's hard. When you're rooted in love, you don't run empty, you draw from an eternal well that never runs dry.

Today, open yourself to that flow. Let love fill your thoughts, your actions, your presence. Let it pour out of you in smiles, in forgiveness, in kindness, and in truth. You are a vessel of love—and the more you give, the more you are filled.

Meditative Prayer

Divine Love,
Fill me until I overflow.
Let Your love rise within me,
And spill into every part of my life.

Teach me to love without limits,
To give without fear,
And to serve from a full heart.

Where I feel guarded,
Open me.
Where I feel empty,
Restore me.

Let my life be a reflection
Of Your boundless grace.
I choose to live with overflowing love,
Today and always.

DAY 239:
A Soul that Smiles with Gratitude

Lesson for the Day

There is a certain radiance that comes from a soul anchored in gratitude—a quiet glow, a soft joy, a peace that doesn't waver with the winds of life. A soul that smiles with gratitude doesn't wait for perfection to feel thankful. It finds beauty in the present and gives thanks for what is.

When your heart turns toward gratitude, your entire energy shifts. You begin to see differently, speak gently, and live more fully. Gratitude becomes not just a momentary emotion but a state of being—a posture of the soul that welcomes grace into every corner of life.

Today, smile with your soul. Let gratitude lift your spirit and open your heart. Give thanks for the simple, the sacred, the seen and unseen. In that space, you'll find that the more you smile with gratitude, the more life smiles back.

Meditative Prayer

Gracious Spirit,
Fill my heart with gentle gratitude.
Let my soul smile today,
With thanks for all that is.

For the light in my life,
And the lessons in the dark,
I give thanks.
For the breath in my body,
And the love I feel,
I give thanks.

Teach me to see blessings in every moment,
To greet life with wonder,
And to rest in appreciation.

May my soul smile freely,
From the joy of knowing I am blessed.

DAY 240:
The Sacred Art of Appreciation

Lesson for the Day

Appreciation is more than noticing something good—it is the sacred art of recognizing the divine presence in all things. When you live with appreciation, you engage life with reverence. You see not just what is useful or beautiful, but what is meaningful, what is worthy of your full attention and gratitude.

To appreciate is to slow down and honor the present. It's an act of love that says, *I see this, I value this, and I'm thankful for it.* Whether it's a person, a moment, a breath, or a lesson—when you appreciate it, you deepen your connection with it. This is how appreciation becomes sacred. It opens the heart and invites peace.

Today, practice the sacred art of appreciation. Let your thankfulness be mindful and intentional. Appreciate the life within you, around you, and between you and the Divine. In appreciation, you not only uplift your own soul—you bless everything you touch.

Meditative Prayer

Divine Presence,
Teach me to live with deep appreciation.
Let me see the sacred
In the small,
The quiet,
The everyday.

Where I have rushed,
Slow me.
Where I have overlooked,
Open my eyes.

Let my heart whisper,
Thank You
Again and again,
Until gratitude becomes my way of being.

I choose to honor this life
Through the art of appreciation.
Let it be my prayer today.

DAY 241:

The Joy That Comes from Trust

Lesson for the Day

Trust is the soil where joy can truly grow. When you release the need to control every outcome and lean into faith, you create space for lightness, ease, and unexpected blessings to enter. The joy that comes from trust isn't dependent on circumstances—it comes from knowing that you are held, guided, and supported by something greater than yourself.

Trust transforms fear into peace and doubt into wonder. It allows you to rest, even in the unknown, and to celebrate the present moment without needing all the answers. When you trust the Divine plan, joy begins to bubble up—not from what you see, but from what you *believe.*

Today, breathe deeply and lean into trust. Let go of what weighs you down and choose to walk in faith. In that sacred surrender, joy will rise—and you will feel the quiet assurance that all is unfolding exactly as it should.

Meditative Prayer

Faithful Divine,
Help me trust You fully today.
Where I feel uncertain,
Anchor me in peace.

Let me find joy
Not just in what I know,
But in what I trust.

Fill me with lightness,
With hope,
With quiet confidence.

I release the weight of worry,
And receive the gift of joyful faith.
I am held,
I am guided,
And I choose to trust.

DAY 242:
Embracing the Flow of Life

Lesson for the Day

Life moves in cycles—expansion and rest, clarity and mystery, beginnings and endings. To embrace the flow of life is to trust its rhythm and allow yourself to move with it rather than resist it. When you stop trying to force or control, you begin to experience the grace and ease that comes with alignment.

The flow of life is not always predictable, but it is always purposeful. Even the pauses, detours, and unexpected currents are part of your sacred unfolding. When you surrender to the flow, you say yes to being guided by something wiser and more loving than your plans alone.

Today, soften your grip. Breathe deeply. Let go of what you've been trying to push or fix. Let life carry you forward—gently, wisely, and in perfect timing. The current of Divine grace is already moving—you only need to allow it.

Meditative Prayer

Wise and Loving Presence,
Help me surrender to the flow of life today.
Where I resist,
Teach me to release.
Where I fear,
Remind me of Your peace.

Let me trust the rhythm,
Even when I don't understand it.
Let me move with grace,
And rest when called.

I flow with faith,
I walk with ease,
And I trust that life is leading me
Exactly where I need to go.

DAY 243:
The Dance of Divine Abundance

Lesson for the Day

Abundance is not just about material wealth—it is a state of being, a sacred flow of energy rooted in trust, gratitude, and openness. The dance of Divine abundance is joyful, generous, and free. It invites you to live with a mindset of plenty, knowing that you are always supported, always connected, and always enough.

When you align with Divine abundance, you stop striving and start receiving. You begin to notice the beauty, the blessings, and the opportunities that surround you. This dance asks you to give and receive with equal grace—to circulate your gifts, your love, your energy, and allow the universe to respond in kind.

Today, step into this dance with faith. Give freely. Receive joyfully. Trust that there is more than enough, and that you are part of an abundant, ever-giving flow. The Divine delights in your joy—and abundance grows when you let yourself move with it.

Meditative Prayer

Abundant and Loving Source,
Thank You for the flow of blessings in my life.
Help me step into the dance of Your abundance
With joy,
With trust,
With grace.

Where I feel lack,
Fill me with faith.
Where I hold back,
Help me open.

Let me give freely,
Receive gratefully,
And move with the rhythm of Divine generosity.

I live in the flow.
I trust in the plenty.
And I dance with abundance today.

DAY 244:
Stepping Into the Overflow

Lesson for the Day

There comes a time in your journey when you're not just surviving—you're ready to thrive. *Stepping into the overflow* means trusting that the Divine has more for you—more peace, more clarity, more purpose, more love. It's the moment when you stop shrinking, stop settling, and start expanding into all that you're meant to be.

Overflow doesn't happen through striving—it happens through surrender, alignment, and belief. When you root yourself in gratitude and open your heart in trust, the flow begins to rise. The more you give, the more you receive. The more you honor your path, the more you are poured into.

Today, take that sacred step into the overflow. Release the fear that you are not enough or that there won't be enough. You were made for this abundance. Let it spill into every area of your life—and let it bless others through you.

Meditative Prayer

Divine Overflow,
I open my heart to receive
All that You are pouring into me.
Let my life be filled
With peace, purpose, and grace.

I release thoughts of lack,
And I step boldly into abundance.
Let blessings rise like a river,
And love spill over every edge.

Use me as a vessel,
Not just to be filled,
But to pour out Your goodness
Wherever I go.

Thank You for the overflow.
More than enough,
Always enough,
Forever flowing.

DAY 245:
A Heart That Knows True Wealth

Lesson for the Day

True wealth is not measured by what you own but by what you hold within. A heart that knows true wealth recognizes the richness of connection, the value of peace, and the abundance found in love, joy, and purpose. It is a heart that sees contentment not as settling, but as a sacred knowing that *this is enough.*

When your wealth is defined by what you give, how you love, and who you become, you begin to walk through life differently. You worry less about accumulation and focus more on impact. You realize that generosity, gratitude, and presence are currencies that never run out.

Today, measure your wealth not by what's in your hands, but by what's in your heart. Celebrate the richness of your life—your relationships, your breath, your spirit, your dreams. You are already deeply abundant in all the ways that matter most.

Meditative Prayer

Divine Source of All,
Thank You for the true wealth in my life.
Fill my heart with deep contentment,
And remind me of what truly matters.

Let me see richness in love,
Abundance in peace,
And prosperity in presence.

Teach me to give freely,
Live simply,
And love deeply.

I am rich in spirit,
Overflowing in grace,
And wealthy in all that is eternal.

Day 246:
Embracing the Gifts of the Universe

Lesson for the Day

The universe is constantly offering you gifts—moments of insight, people who uplift you, lessons that stretch you, and quiet reminders that you are loved. To embrace these gifts is to live with an open heart and a spirit willing to receive. Sometimes they come wrapped in joy, and other times in challenge—but always with purpose.

When you attune yourself to the rhythm of the universe, you begin to see blessings everywhere. What once felt like coincidence becomes divine alignment. What once seemed like a detour becomes redirection. Life opens when you open. The more receptive you are, the more you discover that the universe is not working against you—it's always working for your highest good.

Today, soften your expectations and lift your awareness. Say yes to the gifts waiting to be received—seen and unseen, big and small. Trust that the universe is generous, and that you are worthy of every blessing it longs to give.

Meditative Prayer

Generous Universe,
I open my heart to receive
The gifts You are sending my way.
Help me notice the blessings,
Even in disguise.

Let me accept with gratitude,
Respond with grace,
And trust in Your divine timing.

Where I have resisted,
Let me now allow.
Where I have doubted,
Let me now believe.

I am ready to receive
The love, guidance, and abundance
You are offering me now.

DAY 247:
Trusting That Life is Always Providing

Lesson for the Day

There is a quiet truth that can bring deep peace to your soul. Life is always providing. Even when it doesn't look the way you expected, even when you can't yet see the outcome—something is unfolding on your behalf. The Divine is always working behind the scenes, aligning people, opportunities, and moments to support your growth and your becoming.

Trusting that life is always providing requires faith. It means releasing the need to control, rushing less, and receiving more. When you believe that your needs are known, and your path is supported, you begin to notice the provisions already surrounding you—both physical and spiritual.

Today, shift your focus from lack to trust. Say thank you for what's here, and thank you for what's on the way. You are not forgotten. You are not behind. You are being provided for—in ways both seen and unseen.

Meditative Prayer

Faithful Provider,
Thank You for always giving me what I need,
Even before I ask.
Even when I don't understand.

Help me to trust Your timing,
Your wisdom,
And Your love.

Where I feel lack,
Let me see abundance.
Where I feel fear,
Let me rest in trust.

I open my hands,
I soften my heart,
And I receive all that You are giving.

Life is providing.
You are providing.
And I am deeply supported.

DAY 248:

The Power of an Abundant Mindset

Lesson for the Day

Your mindset shapes the way you experience life. When you shift from scarcity to abundance, you begin to see the world through a lens of possibility, grace, and trust. An abundant mindset doesn't mean denying difficulty—it means choosing to believe that you are supported, that there is enough, and that more goodness is always on its way.

Living with an abundant mindset helps you release comparison, fear, and grasping. It allows you to celebrate others' successes, take inspired risks, and give generously. When you believe that there is more than enough—for you and for everyone—you stop operating from lack and start creating from love.

Today, notice your thoughts. Choose to align with abundance. Affirm that you are worthy of joy, opportunity, connection, and peace. The power of abundance begins within—and the more you think it, speak it, and live it, the more it flows into your life.

Meditative Prayer

Abundant Source of All,
Shift my thoughts today
From fear to faith,
From lack to love.

Fill my mind with thoughts of plenty,
With trust in what's possible,
And with peace in what already is.

Where I have seen not enough,
Help me see overflow.
Where I've held tight,
Teach me to release.

I think abundantly,
I give generously,
I live joyfully.

Because You are my Source,
And You are limitless.

DAY 249:
Finding Fulfillment in the Simple

Lesson for the Day

In a world that often pushes for more, faster, louder—it is in the simple where the soul often feels most fulfilled. A quiet moment of breath, a shared smile, the sound of birdsong, the warmth of morning light—these small moments hold great meaning when you allow yourself to truly receive them.

Fulfillment doesn't have to be found in grand achievements or perfect outcomes. It lives in your awareness, your presence, and your ability to appreciate what already is. When you tune into the simple, your heart softens, your mind quiets, and your spirit begins to rest.

Today, seek the simple. Let it nourish you. Let it be enough. There is richness in this moment, right here, right now. And when you embrace the simple, you discover that peace and purpose were never far—they've been here all along.

Meditative Prayer

Divine Stillness,
Help me slow down today.
Let me find joy
In the quiet,
Peace in the ordinary,
And fullness in the now.

Teach me to see the sacred
In the simple things,
A kind word,
A deep breath,
A moment of stillness.

Where I have chased more,
Bring me home to enough.
Where I have overlooked beauty,
Open my eyes.

I choose fulfillment over frenzy,
Presence over pressure,
And gratitude for what already is.

DAY 250:
Embracing the Spirit of Generosity

Lesson for the Day

Generosity is more than an act—it's a way of being. It flows from a heart that knows there is always enough, and that giving does not diminish you, but expands you. When you embrace the spirit of generosity, you create ripples of light and kindness that touch lives far beyond what you can see.

True generosity isn't only about material things. It's sharing your time, your attention, your encouragement, your presence. It's giving with joy and without expectation. The generous heart knows that love multiplies when it is given, and that grace flows freely when it is shared.

Today, look for ways to give—of yourself, your gifts, your kindness. Whether small or great, every act of generosity is a seed of abundance sown into the world. As you give, you open yourself to receive—and step deeper into the sacred flow of life.

Meditative Prayer

Generous Spirit,
Open my heart to give freely today.
Let me share from a place of love,
Trusting that there is always enough.

Where I see need,
Let me respond with kindness.
Where I see hurt,
Let me offer compassion.

Teach me to give my time,
My care,
My presence,
As sacred offerings.

May I live generously,
Love fully,
And know the joy of blessing others
As I, too, am blessed.

DAY 251:
Walking in the Flow of Prosperity

Lesson for the Day

Prosperity is not only about financial wealth—it's about living in the fullness of what the Divine longs to give you: peace, purpose, connection, and spiritual richness. When you walk in the flow of prosperity, you align yourself with trust and openness, knowing that you are supported by a limitless source.

Walking in this flow means releasing scarcity thinking and embracing the belief that abundance is your birthright. It is choosing to live generously, speak with gratitude, and act with faith. Prosperity flows when you live with alignment, integrity, and a heart willing to receive as much as it gives.

Today, take a step into that divine flow. Walk with confidence, with clarity, and with joy. Let prosperity be more than something you seek—let it be something you embody. The path is already beneath your feet, and the blessings are already on their way.

Meditative Prayer

Abundant Source of All,
Today I walk in the flow of prosperity.
I release fear,
And welcome faith.

Let my steps be guided
By trust and gratitude.
Let my heart remain open
To receive every blessing
Meant for me.

Help me give freely,
Receive joyfully,
And live in harmony
With the abundance of life.

I am provided for,
I am aligned,
I am walking in prosperity.

Day 252:
Receiving with an Open Heart

Lesson for the Day

So often, we are taught how to give—but receiving is equally sacred. To receive with an open heart is to allow the Divine to pour into you, to say yes to love, support, abundance, and healing without guilt or resistance. Receiving is not weakness—it is trust. It is the knowing that you are worthy of being filled.

An open heart does not grasp or demand. It softens. It breathes. It welcomes. When you receive with grace, you honor the flow of life and complete the sacred exchange between giving and receiving. You make space for blessings to land, and you affirm that your needs matter too.

Today, let your heart open wider. Say yes to help, to compliments, to rest, to kindness. Allow yourself to be cared for, supported, and loved. Receiving is holy—and today, you are invited to open your hands and receive all that is being offered.

Meditative Prayer

Loving Source,
Help me receive with an open heart today.
Soften the walls I've built,
And make space for grace.

Where I resist,
Let me allow.
Where I feel unworthy,
Remind me I am enough.

I welcome love,
Support,
Abundance,
And peace.

I open my heart to Your goodness,
And I receive with joy and gratitude.
Thank You for all that flows to me now.

DAY 253:
Knowing That You Are Always Supported

Lesson for the Day

You are never walking alone. Even in moments when it feels quiet or uncertain, there is a deep and steady presence that surrounds you. The Divine, your guides, your inner wisdom—all are gently holding you, guiding your steps, and offering unseen support every day.

To know that you are always supported is to live with trust in something greater than your own efforts. It is to lean into peace when your plans shift, to rest in grace when your strength feels low, and to remember that your worth and your journey are held in sacred care.

Today, breathe into that knowing. Release the need to carry everything alone. Open your heart to the support that surrounds you—seen and unseen. The more you trust in that support, the more clearly you will feel it. You are guided. You are held. You are deeply supported.

Meditative Prayer

Ever-Present Divine,
Thank You for the support that surrounds me.
Even when I cannot see it,
Help me feel it.
Even when I doubt,
Let me trust.

I am not alone in this journey.
You walk with me,
Hold me,
And guide my every step.

Let me rest in Your strength,
And lean into Your grace.
Today, I let go of the need to do it all myself,
And I receive the love,
Support,
And presence that never leaves me.

DAY 254:
The Joy of Sharing Your Light

Lesson for the Day

Your light was never meant to be hidden. It was placed within you to shine—to uplift, to inspire, to heal, and to remind others of their own radiance. When you share your light, you're not seeking attention, you're offering a gift. And in that act of offering, joy expands within you and around you.

Sharing your light doesn't have to be loud. It can be found in a kind word, a compassionate act, a quiet strength, or simply being fully yourself. The more you live in your truth, the brighter your light becomes. And the brighter you shine, the more you awaken that light in others.

Today, share your light without fear. Don't wait for the perfect moment. Shine in small ways, in soft spaces, and in the ordinary moments of your day. The joy of sharing your light is not just in how it touches others—but in how it reminds you who you truly are.

Meditative Prayer

Radiant Creator,

Thank You for the light You've placed within me.

Let it shine freely today,

Not for praise,

But for purpose.

Where I've dimmed myself,

Ignite my courage.

Where I've held back,

Unfold my heart.

Let every word I speak,

Every action I take,

Be filled with light,

And rooted in love.

I share my light with joy,

With grace,

And with the knowing

That it is meant to shine.

DAY 255:

Abundance in Every Form

Lesson for the Day

Abundance is all around you—woven into the sunlight, the laughter of a friend, the breath in your lungs, and the love that meets you when you least expect it. It isn't limited to material wealth. It shows up in peace of mind, opportunities for growth, moments of beauty, and the presence of the Divine in your everyday life.

When you open yourself to abundance in all its forms, you begin to recognize that you are always being provided for. You shift your mindset from *not enough* to *more than enough,* and you create space for miracles to unfold. Abundance is a frequency—and when you align with it, life rises to meet you.

Today, let your heart expand with gratitude. Notice the richness of your life—the connections, the quiet blessings, the wisdom gained. Trust that the universe is generous and that you are aligned with a flow of goodness that never runs out.

Meditative Prayer

Generous Universe,
Help me see the abundance
That surrounds me in every form.

Open my eyes to the beauty,
The blessings,
The overflowing grace
That fills my life.

Where I have focused on lack,
Let me now see plenty.
Where I have closed myself off,
Help me open and receive.

I welcome abundance,
In peace,
In love,
In opportunities,
In joy.

Thank You for all the ways
You provide for me.

DAY 256:
Trusting That More is Always Coming

Lesson for the Day

There is a divine rhythm to life, and it is always moving you toward more—more wisdom, more connection, more alignment with your purpose. Trusting that more is always coming means living with hope, expectancy, and a deep knowing that your journey is unfolding in sacred timing.

This trust doesn't mean you are ungrateful for what you have—it means you are open to expansion. You understand that the Divine is generous, and that the path ahead is filled with possibilities you can't yet see. When you walk in trust, you walk in peace, knowing that every season prepares you for the next.

Today, rest in the truth that *this is not the end of your blessings.* Say thank you for what is, and welcome what's on the way. Let anticipation lift your spirit and faith open your heart. More is always coming—and you are ready to receive it.

Meditative Prayer

Faithful Source of All,
Thank You for all that is,
And all that is yet to be.

Help me trust in the unseen,
And believe in the abundance ahead.

Where I feel stuck,
Plant hope.
Where I feel uncertain,
Whisper Your promises.

I open my heart to more.
More joy,
More peace,
More purpose,
More love.

I trust that life is expanding for me,
And that more is always on the way.

DAY 257:

Living with Open Hands and an Open Heart

Lesson for the Day

To live with open hands and an open heart is to walk through life with trust, surrender, and generosity. Open hands let go of control, release fear, and make space to receive. An open heart welcomes love, connection, and divine guidance without resistance. Together, they create a posture of spiritual alignment—ready to give, ready to receive, and ready to be transformed.

When your hands are clenched tightly, nothing new can enter. When your heart is guarded, love has nowhere to land. But when you soften, you step into the flow of grace. You begin to live in rhythm with the universe—trusting that what is meant for you will come, and what is no longer needed will gently fall away.

Today, practice openness. Let your grip loosen. Let your heart breathe. Be present with what is, and allow blessings to move through you freely. Life becomes more beautiful, more peaceful, and more abundant when you live wide open.

Meditative Prayer

Loving Presence,
Today I open my hands
And my heart to You.

I release what I cannot control,
And I welcome what You are sending.

Where I've held tight in fear,
Let me loosen in faith.
Where I've closed off in pain,
Let me open in trust.

May I give with joy,
Receive with gratitude,
And live with sacred openness.

Let my life be a channel
For love, for peace, for grace.

Day 258:

Releasing Fear of Lack

Lesson for the Day

Fear of lack can keep you small—it can cloud your vision, tighten your heart, and make you feel disconnected from the truth of who you are and what you're worthy of. But scarcity is not your spiritual reality. The Divine is abundant, ever-giving, and deeply aware of your needs. You were not created to live in fear—you were created to trust, receive, and flourish.

Releasing the fear of lack is an act of courage and faith. It means choosing to believe in provision, even when you can't yet see it. It means shifting your focus from "not enough" to "more is coming." Lack is a lie, abundance is the truth. When you remember that, you begin to live in a way that attracts what your heart truly desires.

Today, speak to the fear and let it go. Breathe into trust. Root yourself in gratitude for what is, and allow that energy to expand. You are not forgotten. You are not behind. You are supported, seen, and surrounded by more than enough.

Meditative Prayer

Abundant and Loving Source,
Today I release my fear of lack.
I surrender the stories
That tell me I am not enough
Or that there won't be enough.

Remind me of Your provision,
Your presence,
Your promises.

Fill my heart with peace,
My mind with faith,
And my life with the knowing
That I am supported in all ways.

I let go of fear,
And I welcome abundance.
I trust in You completely.

Day 259:
The Energy of Divine Blessings

Lesson for the Day

Divine blessings are not just things you receive—they are energies you align with. They move with grace, intention, and timing, flowing through your life in ways both seen and unseen. When you open yourself to these blessings, you begin to feel their presence all around you—in the quiet answers, the unexpected support, the peace that settles in your spirit.

To live in the energy of divine blessings is to stay rooted in trust and gratitude. It means recognizing that you don't have to strive for what is already yours. Blessings find you when your heart is open, your spirit is soft, and your life becomes a space where grace is welcome.

Today, attune yourself to that sacred energy. Expect blessings. Speak blessings. Be a blessing. As you align with divine love and guidance, you'll realize the flow has always been there—waiting for you to receive it with joy and faith.

Meditative Prayer

Divine Giver of All Good,
I open myself to the energy of Your blessings today.
Let them flow freely through my life,
Filling every corner of my being.

Where I have doubted,
Replace it with trust.
Where I have longed,
Let me receive.

Help me walk in gratitude,
Speak with faith,
And live as one who is already blessed.

May I carry this energy with me,
A magnet for goodness,
A vessel for grace,
A light in the world.

Day 260:

Living a Life of Overflow

Lesson for the Day

A life of overflow begins with an inner well that is full—nourished by peace, rooted in gratitude, and aligned with divine abundance. This isn't about excess or striving for more. It's about having so much love, joy, and spiritual richness within you that it naturally spills into the world around you.

When you live in overflow, your giving is effortless, your presence is healing, and your energy uplifts others without draining you. It comes from trusting that you are constantly being refilled by the Source. You don't give to earn—you give because you are already full.

Today, tend to your spirit. Fill your own well with silence, joy, connection, and care. Let your overflow bless others—not through effort, but through alignment. You were created to live abundantly, not barely getting by. Allow yourself to thrive, and let that overflow become your offering to the world.

Meditative Prayer

Loving and Abundant Source,
Fill me today until I overflow.
Let my heart be so full of Your peace
That it touches everything I do.

Where I have felt empty,
Pour into me.
Where I've given without receiving,
Restore my balance.

May I live with joy,
Give with ease,
And love from a place
Of divine fullness.

I welcome a life of overflow.
Not for status,
But for service.
Not for gain,
But for grace.

DAY 261:

The Joy Found in Giving

Lesson for the Day

Giving is a sacred act of love—an expression of your heart, your presence, and your belief in abundance. When you give freely and without expectation, you step into the flow of joy. This joy isn't tied to the outcome—it comes from knowing you've shared something meaningful, something divine.

Whether it's your time, your attention, your resources, or your kindness, giving allows you to participate in something bigger than yourself. It opens your spirit, deepens your connection to others, and reminds you that love is meant to move through you, not just to you.

Today, give from your heart. Let your giving be light, intentional, and full of grace. Even the smallest gesture can carry great power. And as you give, notice how joy returns—not because you expect it, but because it is the natural rhythm of a generous soul.

Meditative Prayer

Generous Spirit,
Thank You for the joy of giving.
Let me share freely today,
From a heart full of love.

Where I have held back,
Help me open.
Where I have feared not enough,
Remind me of divine abundance.

Let my giving be sacred,
Led by kindness,
And rooted in joy.

May I give without expectation,
And receive the quiet joy
That comes from being a vessel
Of Your love.

DAY 262:

Creating a Life of Limitless Possibilities

Lesson for the Day

You are a co-creator with the Divine, and within you is the power to shape a life filled with purpose, wonder, and expansion. Creating a life of limitless possibilities begins with belief—believing that you are not confined by your past, your circumstances, or your fears. What you can envision, you can move toward.

When you align your thoughts, actions, and energy with faith, you begin to unlock doors you didn't even know existed. Possibilities aren't something you chase—they're something you *invite* by choosing trust, clarity, and openness each day. The more you say yes to what lights you up, the more your life expands.

Today, release limitation. Let go of the old story that says you're not ready or not worthy. Open yourself to new ideas, unexpected paths, and divine inspiration. You were created to grow, to dream, and to rise. The life you long for begins with the possibility you believe in today.

Meditative Prayer

Infinite Creator,
Thank You for the possibilities
That unfold before me each day.

Clear my vision,
Expand my heart,
And awaken my spirit
To what is truly possible.

Where I've doubted,
Plant new belief.
Where I've feared,
Shine Your light of courage.

I am open to ideas,
Aligned with purpose,
And ready to co-create
A life beyond limits.

Let my journey reflect the truth of who I am,
Empowered,
And divinely supported.

533

DAY 263:

The Sacred Balance of Receiving and Giving

Lesson for the Day

Life is a sacred dance between giving and receiving—a flow of energy that nurtures both the soul and the world. When you give from an open heart and receive with humility and gratitude, you honor this divine rhythm. True balance is not found in doing more, but in allowing both directions of love to move freely through you.

If you only give, you may become depleted. If you only receive, the energy becomes stagnant. But when you open yourself to both, you create harmony. Giving becomes joyful, and receiving becomes sacred. You begin to understand that each act—whether offering or accepting—is part of a holy exchange rooted in love.

Today, check in with the flow within your life. Where do you need to give more freely? Where do you need to receive without guilt? As you move in this balance, trust that the Divine is guiding both your hands and your heart.

Meditative Prayer

Divine Source of Flow,
Teach me the sacred rhythm
Of giving and receiving.

Let my heart be generous,
And my spirit be open.

When I give,
Let it be with joy and love.
When I receive,
Let it be with grace and gratitude.

Balance me,
Fill me,
And flow through me,
So that I may live in harmony
With the rhythm of Your abundance.

May I honor this holy exchange
Each day with presence and peace.

DAY 264:

Allowing Your Heart to Expand with Gratitude

Lesson for the Day

Gratitude is not just a feeling—it is a spiritual opening. When you allow your heart to expand with gratitude, you begin to see the world with new eyes. The ordinary becomes miraculous, the challenges become teachers, and the present moment becomes a sacred gift.

Gratitude stretches your heart beyond limitation. It softens fear, dissolves resentment, and connects you more deeply to the Divine and to life itself. In that expansion, you make room for joy, peace, and deeper love. Gratitude doesn't just change how you feel—it transforms how you *live.*

Today, breathe into gratitude. Let it widen the space within your chest. Let it rise in whispers of *thank you* throughout the day. The more your heart expands in appreciation, the more aligned you become with the beauty, grace, and abundance that surround you.

Meditative Prayer

Gracious Spirit,
Today I open my heart in gratitude.
Let thankfulness flow through me
Like breath—gentle and constant.

Where I've felt closed,
Expand me.
Where I've held back,
Release me.

Let every moment
Be touched by appreciation.
Let every blessing
Be honored with joy.

May my heart grow wide
With love,
With presence,
And with the sacred power of gratitude.

DAY 265:
A Soul Aligned with Divine Prosperity

Lesson for the Day

Divine prosperity is not merely about wealth—it is a sacred harmony between your soul's purpose and the abundant flow of the universe. When your soul is aligned with divine prosperity, you begin to live with ease, clarity, and trust. You recognize that everything you need is already finding its way to you.

Alignment means choosing faith over fear, purpose over pressure, and gratitude over grasping. It's the quiet confidence that you are walking in the right direction, and that the Divine will meet you at every step with resources, support, and blessings. When your inner world is in balance, your outer world reflects that abundance.

Today, align your soul with prosperity by stepping into your truth and trusting the path ahead. Let your thoughts, actions, and energy reflect the belief that you are divinely provided for. There is more than enough, and you are more than worthy to receive it.

Meditative Prayer

Prospering Presence,
Align my soul with Your divine flow today.
Let my heart trust,
Let my mind believe,
And let my spirit open to receive.

Where I've feared not enough,
Remind me of Your endless supply.
Where I've strayed from purpose,
Guide me gently home.

I choose prosperity.
Not just in things,
But in peace, in purpose, in joy.

May I walk in truth,
Live in trust,
And receive with grace
The abundance You have prepared for me.

Day 266:

Embracing the Limitlessness of Spirit

Lesson for the Day

You are not confined by your past, your fears, or the labels the world places upon you. Your spirit is vast, radiant, and limitless—connected to the Divine in every breath. When you embrace the limitlessness of Spirit, you begin to live from your highest truth, no longer bound by what *has been*, but inspired by what *can be*.

Living from this limitless space is an act of deep trust. It asks you to stretch beyond comfort, dream beyond logic, and move beyond doubt. The Divine within you holds infinite creativity, strength, wisdom, and love. You were never meant to shrink—you were made to soar.

Today, remind yourself of your vastness. Release the need to stay small or safe. Step into the freedom of Spirit, where anything is possible and everything is guided. You are not just a part of the universe—you are woven into its expansion.

Meditative Prayer

Infinite Spirit,
Help me remember who I truly am,
Limitless,
Free,
And filled with Divine light.

Break the walls I've built in fear,
And expand my heart in trust.

Let me dream without boundaries,
Love without hesitation,
And move through life
With courage and grace.

I embrace the vastness within me.
I walk in the truth of my spirit.
And I say yes
To the boundless possibilities You've placed before me.

DAY 267:

Walking in the Freedom of Abundance

Lesson for the Day

Abundance isn't just about having more—it's about feeling free. Free to live in alignment with your soul, free to give without fear, and free to receive without guilt. When you walk in the freedom of abundance, you release the weight of scarcity and step into the truth that you are fully supported by the Divine.

This freedom allows you to live with open hands and an open heart. It shifts your focus from grasping to trusting, from hoarding to sharing, from worrying to resting. You no longer feel bound by what you don't have—you are empowered by what already flows through and around you.

Today, choose to walk in that freedom. Let go of the idea that you must earn your worth or prove your value. You are already worthy of a life filled with joy, connection, and provision. Trust that abundance is not just available—it's already here, and it walks beside you.

Meditative Prayer

Abundant and Loving Source,
Thank You for the freedom that comes
From trusting in Your provision.

Help me walk today
With peace in my heart,
Faith in my steps,
And gratitude in my spirit.

I release fear,
I release striving,
And I rest in the flow of Your abundance.

Let me give freely,
Receive joyfully,
And live fully in the freedom
Of knowing I am always supported.

DAY 268:

The Power of Seeing Life as a Gift

Lesson for the Day

When you begin to see life as a gift, everything changes. Each breath becomes a blessing. Each sunrise becomes a miracle. Even the challenges become opportunities for growth and grace. This perspective grounds you in gratitude and elevates the ordinary into something sacred.

Life isn't always easy—but it is always meaningful. When you see life through the eyes of wonder, your heart softens, your spirit awakens, and joy begins to rise. This shift doesn't deny hardship—it simply invites you to look deeper, to find the light within the moment, and to remember that every day is a chance to begin again.

Today, pause and look around with reverence. Let your eyes, your heart, your soul whisper *thank you.* Allow this awareness to shape your choices and your energy. The more you see life as a gift, the more life opens itself to you.

Meditative Prayer

Giver of Life,
Thank You for the gift of today.
Let me receive it
With wonder,
With gratitude,
With joy.

Open my heart to see
The sacred in the simple,
The miracle in the mundane,
The blessing in every breath.

Where I have taken life for granted,
Awaken my soul.
Where I have rushed past beauty,
Slow me down.

Let me live today
As one who knows,
Life is a gift,
And I am here to cherish it.

Day 269:
A Heart Overflowing with Joy

Lesson for the Day

Joy is a sacred current that flows from within—it isn't dependent on external circumstances, but on your willingness to receive the moment as it is. A heart overflowing with joy is one that has learned to celebrate life not because it is perfect, but because it is *present.* It finds delight in the now, in the breath, in the beauty tucked within the ordinary.

Joy is not the absence of pain—it is the presence of hope. It lives alongside sorrow and gently lifts your spirit when the weight of the world feels too heavy. When your heart opens to joy, it becomes contagious. You become a vessel of light, lifting others simply by existing in your truth.

Today, choose joy—not as a reaction, but as a way of being. Let it fill you, surprise you, and spill out of you in laughter, gratitude, and quiet moments of awe. A joyful heart is a radiant heart—and you were made to shine.

Meditative Prayer

Divine Joy,
Fill my heart until it overflows.
Let it rise gently within me,
Like sunlight through the clouds.

Help me see the beauty,
Even in the in-between.
Let laughter be my healing,
And gratitude be my song.

Where heaviness lingers,
Lift it with joy.
Where fear whispers,
Let joy speak louder.

I welcome joy into my being,
Into my breath,
Into this sacred day.
Let my heart overflow
And bless the world around me.

DAY 270:
Trusting That You Are Always Provided For

Lesson for the Day

Trust is the foundation of peace. When you trust that you are always provided for, you let go of fear and control. You release the worry that there won't be enough and instead open yourself to the knowing that the Divine is constantly supporting you, guiding you, and meeting your needs in ways both seen and unseen.

To trust in provision is to believe that you are always being held—whether in abundance or in challenge. Life's flow is not about taking more; it's about receiving what you need at the perfect moment. Trusting in this provision frees your spirit to rest, to receive, and to move forward with confidence, knowing you are never alone.

Today, breathe into that trust. Let go of any tension around what you don't have or what you might lack. Trust that what you need will always come, and you are fully supported on this journey.

Meditative Prayer

Divine Provider,
Thank You for Your constant care.
Help me trust that I am always supported,
That what I need will always come at the perfect time.

Where I have feared scarcity,
Fill me with peace.
Where I have doubted,
Reassure me with Your love.

Let me walk through this day knowing
I am provided for in all ways,
In my heart, in my mind, in my body,
And in my spirit.

I release fear and welcome trust.
I trust in Your provision,
And I am at peace.

Day 271:

The Season of Reflection

Lesson for the Day

Life moves in seasons, and each season has its own rhythm and purpose. The season of reflection is a sacred time—one that invites you to pause, look back, and honor the journey. It's a time to review the lessons, acknowledge the growth, and appreciate how far you've come. Reflection isn't about regret or dwelling on the past, but about understanding its role in shaping your present.

In the quiet moments of reflection, you are given the space to reconnect with your inner wisdom, to realign with your purpose, and to adjust your path if needed. It is here, in stillness, that clarity often arises, and you can move forward with renewed intention and peace.

Today, take time for reflection. Sit in gratitude for your journey, honor the growth you've experienced, and open your heart to the lessons still waiting to unfold. In this season, there is no rush—only the gentle unfolding of what is already within you.

Meditative Prayer

Divine Guide,
Thank You for the gift of reflection.
Help me see clearly the steps I've taken,
The lessons I've learned,
And the strength I've gained.

Where I've stumbled,
Help me find peace.
Where I've grown,
Help me honor the growth.

Give me the courage to look within,
To hear Your whispers of wisdom,
And to trust that all is unfolding in perfect timing.

In this season of reflection,
Let me find clarity,
Let me find peace,
And let me find the joy of knowing I am exactly where I need to
be.

DAY 272:
Gathering the Lessons of the Year

Lesson for the Day

Each year offers its own lessons—sometimes subtle, sometimes profound, but always purposeful. The act of gathering these lessons is not one of judgment but of gratitude, seeing the growth that has taken place even through challenges. As you reflect on the past year, gather the wisdom that it has offered you—whether in moments of joy, sorrow, success, or struggle.

The lessons you've gathered are treasures, pieces of the puzzle that create the fullness of your journey. They are the tools you carry with you into the new year, helping you navigate the path ahead with deeper wisdom and a heart open to new possibilities.

Today, take time to gather these lessons. Write them down, reflect on them, and honor them as part of your spiritual evolution. There is power in acknowledging how far you've come, and in knowing that every experience, every moment, has been an integral part of your growth.

Meditative Prayer

Divine Teacher,
Thank You for the lessons this year has brought.
Help me gather them with gratitude,
And carry them forward with grace.

Where I have struggled,
Let me find strength.
Where I have faltered,
Let me discover wisdom.

Help me see the value in every moment,
Every victory,
Every setback,
Every lesson learned.

I honor my journey,
I trust in the growth,
And I am ready for what the new year holds.

Day 273:
Embracing the Wisdom Within

Lesson for the Day

The greatest wisdom you can ever seek is already within you. It is not hidden or distant—it lives in your heart, in your intuition, and in the quiet whispers of your soul. To embrace the wisdom within is to trust yourself deeply, to listen to your inner voice, and to honor the guidance that arises from a place of peace and clarity.

We often look outside ourselves for answers, but the truth is, you have everything you need inside of you. When you stop, pause, and listen, your soul speaks in ways that are subtle, yet profound. Embracing this wisdom requires patience, faith, and the courage to act from a place of knowing.

Today, give yourself permission to trust what arises from within. Let your inner wisdom guide your choices, your actions, and your energy. You are more capable than you may realize—and the answers you seek are already part of your being.

Meditative Prayer

Divine Wisdom,

Help me listen deeply to the guidance within me.

Let my heart be open,

My mind be still,

And my soul be receptive to the truth you speak.

Where I doubt myself,

Fill me with confidence.

Where I feel lost,

Lead me back to my center.

I trust in the wisdom I carry,

And I choose to live from that place today.

I honor the truth within me,

And I walk with it as my guide.

DAY 274:
Walking the Path of Understanding

Lesson for the Day

The path of understanding is not about having all the answers. It is about embracing curiosity, compassion, and patience as you seek to see the world from multiple perspectives. It is about stepping into the shoes of others, listening without judgment, and seeking the deeper truths that connect us all. Understanding requires openness—a willingness to learn and grow beyond your current views and experiences.

Walking this path means embracing humility and recognizing that there is always more to discover. You don't need to have all the knowledge to be wise. Instead, wisdom is found in your openness to understanding, both of yourself and of others. When you walk the path of understanding, you build bridges where there were once walls.

Today, open your heart and mind to understanding. Seek to understand others without trying to change them. Allow yourself to be open to new insights and truths. The more you understand, the more deeply you connect, and the more peace you will find.

Meditative Prayer

Divine Source of Wisdom,
Guide me along the path of understanding.
Help me listen with patience,
Speak with compassion,
And see the world with clarity and grace.

Where I have judged,
Help me soften.
Where I have misunderstood,
Open my eyes.

Let me walk today with empathy,
With kindness,
And with a heart open to learning.

May I meet others where they are,
And may my understanding bring peace to myself and the world.

DAY 275:
The Beauty of a Reflective Heart

Lesson for the Day

A reflective heart is one that looks inward with clarity, compassion, and honesty. It is not about self-judgment but self-awareness—about recognizing the lessons that life offers, the growth that occurs in stillness, and the wisdom that arises in moments of pause. The beauty of a reflective heart lies in its openness to understanding itself and its ability to learn and evolve.

When you reflect, you give yourself the gift of growth. You take the time to observe, to understand, and to integrate your experiences. This reflection fosters peace within, as you begin to understand your own motivations, desires, and fears. With a reflective heart, you learn to embrace both the light and shadow within, allowing each to inform your path forward.

Today, give yourself the space to reflect. Look inward without haste. Honor the beauty of the journey, the lessons you have learned, and the person you are becoming. A reflective heart is a peaceful heart, grounded in wisdom and grace.

Meditative Prayer

Loving Source,
Help me cultivate a reflective heart today.
Guide me inward to see with clarity,
To learn with love,
And to grow with patience.

Where I have been too quick to judge,
Let me pause and understand.
Where I have been too hard on myself,
Let me offer compassion.

Let my heart be open to the lessons
That each moment holds,
And may I move forward with peace,
Wisdom, and grace.

I embrace the beauty of reflection,
The stillness, the learning, the growth.

Day 276:

Learning from Every Experience

Lesson for the Day

Every experience, whether joyful or challenging, holds a lesson. Life is constantly inviting you to learn—to deepen your understanding, to grow in wisdom, and to evolve into the highest version of yourself. The key is to approach each experience with openness, curiosity, and a willingness to receive the lesson it carries.

When you learn from every experience, you transform the ordinary into the extraordinary. You stop viewing difficulties as obstacles and begin to see them as opportunities for growth. Even the moments of pain or confusion serve a purpose—they refine you, teach you resilience, and help you move forward with greater strength.

Today, embrace each experience as a teacher. Let go of expectations and judgment, and instead, ask yourself, *What is this here to show me?* The more you approach life with this mindset, the more you will see the beauty and wisdom in all things.

Meditative Prayer

Divine Teacher,

Thank You for the lessons woven into every experience.

Help me see each moment as an opportunity to learn,

To grow,

And to deepen my understanding.

Where I've resisted,

Help me open.

Where I've feared,

Help me trust.

Let me find wisdom in every situation,

Peace in every challenge,

And strength in every lesson.

May my heart remain open,

And my mind be receptive to the gifts each experience brings.

DAY 277:
The Sacredness of Inner Knowing

Lesson for the Day

Your inner knowing is a sacred gift—a quiet, unwavering voice that guides you toward truth, peace, and alignment with your higher self. It is the wisdom that comes from within, from the depth of your soul, and it connects you to something greater than your own mind. The sacredness of this inner knowing is found in its purity, its authenticity, and its ability to lead you on the path that is meant for you.

Learning to trust your inner knowing requires faith in yourself and in the guidance of the Divine. It means listening beyond the noise of the world, tuning into your heart, and allowing that deeper voice to guide your choices. This knowing doesn't require evidence or proof—it simply asks for your trust and your willingness to follow its lead.

Today, give yourself permission to listen to your inner wisdom. Quiet the external distractions and tune into the subtle truths that arise within. Trust that your soul already knows the way, and follow the gentle guidance that speaks from a place of deep knowing.

Meditative Prayer

Divine Source of Wisdom,
Help me tune into the sacred knowing within me.
Let my heart listen closely,
Let my mind quiet enough to hear.

Guide me to trust what arises from within,
To trust the wisdom that already knows the way.
Where I've doubted,
Fill me with faith.

Let me walk today in alignment with my soul,
Guided by the truth that lives inside of me.
I honor the sacredness of my inner knowing,
And I trust it will lead me to all that is meant for me.

Day 278:

Trusting Your Intuition

Lesson for the Day

Your intuition is your inner compass, a direct connection to your higher self and to the Divine. It speaks softly, guiding you toward choices that align with your truth and purpose. Trusting your intuition is an act of faith—it's trusting the whispers of your soul even when they don't fit the logic of the mind or the expectations of others.

When you trust your intuition, you begin to live with more clarity and confidence. It becomes a powerful tool for decision-making, offering you guidance when the path ahead is unclear. Intuition doesn't always make sense to the outer world, but it always leads you closer to your authentic self.

Today, practice listening to your inner voice. Trust the subtle nudges and the gut feelings. Let your intuition be your guide, and know that it will always lead you in the direction that is best for you. The more you trust it, the more it will guide you with clarity and ease.

Meditative Prayer

Divine Wisdom,
Help me trust my intuition today.
Guide me to listen deeply to my inner voice,
And to follow the wisdom that speaks from within.

Where I have doubted myself,
Help me trust my knowing.
Where I have questioned my path,
Let my intuition lead me forward.

Let me move with clarity and confidence,
Knowing that my soul knows the way.
I trust in the guidance within me,
And I am open to the direction it offers.

DAY 279:

Honoring the Past Without Holding On

Lesson for the Day

The past holds wisdom, memories, and lessons that have shaped who you are today. Honoring the past means acknowledging its role in your life and finding peace in the journey it led you on. It is a gentle acceptance that your experiences—both joyful and painful— have all contributed to your growth and understanding.

However, honoring the past does not mean holding on to it. When you hold on too tightly, you block the flow of the present moment and the possibilities of the future. To move forward, you must release what no longer serves you, holding only the lessons and gratitude. The past has its place in your story, but it is the present that holds the power to create the life you are meant to live.

Today, take time to reflect on the past with gratitude, but let go of any attachment that limits your growth. Honor it, but choose to step into the fullness of the present moment. You are ready to live in the now and trust the future with an open heart.

Meditative Prayer

Divine Healer,
Thank You for the lessons of the past.
Help me honor what has shaped me,
And release what no longer serves me.

Where I have held on too tightly,
Give me the strength to let go.
Where I have carried burdens,
Help me release them with grace.

May I find peace in what was,
And freedom in what is to come.
Let me walk forward with an open heart,
Ready to embrace the future.

DAY 280:

The Lessons of the Changing Seasons

Lesson for the Day

Just as the seasons change, so do the seasons of your life. Each shift offers its own lessons—some subtle, some profound. Spring teaches renewal and growth, summer offers abundance and warmth, autumn reminds us of release and transformation, and winter brings rest and reflection. Life mirrors these rhythms, inviting you to flow with the natural cycles of growth, release, and renewal.

The changing seasons remind us that nothing is permanent, and yet, everything has purpose. The beauty of each season is found in its impermanence. In this, we are called to embrace change, to find peace in the cycles of our own lives, and to trust that each stage has its own wisdom to offer.

Today, reflect on the season of your life. What lessons are you learning in this moment? What are you being invited to release, to embrace, or to nurture? Trust that each season brings its own gifts, and that in each phase, you are exactly where you need to be.

Meditative Prayer

Divine Creator,
Thank You for the lessons found in every season.
Help me embrace each phase of life,
The growth, the release, the rest, and the renewal.

Where I resist change,
Help me surrender with trust.
Where I fear the unknown,
Fill me with peace.

May I find beauty in each season,
And wisdom in each moment.
Guide me through the rhythms of life,
Knowing that all is unfolding perfectly.

DAY 281:
A Heart That Seeks Understanding

Lesson for the Day

A heart that seeks understanding is open, patient, and compassionate. It doesn't rush to judge or make assumptions—it takes the time to listen, to learn, and to connect. Seeking understanding requires humility and curiosity, recognizing that every person, every experience, and every situation has layers of depth to uncover.

When you seek understanding, you create bridges instead of walls. You open yourself to the possibility that there is more to a situation than meets the eye, and that each encounter holds an opportunity for growth. Understanding doesn't mean agreement—it means honoring someone else's perspective, experiences, and truth.

Today, choose to seek understanding rather than judgment. Let your heart remain open, and practice listening deeply, not only to others but also to yourself. There is wisdom in every person and situation, and by seeking understanding, you create more peace in your life and in the world around you.

Meditative Prayer

Divine Source of Wisdom,
Help me seek understanding today.
Open my heart to listen with compassion,
And my mind to receive with patience.

Where I have rushed to judge,
Help me pause and open.
Where I have closed myself off,
Help me see with fresh eyes.

Let me understand not only with my mind,
But with my heart,
So I may walk with grace and connection.

Guide me to see the truth in every situation,
And to honor each person's unique journey.

DAY 282:

The Gift of Stillness in Reflection

Lesson for the Day

In the hustle and bustle of daily life, stillness is often overlooked. Yet, in the quiet moments of reflection, we find the clarity and peace that can transform our perspective. Stillness allows us to pause, to reconnect with our inner wisdom, and to evaluate the lessons life has offered. It is in stillness that we make space for understanding, healing, and insight.

The gift of stillness is found in the ability to stop, breathe, and listen deeply. It is a sacred pause that invites us to reflect on our journey, to appreciate how far we've come, and to release what no longer serves us. When we allow ourselves the space to reflect in stillness, we open ourselves to the divine guidance that is always available, but often drowned out by noise.

Today, take time for stillness. Let it be a time of deep reflection, a chance to evaluate where you are, where you've been, and where you're going. In this quiet, sacred space, trust that clarity and peace will follow.

Meditative Prayer

Divine Source of Peace,
Thank You for the gift of stillness.
Help me find rest in the quiet,
And clarity in the pause.

Where my mind is restless,
Help me calm it.
Where my heart is heavy,
Help me soften it.

Let me reflect with patience and grace,
And trust in the wisdom that comes from silence.
Guide me to listen deeply to Your whispers,
And to move forward with peace and clarity.

DAY 283:
The Power of Perspective

Lesson for the Day

Perspective shapes how we experience the world. It colors our emotions, influences our decisions, and determines how we respond to challenges. A shift in perspective can turn a difficult situation into an opportunity for growth, or transform a moment of discomfort into a lesson of resilience. The power of perspective is that it is entirely within our control—we can choose how we view a situation, and that choice determines how we navigate through life.

When we choose to see life through the lens of gratitude, compassion, or possibility, our experiences change. Even in adversity, there are opportunities to learn, grow, and evolve. Perspective is the key to finding peace in the chaos and hope in the uncertainty.

Today, consider how you are viewing the world around you. How can you shift your perspective to invite more peace, joy, and growth? Know that you have the power to change how you experience life by simply changing how you choose to see it.

Meditative Prayer

Divine Guide,
Open my eyes to the power of perspective.
Help me see the world with compassion,
With gratitude,
And with an open heart.

Where I have been focused on lack,
Shift my vision to abundance.
Where I have seen challenge,
Help me see opportunity.

Let me embrace the fullness of each moment,
And choose to respond with clarity and grace.
Thank You for the power of perspective,
And for the peace it brings when I trust in it.

DAY 284:
Holding Onto What Matters Most

Lesson for the Day

In life, we are often faced with distractions, pressures, and fleeting desires that pull our attention away from what truly matters. Holding onto what matters most is an act of clarity, intention, and purpose. It means focusing on the things that nourish your soul, the relationships that lift you, and the values that guide your heart.

What matters most is unique to each of us, and it's important to define what those things are in your life—whether it's love, integrity, peace, or service. By holding onto what truly matters, you create a life filled with meaning, connection, and fulfillment. This practice of intentional focus allows you to weather life's storms with a steady heart and unshakable grounding in your values.

Today, take a moment to evaluate what matters most to you. Release what no longer serves, and give your energy to the people, passions, and practices that align with your highest self. Hold them close and cherish them as the true treasures of your life.

Meditative Prayer

Divine Source of Clarity,
Help me focus on what truly matters today.
Let my heart be centered on love,
Peace,
And purpose.

Where I have been distracted,
Help me refocus.
Where I have been pulled away,
Help me return to what is sacred.

Let me hold tightly to what nourishes my soul,
And release what drains my spirit.
Guide me to live with intention,
And to cherish what is most precious to me.

DAY 285:
The Sacred Pause Before the Next Chapter

Lesson for the Day

Before every new beginning, there is a sacred pause—a moment of stillness where we reflect, recharge, and honor the space between what was and what will be. This pause is not empty or wasted, it is filled with the wisdom of the past and the anticipation of what is to come. It is the space where you acknowledge your growth, release what needs to be let go of, and prepare yourself to step into the next chapter of your life with clarity and grace.

The sacred pause gives you the opportunity to recalibrate, to listen deeply, and to align your heart with your next steps. It allows you to enter the future with a sense of calm, knowing that you are ready for what lies ahead, but also honoring where you are right now.

Today, embrace this sacred pause. Give yourself permission to reflect, rest, and recalibrate. Trust that the next chapter of your life is unfolding in perfect timing, and that this moment of stillness is a vital part of your journey.

Meditative Prayer

Divine Presence,
Help me honor the sacred pause in my life.
Let me reflect with gratitude,
And rest with peace.

Where I feel rushed or uncertain,
Fill me with calm.
Where I feel unprepared,
Guide me to the clarity I need.

Let me release what no longer serves,
And make space for the new.
In this moment of stillness,
I trust that the next chapter is unfolding with grace.

DAY 286:

Seeing the Patterns in Your Journey

Lesson for the Day

Life often presents itself in patterns—recurring themes, cycles, and lessons that appear at different points on your journey. These patterns are not random. They are opportunities for growth and healing, each one designed to bring you closer to your authentic self. When you learn to recognize these patterns, you gain insight into the deeper workings of your life and the wisdom that has been guiding you all along.

By seeing the patterns in your journey, you can identify the lessons that you are being invited to learn. You can release old cycles that no longer serve you, and step into new ways of being. Recognizing these patterns allows you to move forward with intention, making conscious choices that align with your soul's purpose.

Today, take time to reflect on the patterns in your life. What lessons have shown up repeatedly? What themes keep emerging? Trust that the patterns in your journey are here to help you evolve, and that each one is a stepping stone toward the highest version of yourself.

Meditative Prayer

Divine Teacher,
Help me see the patterns in my life with clarity.
Guide me to recognize the lessons
That have been showing up for me.

Where I have missed the message,
Help me open my eyes.
Where I have resisted growth,
Fill me with understanding.

Let me embrace the lessons,
Release the cycles that no longer serve me,
And step into the new patterns of wisdom and peace.

I trust that everything is unfolding in divine order,
And that each pattern has a purpose on my journey.

Day 287:

The Wisdom of the Soul's Journey

Lesson for the Day

The soul's journey is not linear—it is an expansive, evolving experience filled with growth, discovery, and transformation. Every step, every challenge, and every triumph is part of your soul's unfolding path. The wisdom of this journey is found in the lessons you learn, the strength you develop, and the peace that comes when you surrender to the process.

Your soul carries within it the memory of its past experiences and the clarity of its true purpose. It knows the way, even when the mind is uncertain. The wisdom of your soul speaks through your intuition, your heart, and your deepest truths. When you listen to this inner guidance, you align with the divine flow that moves through every part of your being.

Today, honor the wisdom of your soul's journey. Trust that each experience—whether joyful or difficult—has shaped you into who you are today. Let your soul guide you forward, knowing that you are always supported, always growing, and always moving toward your highest good.

Meditative Prayer

Divine Soul of Wisdom,
Thank You for the guidance of my soul.
Help me trust the journey,
And honor the wisdom I carry within me.

Where I have doubted,
Fill me with confidence.
Where I have struggled,
Give me the strength to continue.

Let me listen to the whispers of my soul,
And walk with peace,
With trust,
And with love.

I embrace the wisdom of my journey,
And trust that I am always exactly where I need to be.

DAY 288:

Honoring the Cycles of Growth

Lesson for the Day

Growth is not a straight path, but a series of cycles—each with its own timing, rhythm, and purpose. There are seasons of expansion, times of rest, moments of challenge, and periods of quiet reflection. Honoring the cycles of growth means embracing each phase with patience, knowing that each one has its role in your overall journey.

Just as nature goes through cycles of planting, growing, and resting, so does your soul. The growth you experience is not always immediate—it may take time to blossom. When you honor these cycles, you release the pressure to rush and instead allow yourself to be nurtured by each phase. Trust that all growth, even the quiet or hidden moments, is leading you toward your highest self.

Today, reflect on where you are in your own cycle. Are you in a period of rest, or are you in a time of growth and transformation? Honor wherever you are, and trust that every cycle is necessary for your evolution.

Meditative Prayer

Divine Creator,
Thank You for the sacred cycles of growth.
Help me honor each phase,
Whether in rest, in expansion, or in challenge.

Where I feel impatient,
Fill me with peace.
Where I feel unsure,
Fill me with trust.

Let me be present in each moment,
And embrace the rhythm of my journey.
I trust that every cycle leads me toward greater wisdom,
And that growth is always happening, even in the stillness.

Day 289:
Seeing the Divine's Hand in Every Step

Lesson for the Day

Every step you take is part of a sacred dance with the Divine. When you open yourself to seeing the hand of the Divine in each moment, you begin to trust that you are being guided, loved, and supported at every turn. There are no coincidences—only divine alignments that bring you closer to your highest good.

Recognizing the Divine's hand in every step is an act of surrender and trust. It means knowing that the timing of your life, the people you meet, and the challenges you face are all part of a greater plan. Even when things don't seem to go as expected, trust that the Divine is leading you exactly where you need to be.

Today, take a moment to pause and reflect on the steps you've taken. See the Divine's presence in every experience, every lesson, and every encounter. Trust that you are always being guided and that every step, no matter how small, is leading you toward greater understanding and fulfillment.

Meditative Prayer

Divine Presence,
Help me see Your hand in every step I take today.
Let me feel Your guidance in every decision,
And Your love in every experience.

Where I have questioned the path,
Fill me with trust.
Where I have felt lost,
Fill me with peace.

I choose to walk with faith,
Knowing You are with me always,
Guiding me toward the highest good.
I trust in the divine timing of my life,
And I am grateful for every step.

DAY 290:

Trusting the Wisdom Gained Through Time

Lesson for the Day

With time comes wisdom—an accumulation of experiences, insights, and lessons learned. Each moment, no matter how small, offers you the opportunity to grow, and over time, this growth deepens your understanding of yourself and the world around you. Trusting the wisdom gained through time means honoring the lessons you've learned and using them to guide your future decisions.

It's easy to forget that the challenges you've faced and the victories you've celebrated have shaped you into the person you are today. When you trust the wisdom gained through time, you acknowledge that every experience has played a role in preparing you for the next step on your journey. You become grounded in the understanding that you have everything within you to navigate whatever comes next.

Today, reflect on the wisdom you have gathered. Trust that this wisdom is not only valid, but a powerful tool for your continued growth. Allow yourself to lean on the insights you've gained through time as you move forward with confidence and clarity.

Meditative Prayer

Divine Source of Wisdom,
Thank You for the lessons that time has taught me.
Help me trust the wisdom gained through every experience,
The challenges, the triumphs, the quiet moments.

Where I have questioned the past,
Fill me with peace.
Where I have doubted my journey,
Fill me with clarity.

Let me trust that every step has led me here,
And that I am always growing, always learning.
Guide me to use this wisdom with love,
To move forward with faith,
And to honor the truth I've gained along the way.

DAY 291:

The Gift of Maturity in Spirit

Lesson for the Day

Maturity in spirit is the deepening of your understanding, compassion, and connection with the Divine. It is not about age or time—it is about growth, transformation, and the ability to see beyond the surface of life's experiences. Maturity in spirit allows you to move through challenges with grace, understanding, and the ability to let go of what no longer serves you.

As your spirit matures, you become more grounded in your values, more aware of your inner wisdom, and more aligned with your soul's purpose. Maturity doesn't mean perfection—it means knowing when to speak and when to be silent, when to hold on and when to let go, when to give and when to receive. It is a quiet strength, a balanced peace that comes from knowing who you are and trusting that you are always supported by the Divine.

Today, honor the maturity of your spirit. Reflect on how you've grown, how you've learned, and how your soul has deepened. Trust that as you continue to evolve, you will be guided by the wisdom of your heart and the strength of your spirit.

Meditative Prayer

Divine Presence,
Thank You for the gift of spiritual maturity.
Help me grow with grace,
And learn with love,
As I walk this journey of becoming.

Where I have struggled,
Help me find wisdom.
Where I have resisted growth,
Help me surrender with trust.

Let me move forward today,
Grounded in my values,
Aligned with my soul's purpose,
And confident in the guidance of my spirit.

I honor the strength, the peace, and the wisdom
That comes with maturity.

Day 292:

The Peace That Comes from Understanding

Lesson for the Day

Understanding brings peace—it is the key that unlocks the door to harmony within. When we understand ourselves, others, and the circumstances of our lives, we create a space for compassion and calm to enter. Understanding doesn't mean we always agree or have all the answers, but it allows us to approach life with an open heart and a clearer mind.

The peace that comes from understanding is rooted in acceptance. It is about embracing the truths that we may not yet fully grasp, trusting that everything unfolds in divine order. When we seek to understand, we release judgment and allow the flow of grace to guide us. This peace helps us navigate challenges with ease and move through life with a heart that is both grounded and open.

Today, take time to reflect on where you can seek deeper understanding. Who or what needs more compassion from you? What in your life can be approached with more awareness and patience? Trust that as you embrace understanding, peace will follow.

Meditative Prayer

Divine Source of Clarity,
Grant me the peace that comes from understanding.
Help me see with compassionate eyes,
And listen with an open heart.

Where I have judged,
Help me open to understanding.
Where I have misunderstood,
Guide me to see the deeper truth.

Let me find peace in the moments of uncertainty,
And trust that understanding leads me to greater love.
May my heart be a vessel of compassion,
And my mind a space of clarity.

DAY 293:
A Heart Open to Lifelong Learning

Lesson for the Day

Life is a continuous journey of learning, growth, and discovery. The key to staying vibrant, connected, and evolving is to approach each day with a heart open to lifelong learning. This mindset allows you to embrace new experiences, ideas, and perspectives, knowing that every moment offers an opportunity to expand your understanding.

Lifelong learning is not just about acquiring knowledge, but about evolving spiritually, emotionally, and mentally. It requires humility, curiosity, and a willingness to remain open to change. When you approach life with a learner's heart, you create space for transformation and deeper insight, and you remain adaptable to the ebb and flow of your journey.

Today, approach your day with openness. Ask yourself, *What can I learn from this experience?* and, *How can I grow from this moment?* By embracing the opportunity to learn in every circumstance, you will open your heart to the richness and depth of life.

Meditative Prayer

Divine Teacher,
Thank You for the gift of learning.
Help me remain open to new wisdom,
New experiences,
And new opportunities for growth.

Where I have become stagnant,
Fill me with curiosity.
Where I have resisted change,
Help me embrace transformation.

Let me learn with humility,
Grow with grace,
And remain open to the lessons life offers.

Guide me today in all I do,
And help me see each moment as an opportunity to evolve.

Day 294:
Walking with the Grace of Experience

Lesson for the Day

Experience is a powerful teacher. Every moment you've lived, every challenge you've faced, and every joy you've celebrated has contributed to the person you are today. Walking with the grace of experience means carrying those lessons with you—allowing them to inform your choices, guide your actions, and deepen your connection with life.

Grace in experience is not about perfection, it's about accepting the past with love, embracing the wisdom gained, and moving forward with a sense of ease. When you walk with grace, you honor your journey without being weighed down by it. You trust that the experiences you've had were necessary for your growth, and you let them unfold into strength, compassion, and peace.

Today, allow your experiences to guide you gently. Walk with confidence, knowing that you are carrying the wisdom of all you've learned, and trust that you are always evolving toward greater understanding and grace.

Meditative Prayer

Divine Teacher,
Thank You for the grace that comes with experience.
Help me carry the lessons of my journey
With peace and wisdom,
Not burdened, but strengthened by them.

Where I have struggled,
Help me find peace.
Where I have learned,
Help me share that wisdom.

Let me walk today with the grace
Of knowing I am always growing,
Always learning,
And always evolving into my highest self.

Day 295:

Recognizing the Search in the Ordinary

Lesson for the Day

The sacred is not confined to extraordinary moments or grand experiences. It resides in the ordinary—the quiet moments, the simple acts, and the everyday blessings that often go unnoticed. When you begin to recognize the sacred in the ordinary, you realize that every moment is imbued with meaning, and every experience holds the potential for connection to something greater.

Whether it's the warmth of the sun, the sound of a loved one's voice, or the peaceful rhythm of your breath, the Divine is present in the smallest details of your life. When you open your heart to see the sacred in the ordinary, you begin to live with a sense of awe and appreciation for the gifts that surround you. Life becomes more meaningful, more alive, and more connected to the Divine.

Today, take time to look for the sacred in your day. Whether in nature, in relationships, or in a quiet moment of solitude, recognize that the Divine is present in every corner of your life. The more you see it, the more it will appear.

Meditative Prayer

Sacred Presence,
Help me see the Divine in every moment today.
Let me recognize Your love in the smallest details,
And find meaning in the ordinary.

Where I have rushed through my day,
Help me slow down and see with new eyes.
Where I have overlooked beauty,
Help me notice and appreciate it.

Let my heart be open to the sacredness of the now,
And may I carry the awareness of Your presence
In all that I do.

DAY 296:

Learning to Listen to the Soul's Whisper

Lesson for the Day

The soul speaks in whispers—subtle, gentle nudges that guide you toward your highest path. These whispers are often drowned out by the noise of daily life, yet they carry the truest form of guidance. Learning to listen to the soul's whisper requires quieting the mind and tuning into the deeper rhythms of your heart. When you listen, you connect with a wisdom that transcends logic and reason, guiding you to make choices that are in alignment with your true self.

The soul's whispers are not always loud or dramatic, but they are always there, guiding you toward peace, growth, and authenticity. Learning to trust these whispers is an act of faith. It means moving beyond external influences and relying on your inner knowing. As you cultivate this connection, you deepen your trust in yourself and in the divine flow of life.

Today, take time to listen. Quiet your mind, slow your breath, and tune into the subtle messages of your soul. Trust that the whispers are leading you exactly where you need to be.

Meditative Prayer

Divine Whisper,
Help me quiet my mind so I can hear the soft voice of my soul.
Guide me to listen deeply to the wisdom that comes from within.

Where I have ignored my intuition,
Help me tune in.
Where I have doubted myself,
Fill me with trust.

Let me follow the path my soul whispers to me,
With courage, clarity, and peace.
I trust in Your guidance,
And in the gentle wisdom that speaks to my heart.

DAY 297:
The Power of Spiritual Discernment

Lesson for the Day

Spiritual discernment is the ability to distinguish between what resonates with your highest truth and what does not. It is an inner wisdom that guides you in making decisions, interpreting experiences, and understanding the messages of your soul. Discernment is not about judgment, it is about clarity—an ability to see situations, people, and ideas through the lens of your spiritual wisdom, free from ego or bias.

When you cultivate spiritual discernment, you align yourself with divine guidance. It helps you to know when to say yes and when to say no, when to act and when to wait. It is an empowering practice, allowing you to walk confidently on your path, knowing you are being guided by a higher wisdom.

Today, practice discernment in your thoughts, actions, and choices. Tune into your inner voice and trust the clarity that arises from within. Trust that your spiritual discernment will guide you to what is in alignment with your highest good.

Meditative Prayer

Divine Guide,
Help me cultivate the gift of spiritual discernment.
Let me listen deeply to Your guidance
And trust the wisdom that comes from within.

Where I am unclear,
Bring me clarity.
Where I am uncertain,
Fill me with peace.

Guide me to see the truth in every situation,
And to act with wisdom and grace.
I trust in the discernment You offer me,
And I walk in alignment with Your will.

Day 298:

Embracing the Wisdom of the Ancestors

Lesson for the Day

The wisdom of the ancestors is a rich, sacred legacy that connects you to a deeper sense of self and belonging. Our ancestors lived lives filled with their own challenges, triumphs, and lessons, and the wisdom they gained has been passed down through generations. Embracing this wisdom means honoring the paths they walked, the values they held, and the teachings they passed on, whether consciously or unconsciously.

By tapping into this ancestral wisdom, you gain a deeper understanding of your own life, your place in the world, and your personal journey. The ancestors offer guidance, healing, and support, helping you navigate your own challenges with the strength, resilience, and knowledge they imparted. They are always with you, offering their wisdom and love from beyond the veil.

Today, take a moment to reflect on the wisdom of your ancestors. What teachings can you carry forward in your own life? How can you honor their legacy? Trust that their wisdom is always available to guide you on your path.

Meditative Prayer

Ancestors of my bloodline,
Thank You for the wisdom you have passed down.
I honor the paths you walked,
And the lessons you learned along the way.

Help me hear your voices,
Feel your presence,
And carry your teachings forward in my life.

Where I need strength,
Give me the resilience you embodied.
Where I seek guidance,
Illuminate the path with your wisdom.

I am deeply connected to your legacy,
And I walk with gratitude,
Listening to the wisdom of the ancestors
Who guide me through each step of my journey.

DAY 299:

Carrying the Light of Knowledge

Lesson for the Day

Knowledge is a powerful tool, but it is even more transformative when paired with wisdom and compassion. The light of knowledge illuminates the way forward, helping you navigate through life with clarity, purpose, and insight. However, knowledge alone is not enough. To carry the light of knowledge means to integrate it into your life in ways that serve the greater good, to use it with humility and love, and to share it with others without expectation or ego.

When you carry the light of knowledge, you also carry responsibility—the responsibility to continue learning, to question, and to grow. Knowledge expands the mind, but wisdom opens the heart. By combining both, you become a beacon of light to others, sharing what you've learned while allowing space for others to learn as well.

Today, reflect on how you can carry the light of knowledge in a way that serves both your own growth and the wellbeing of those around you. Use your insights to uplift, to guide, and to offer clarity, all while remaining humble and open to new discoveries.

Meditative Prayer

Divine Source of Wisdom,
Thank You for the gift of knowledge.
Help me carry it with humility,
Use it with compassion,
And share it with love.

Where I have learned,
Let me teach with grace.
Where I have grown,
Let me offer my growth to others.

Guide me to seek knowledge with an open heart,
And to carry it as a light to illuminate the path of others.
May I be a source of wisdom and peace,
Sharing the light I have received.

DAY 300:

Knowing When to Hold On and When to Release

Lesson for the Day

Life is a delicate balance between holding on and letting go. Sometimes, it is necessary to hold on to what is dear, what brings you joy, and what is in alignment with your values and purpose. Other times, it is just as important to release what no longer serves you—whether it's a situation, a belief, a relationship, or an attachment. Knowing when to hold on and when to release is an art of discernment, requiring deep self-awareness and trust in the flow of life.

Holding on with love and wisdom means being grounded in what is essential and true for you. Releasing, on the other hand, requires trust—trust that when you let go, you create space for something new and more aligned with your growth. It is not about giving up, it is about making room for the next chapter of your journey.

Today, reflect on what in your life you need to hold on to, and what it is time to release. Trust that your inner wisdom will guide you in knowing the difference, and that in both holding and releasing, you are creating a life that is in harmony with your soul's purpose.

Meditative Prayer

Divine Source of Wisdom,
Guide me in knowing when to hold on
And when to release.

Where I need strength,
Help me hold on with love.
Where I need freedom,
Help me release with trust.

Let me recognize what nourishes my soul,
And let me release what limits my growth.
May I trust that in every act of release,
I am making space for new blessings to flow.

Day 301:

The Art of Letting Go

Lesson for the Day

Letting go is a sacred art—a practice of surrender, trust, and release. It is not about giving up, but about creating space for new growth, new experiences, and new possibilities. Letting go of old attachments, resentments, fears, or outdated beliefs allows you to move forward with a lighter heart, a clearer mind, and a more open spirit.

The art of letting go requires courage. It means facing the discomfort of uncertainty and stepping into the unknown with faith that what is meant for you will always find its way. When you let go, you make room for divine alignment—trusting that the universe, your soul, and the Divine are working in harmony for your highest good.

Today, ask yourself, *What do I need to release in order to move forward? What is no longer serving me?* Allow yourself to let go, trusting that you are not losing anything, but instead making space for the new, the meaningful, and the aligned.

Meditative Prayer

Divine Source of Release,
Help me practice the art of letting go today.
Where I am holding on too tightly,
Guide me to release with love.
Where I am afraid to surrender,
Fill me with trust.

Let me let go of what no longer serves me,
Old patterns, old hurts, old fears.
And may I make space for what is meant to come,
For the new blessings, new opportunities,
And new growth that awaits me.

I trust in Your guidance as I release
And step into the freedom of surrender.

DAY 302:
Releasing What No Longer Serves You

Lesson for the Day

Releasing what no longer serves you is an essential step in your personal growth and spiritual journey. Over time, we accumulate things—whether thoughts, beliefs, relationships, or material possessions—that hold us back or weigh us down. These attachments, even though once valuable, can become hindrances if they no longer align with who we are becoming. Releasing them is a conscious act of making room for new experiences, healthier relationships, and more positive energy to enter your life.

Letting go doesn't mean you've failed or that what you've held onto was wrong, it simply means that you are ready for something better, something more aligned with your current self. The act of release is a powerful affirmation of your trust in the flow of life and in the process of transformation.

Today, take a moment to reflect on what you need to release. Whether it's a limiting belief, a past experience, or a relationship that no longer serves your growth, give yourself permission to let go. Trust that what you release will make space for what is truly meant for you.

Meditative Prayer

Divine Source of Freedom,
Help me release what no longer serves me today.
Where I have held on out of fear,
Help me release with love.
Where I have resisted change,
Fill me with courage to surrender.

I let go of what weighs me down,
Old beliefs, old hurts, old attachments.
And I trust that in this release,
I create space for growth, for peace,
For what is meant to come into my life.

Guide me as I step into the flow of new possibilities,
And may I walk forward lightened, open, and free.

DAY 303:
Trusting in the Process of Change

Lesson for the Day

Change is a natural part of life, but it often brings uncertainty and discomfort. Trusting in the process of change is about surrendering to the flow of life and accepting that everything is unfolding in divine timing. While change may feel unsettling, it is always leading you to growth, transformation, and new opportunities. Every shift, whether big or small, is helping you become the person you are meant to be.

The key to trusting in change is knowing that, even when the path ahead seems unclear, you are always being guided toward something better. The process may not always be linear, and there may be moments of doubt, but trust that each experience—each step—is a part of your unfolding journey.

Today, allow yourself to release the fear of change and trust the process. Understand that change, though uncomfortable at times, is an essential part of your spiritual and personal evolution. Trust that you are always being supported, and that each transition is guiding you toward the life you are meant to live.

Meditative Prayer

Divine Source of Transformation,
Help me trust in the process of change today.
Where I feel uncertain,
Fill me with peace.
Where I fear the unknown,
Fill me with trust.

I surrender to the flow of life,
And trust that every change is leading me toward growth.
Help me embrace each transition with grace,
And understand that all is unfolding for my highest good.

Guide me as I step into the unknown,
With faith in Your divine plan,
And peace in my heart.

DAY 304:
Shedding the Old to Make Space for the New

Lesson for the Day

Shedding the old is an essential part of the process of growth and transformation. Just as a tree must release its leaves to prepare for new growth, we too must let go of outdated beliefs, habits, relationships, and even physical clutter in order to make space for the new and the better. Holding on to the past, even if it's no longer serving us, can prevent us from fully embracing the future.

When we shed the old, we create room for new experiences, opportunities, and energy to flow into our lives. This act of release is an affirmation of trust in the future and in the process of evolution. It allows us to move forward with a lighter heart, a clearer mind, and an openness to new possibilities.

Today, reflect on what you may need to release in order to move forward. What no longer serves you—whether it's a thought pattern, a relationship, or an attachment? Trust that shedding the old will make space for something new, something that aligns more deeply with your true self and your highest good.

Meditative Prayer

Divine Source of Renewal,
Help me shed the old today,
And create space for the new.
Where I have held on to what no longer serves me,
Help me release with love.

Let me make room for new growth,
New experiences,
And new blessings.
Fill my heart with trust in the process of change,
And my mind with peace in knowing that all is unfolding as it
should.

I trust that in shedding the old,
I am preparing for the new that is waiting for me.

DAY 305:
The Freedom Found in Surrender

Lesson for the Day

Surrender is not about giving up, it's about letting go of control and trusting in the flow of life. When we surrender, we stop resisting the natural course of things and allow space for peace, clarity, and divine guidance. Surrender is not passive—it is an active choice to release the need to control every outcome and trust that the universe, or the Divine, is working in your favor.

In surrendering, we find freedom. We free ourselves from the weight of expectations, from the anxiety of trying to manage everything, and from the stress of worrying about what's next. Surrender allows us to step into the present moment fully, knowing that whatever happens is for our highest good. It is in letting go that we allow ourselves to experience the true peace and freedom that comes from trusting the journey.

Today, practice surrender. Let go of the need to control or force outcomes. Trust that life is unfolding in perfect timing and that every step, even those that seem uncertain, is part of your divine path. The freedom found in surrender is not in the absence of effort, but in the deep faith that you are being guided every step of the way.

Meditative Prayer

Divine Source of Peace,
Help me surrender today.
Where I have resisted,
Fill me with trust.
Where I have struggled,
Fill me with peace.

Let me release the need to control,
And trust that all is unfolding perfectly.
Guide me to surrender with grace,
And to find freedom in the flow of life.

I trust in the wisdom of the universe,
And in the divine timing of my journey.
Thank you for the peace found in surrender,
And the freedom that comes with trusting You.

Day 306:

The Beauty of Closure

Lesson for the Day

Closure is an essential part of healing and personal growth. It allows you to release the past and move forward with peace, knowing that a chapter has ended and a new one is beginning. The beauty of closure lies in its ability to create space for new experiences, relationships, and opportunities. It is not about forgetting what was, rather, it is about honoring what was while making the conscious decision to let go and step into what's next.

When you embrace closure, you release any lingering attachments to the past that may hold you back. Whether it's a relationship, a job, or a period in your life, closing that chapter creates the emotional and spiritual freedom to move forward with confidence. Closure allows you to look back with gratitude and forward with hope.

Today, reflect on any areas in your life where closure is needed. What do you need to release in order to move forward? Trust that by embracing closure, you are honoring your growth and opening yourself to new beginnings.

Meditative Prayer

Divine Source of Healing,
Help me embrace the beauty of closure today.
Where I have held on to the past,
Fill me with peace.
Where I have clung to what no longer serves me,
Guide me to release it with love.

Let me honor what has been,
And trust that closure makes space for new growth,
New beginnings, and new opportunities.
May I move forward with an open heart,
Grateful for the lessons learned,
And excited for the future ahead.

Day 307:
Walking Through the Doors of Transition

Lesson for the Day

Transitions are natural parts of life, but they can still bring uncertainty and discomfort. Walking through the doors of transition requires courage, trust, and faith in the unknown. These moments often mark a shift—whether it's a change in relationships, careers, or personal growth—and though they may feel challenging, they carry within them the potential for transformation and renewal.

When you embrace transition, you allow yourself to move forward with grace. Rather than resisting change, you step through the door with open hands and an open heart, trusting that this new chapter is part of your divine path. Though the door may seem daunting, it is leading you to a place of growth, understanding, and deeper alignment with your highest good.

Today, reflect on the transitions in your life. Are you standing at the threshold of something new? Trust that these changes, though they may feel uncertain, are part of the grand unfolding of your journey. Walk with confidence through each door, knowing that each step is divinely guided.

Meditative Prayer

Divine Guide,

Help me walk through the doors of transition with trust and

courage.

Where I feel uncertain,

Fill me with peace.

Where I feel afraid,

Fill me with faith.

Let me embrace the changes before me,

Knowing that they are leading me toward growth,

Healing, and new opportunities.

May I trust the path ahead,

And walk forward with an open heart and a clear mind.

Thank you for guiding me through each transition,

And for the wisdom and strength that comes with change.

DAY 308:
Releasing the Weight of the Past

Lesson for the Day

The past can often feel like a heavy burden, weighing us down with regret, guilt, or unhealed wounds. Yet, holding onto the weight of the past prevents us from fully embracing the present and moving forward into the future. Releasing the weight of the past is a powerful act of self-liberation—one that frees your mind, heart, and spirit from the limitations of what has already occurred.

Releasing does not mean forgetting, it means making peace with what has been and choosing to no longer let it define you. It's about accepting the lessons, honoring the journey, and letting go of the emotional or mental heaviness that holds you back. When you release the weight of the past, you allow yourself to step into the freedom of the present moment and the potential of the future.

Today, take a moment to reflect on the past. What are you still carrying that no longer serves you? Whether it's an old wound, an unspoken regret, or a memory that holds you captive, allow yourself to release it. Trust that in letting go, you are making room for new opportunities, peace, and healing.

Meditative Prayer

Divine Healer,
Help me release the weight of the past today.
Where I have carried old wounds,
Fill me with healing.
Where I have held onto regret,
Fill me with peace.

Let me honor my journey,
And forgive myself for what I have held onto.
Guide me to release what no longer serves me,
And to step forward into freedom.

I trust that in releasing,
I am creating space for new blessings,
New experiences,
And new growth.

DAY 309:
A Heart That Moves Forward with Grace

Lesson for the Day

Grace is the ability to move through life's challenges with calm, dignity, and an open heart. It is not about avoiding difficulty, but about how we respond to it. A heart that moves forward with grace acknowledges the struggles, embraces the lessons, and continues on the journey with love, forgiveness, and trust. Moving forward with grace means accepting that change and hardship are part of life, yet still choosing to rise above them with a sense of peace and purpose.

When we approach life with grace, we allow ourselves to move forward, free from the burdens of resentment, guilt, or regret. We trust that each step we take, no matter how small, is part of the unfolding path that leads to growth, understanding, and healing. Grace doesn't deny difficulty, but it transforms how we experience it, allowing us to rise stronger and more centered.

Today, reflect on how you can move forward with grace. What areas in your life need your grace, your forgiveness, and your trust? With each step, carry yourself with the knowledge that grace is within you, ready to guide your heart and actions.

Meditative Prayer

Divine Source of Grace,
Help me move forward today with a heart full of love and peace.
Where I have struggled,
Let me rise with grace.
Where I have felt burdened,
Let me walk with lightness.

Help me carry forgiveness,
And release what no longer serves my soul.
Let my heart be open to the lessons of the journey,
And my spirit strong enough to move forward with grace.

I trust that grace will guide me,
And I am ready to embrace the next step with faith,
Love, and peace.

DAY 310:

Embracing the Flow of Life

Lesson for the Day

Life is like a river—constantly moving, changing, and flowing in its own rhythm. To embrace the flow of life is to let go of the need to control every outcome and to trust that life is unfolding exactly as it should. It is about surrendering to the current, understanding that some parts of the journey may feel smooth, while others may have turbulence, but every moment serves a purpose in your personal growth.

When you resist the flow, you create friction and tension. But when you align yourself with life's rhythm, you move with ease, grace, and trust. Embracing the flow of life means trusting in the timing, trusting in your ability to navigate challenges, and knowing that every twist and turn is an opportunity for growth.

Today, reflect on where you are resisting the flow of life. What areas of your journey are you holding onto too tightly? Surrender to the current, knowing that the flow of life is guiding you exactly where you need to go. Trust in the process and in your ability to adapt to what comes next.

Meditative Prayer

Divine Flow,
Help me embrace the flow of life today.
Where I have resisted,
Fill me with trust.
Where I have struggled,
Fill me with peace.

Guide me to move with the current,
And to release the need to control.
Let me trust in Your divine timing,
And in the unfolding of my journey.

I trust that life is flowing exactly as it should,
And that each step is leading me toward growth and fulfillment.

Day 311:
Finding Strength in Life's Changes

Lesson for the Day

Life is ever-changing—sometimes beautifully, sometimes with difficulty. But in every change, there is an opportunity to grow, learn, and discover new strength within yourself. Finding strength in life's changes means acknowledging that change is not something to fear or resist, but something to embrace as part of the flow of life. Every transition, whether it feels uncertain or challenging, holds within it the potential for transformation and personal growth.

The strength you find in change comes from the belief that you have the resilience to navigate whatever comes your way. It comes from trusting in your inner wisdom, knowing that with each shift, you are evolving into the person you are meant to be. The key is to remain open, grounded, and willing to flow with the changes rather than fighting against them.

Today, reflect on a recent change in your life. How has it made you stronger? How can you embrace future changes with more trust and confidence? Know that with each new change, you are becoming more resilient, more powerful, and more aligned with your highest self.

Meditative Prayer

Divine Source of Strength,
Help me find strength in life's changes today.
Where I have felt fear,
Fill me with courage.
Where I have resisted,
Fill me with peace.

Guide me through each transition,
And help me trust in the process of transformation.
Let me embrace change with grace,
And discover new strength with every step.

I trust that every change is an opportunity for growth,
And I move forward with faith in myself and in the divine plan.

DAY 312:

The Power of a Fresh Start

Lesson for the Day

A fresh start is a powerful gift—an opportunity to release the past and begin again with a clear heart and mind. It's a chance to let go of old patterns, thoughts, and behaviors that no longer serve you, and to step into a new chapter with intention and purpose. A fresh start doesn't require perfection. It simply requires the willingness to begin again, to start where you are, and to trust that the Divine is with you every step of the way.

The power of a fresh start lies in its ability to offer renewal and hope. It's a reminder that no matter how much time has passed, you can always begin anew. Every day is an invitation to choose differently, to act from your highest self, and to create the life you truly desire.

Today, reflect on the fresh starts available to you. Is there an area in your life where you can begin again, with a clean slate? Trust that this moment is the perfect time to take that first step. A fresh start is not just a new beginning—it is a transformative act of empowerment.

Meditative Prayer

Divine Creator,
Thank You for the gift of fresh starts.
Help me release the past with love,
And step into this new moment with trust and hope.

Where I have felt stuck,
Fill me with renewal.
Where I have doubted,
Fill me with courage to begin again.

Let me move forward with intention,
Knowing that every step I take brings me closer to the life I am
meant to live.
Thank you for the power of new beginnings,
And for the chance to start fresh with each new day.

DAY 313:
Accepting What Cannot Be Changed

Lesson for the Day

Acceptance is one of the most powerful forms of peace. There are moments in life when we are faced with circumstances that we cannot change, no matter how hard we try. These situations may bring pain, frustration, or uncertainty, but accepting them is not about giving up—it's about finding peace in the midst of what is. When we release the need to control what cannot be changed, we make room for healing, growth, and clarity.

Acceptance allows us to embrace life as it is, rather than resisting or fighting against what cannot be altered. It doesn't mean we like what has happened or that we agree with it, rather, it's about choosing to live with what is, finding the lessons in it, and moving forward with grace. Through acceptance, we can let go of the emotional weight of resistance and reclaim our inner peace.

Today, reflect on the areas of your life where acceptance is needed. What can you release control over, and allow to simply be? Trust that through acceptance, you will find peace and the strength to continue on your journey with an open heart.

Meditative Prayer

Divine Source of Peace,
Help me accept what cannot be changed today.
Where I have resisted,
Fill me with peace.
Where I have struggled,
Fill me with strength.

Let me embrace what is,
Knowing that in acceptance,
I find freedom.
Guide me to release what I cannot control,
And move forward with grace,
Trusting that all is unfolding in divine order.

DAY 314:

Learning to Trust in What's Ahead

Lesson for the Day

Trusting what's ahead can be one of the most challenging yet liberating aspects of life. We often feel uncertain about the future, and fear or doubt can cloud our path. However, learning to trust in what's ahead is an essential step in embracing the unknown with an open heart and a confident spirit. Trust is not about having all the answers or knowing every step of the journey—it's about believing that the universe, the Divine, or your higher self is guiding you toward what is meant for you.

When you trust in what's ahead, you release the anxiety of trying to control every outcome. You step into the flow of life with faith that each moment is part of a larger plan that is unfolding in perfect timing. Trust allows you to move forward with hope, even when the path seems unclear. It's the belief that no matter what comes, you have everything within you to navigate it with grace.

Today, take a moment to reflect on the future. What aspects of your journey can you surrender to trust? Where can you let go of fear and open yourself to the possibilities ahead? Trust that everything is unfolding exactly as it should.

Meditative Prayer

Divine Source of Guidance,
Help me trust in what's ahead today.
Where I have doubted,
Fill me with faith.
Where I have feared,
Fill me with peace.

Let me release the need to control the future,
And trust that all is unfolding in divine order.
Guide me to move forward with confidence,
And to trust that every step is leading me closer to my highest
good.

Thank you for the strength to trust,
And for the peace that comes from knowing I am supported.

DAY 315:
Walking Away from What No Longer Aligns

Lesson for the Day

There are times in life when we must make the difficult decision to walk away from people, situations, or even beliefs that no longer align with our true selves. Walking away doesn't mean giving up—it means choosing to honor your growth, your values, and your inner peace. It takes courage to step away from what is familiar or comfortable, especially when it no longer serves your highest good.

When you walk away from what no longer aligns, you create space for new opportunities, healthier relationships, and a deeper connection with your purpose. Trust that when you release what no longer fits, you open the door to what is meant for you, and you are affirming your worth and your desire for a life that supports your true essence.

Today, reflect on what may need to be released in your life. What is no longer serving your growth or peace? Trust that walking away from it is an act of self-love and will create room for new blessings that are in alignment with your highest good.

Meditative Prayer

Divine Source of Clarity,
Help me recognize what no longer aligns with my highest good.
Where I am holding on to what no longer serves me,
Give me the courage to walk away.

Let me honor myself and my growth,
And trust that in releasing what no longer fits,
I make space for the life I am meant to live.

Guide me as I move forward,
Confident in my decisions,
And open to the new blessings that await me.

DAY 316:
The Sacredness of Endings and Beginnings

Lesson for the Day

Endings and beginnings are both sacred moments in the cycle of life. Each ending marks the completion of one chapter and the closing of a door, but it also paves the way for a new beginning—a new opportunity, a fresh start, or a new phase of growth. The sacredness of these transitions lies in their ability to guide us toward transformation and renewal. Every ending carries with it a lesson learned and a strength gained, while every beginning holds the promise of possibility and growth.

Embracing both endings and beginnings requires trust in the process of life. When we honor the sacredness of both, we find peace in the knowledge that life is a continuous flow of change and evolution. We understand that each ending makes space for something new, and that every new beginning brings us closer to who we are meant to be.

Today, reflect on the endings and beginnings in your life. What has ended that has made space for new growth? What new beginnings are you being invited to embrace? Trust that these transitions are part of the divine flow of life and honor the sacredness of both.

Meditative Prayer

Divine Source of Creation,
Thank You for the sacredness of endings and beginnings.
Help me honor the completion of what has been,
And embrace the new that is unfolding before me.

Where I have feared endings,
Fill me with peace.
Where I have resisted new beginnings,
Fill me with hope and trust.

Guide me through each transition,
And help me see the beauty in both what has passed
And what is yet to come.
I trust in the divine flow of life,
And in the sacredness of every step.

DAY 317:
Embracing the Cycles of Life

Lesson for the Day

Life moves in cycles—seasons of growth, rest, transformation, and renewal. These natural rhythms are part of the divine flow of existence, reminding us that everything has its time and place. Just as the seasons change, so too do the phases of our lives. There are times of expansion, when we are filled with energy and purpose, and times of contraction, when we are asked to reflect, rest, and rejuvenate.

Embracing the cycles of life means accepting both the ebbs and flows. It's recognizing that each phase has its purpose, even if we don't fully understand it at the time. We cannot rush through the cycles or resist their natural course. Instead, we must learn to flow with them, trusting that each cycle leads us closer to our highest potential.

Today, reflect on the cycles you are currently experiencing. Are you in a season of growth, rest, or transformation? Trust that each cycle is necessary for your evolution, and embrace it with openness and grace. Remember, everything has its time, and every cycle brings you closer to the person you are meant to be.

Meditative Prayer

Divine Source of Life,
Thank You for the gift of the cycles of life.
Help me embrace each season with grace,
Whether in times of growth, rest, or transformation.

Where I have resisted the flow,
Fill me with trust.
Where I have been impatient,
Fill me with patience.

Guide me to move with the rhythm of life,
And to honor each phase of my journey.
I trust that every cycle has its purpose,
And that all is unfolding in divine order.

DAY 318:
Finding Peace in Every Goodbye

Lesson for the Day

Goodbyes are never easy. Whether they are the end of a chapter, a relationship, or a moment in time, they bring with them a sense of loss or sadness. However, finding peace in every goodbye is an act of self-love and spiritual growth. Goodbyes are not just about endings. They are about acknowledging the lessons learned, the memories created, and the space made for new beginnings.

In every goodbye, there is an opportunity for healing and renewal. The peace you seek is not found in avoiding the pain of goodbye, but in accepting it as a natural part of life. Trust that every departure, whether physical or emotional, is creating room for new experiences and growth. Each goodbye is a step toward greater clarity, understanding, and connection with your true self.

Today, reflect on any goodbyes you may be facing or have faced. Allow yourself to honor the emotions that come with them, and then find peace in knowing that every ending makes way for a new chapter. Trust that each goodbye is leading you closer to the life you are meant to live.

Meditative Prayer

Divine Source of Peace,
Help me find peace in every goodbye today.
Where I have resisted change,
Fill me with acceptance.
Where I have feared loss,
Fill me with trust in the new beginnings that follow.

Let me honor the moments that have passed,
And release them with love.
Guide me to walk forward with an open heart,
Knowing that goodbyes are a part of the divine flow of life.

Thank you for the peace that comes from letting go,
And for the new opportunities that await me.

DAY 319:
Letting Go of Fear and Stepping into Faith

Lesson for the Day

Fear is a natural part of the human experience, but it doesn't have to control us. Fear often arises when we face the unknown, when we are on the verge of change, or when we feel out of our comfort zone. However, letting go of fear and stepping into faith is a powerful choice. It is the act of trusting in the unseen, believing that there is a greater plan at work, and that you are supported and guided every step of the way.

Faith allows us to move forward even when the path ahead seems unclear. It is not the absence of fear, but the courage to take action despite it. Stepping into faith means choosing to believe that the universe, the Divine, or your inner wisdom has your back, even when the future feels uncertain. When you embrace faith, you let go of the grip fear has on your heart and open yourself up to limitless possibilities.

Today, reflect on the areas where fear may be holding you back. What would it feel like to step forward with faith instead? Trust that when you let go of fear and embrace faith, you create the space for transformation, growth, and new opportunities.

Meditative Prayer

Divine Source of Faith,
Help me let go of fear today.
Where I feel uncertain,
Fill me with trust.
Where I feel limited,
Fill me with courage to step forward.

Let me release the need to control,
And step into the flow of faith.
Guide me to trust in the path ahead,
Even when I cannot see the way clearly.

I trust that with each step,
I am supported, I am guided,
And I am always exactly where I need to be.

DAY 320:
Releasing Resistance and Trusting the Divine

Lesson for the Day

Resistance often arises when we feel the need to control our circumstances, when things don't go according to our plan, or when we encounter challenges. We resist change because we fear the unknown or the discomfort of letting go. However, releasing resistance and trusting the Divine is a powerful practice of surrender. It's about letting go of the need to control and trusting that life is unfolding exactly as it should.

When we trust the Divine, we acknowledge that we are supported and guided beyond our understanding. The Divine sees the bigger picture and is always leading us toward what is best for our growth, even when it's difficult to see in the moment. By releasing resistance, we make space for peace, clarity, and divine guidance. We allow ourselves to flow with life, rather than fighting against it.

Today, reflect on the areas where you are resisting. What would it feel like to release that resistance and trust that everything is unfolding as it should? Trust that as you let go, you create the space for the Divine to work in your life.

Meditative Prayer

Divine Source of Guidance,
Help me release resistance today.
Where I have fought against the flow,
Fill me with peace.
Where I have feared the unknown,
Fill me with trust.

Guide me to trust that You are always working in my favor,
And that everything is unfolding in divine timing.
Let me surrender to Your plan with an open heart,
And trust that I am always supported by Your love.

I release my need to control,
And step into the flow of Your divine wisdom.

DAY 321:

Learning to Adapt with Grace

Lesson for the Day

Adaptability is a valuable quality, especially in times of change or uncertainty. Life does not always go as planned, and the ability to adapt gracefully allows us to navigate challenges with ease. Adapting with grace means accepting change without resistance, finding peace in the flow, and trusting that each shift is an opportunity for growth. It's not about giving up your desires or goals, but about being flexible and willing to adjust your approach to fit the current circumstances.

When you adapt with grace, you remain centered, grounded, and open, even when faced with the unexpected. You allow yourself to respond to life's twists and turns with confidence, knowing that the process of adaptation is an important part of your journey. Grace in adaptation means letting go of frustration and embracing the opportunity to evolve.

Today, reflect on areas where you can be more adaptable. How can you embrace change with grace and trust in the process of transformation? Allow yourself to be open to new ways of doing things, and trust that your ability to adapt will lead you to a place of greater peace and understanding.

Meditative Prayer

Divine Source of Flexibility,
Help me adapt with grace today.
Where I have resisted change,
Fill me with peace.
Where I have struggled to let go,
Fill me with trust.

Guide me to remain open and flexible,
Allowing life to unfold with ease.
Let me embrace change without fear,
And trust that every shift is leading me toward growth and
wisdom.

May I adapt to each moment with grace,
And move forward with confidence, knowing I am always
supported.

DAY 322:
The Seasons of the Heart

Lesson for the Day

Just as nature goes through cycles of change, so too does the heart. There are seasons of love, joy, and expansion, and there are seasons of sorrow, reflection, and healing. Each season of the heart brings with it unique gifts and challenges. The key is learning to embrace each season for what it is, knowing that each one serves a purpose in the journey of personal growth and emotional well-being.

In the spring of the heart, you may feel vibrant and full of new possibilities. In the winter, you may feel a need for rest, introspection, and quiet healing. No matter what season you are in, trust that it is an important part of your evolution. Each season of the heart offers the chance to connect more deeply with yourself and the world around you.

Today, reflect on the current season of your heart. Are you in a time of growth, rest, or transformation? Honor this season and trust that it is guiding you toward greater understanding, peace, and love. Each phase has its lessons, and the beauty is in the flow.

Meditative Prayer

Divine Source of Love,
Help me honor the season of my heart today.
Where I am in a season of growth,
Fill me with joy and inspiration.
Where I am in a season of healing,
Fill me with patience and peace.

Let me embrace each phase of my emotional journey,
Knowing that all seasons lead me to greater wisdom and love.
Guide me to move through the seasons of my heart
With grace and trust in the divine timing of all things.

Day 323:
Making Peace with the Past

Lesson for the Day

The past is an integral part of who we are, but it no longer defines us. Making peace with the past means releasing the hold it has on our present and future. It is the act of accepting what has happened, forgiving ourselves and others, and choosing to live with an open heart, free from the weight of past regrets or pain. Peace with the past does not require forgetting, it requires understanding, healing, and letting go of the emotional attachments that no longer serve us.

When we make peace with the past, we stop carrying its burdens into our future. We forgive where necessary, learn from the lessons, and accept that the past was simply part of our journey. This peace allows us to embrace the present moment fully, knowing that we are not defined by our past mistakes or experiences, but by our ability to grow and evolve from them.

Today, reflect on any unresolved feelings or memories from your past. What can you release in order to make peace? Trust that by forgiving, letting go, and accepting, you are creating space for new growth, healing, and a more peaceful future.

Meditative Prayer

Divine Source of Healing,
Help me make peace with my past today.
Where I have held on to pain,
Fill me with forgiveness.
Where I have carried regret,
Fill me with understanding.

Guide me to release what no longer serves me,
And to embrace the lessons from my past.
Let me walk forward with a peaceful heart,
Free from the burdens of yesterday,
And open to the possibilities of today and tomorrow.

Thank you for the healing power of peace,
And for the strength to move forward.

DAY 324:
Walking Lightly Into the Future

Lesson for the Day

The future is an unknown, filled with endless possibilities and opportunities. Often, we carry the weight of our past or the anxieties about what is to come, making it difficult to move forward with ease. Walking lightly into the future means releasing the burdens that weigh us down—whether they be fears, regrets, or expectations—and stepping into the unknown with an open heart and a light spirit.

When we walk lightly into the future, we embrace it with curiosity, trusting that life is unfolding in perfect timing. We let go of the need to control the outcomes and instead allow ourselves to flow with the changes that come our way. This approach not only lightens our load but also allows us to experience each moment fully, without the weight of unnecessary worries.

Today, reflect on how you can walk lightly into the future. What can you release to create more space for peace, joy, and possibility? Trust that the future holds exactly what you need for your growth and evolution, and that you are always supported in your journey.

Meditative Prayer

Divine Source of Possibility,
Help me walk lightly into the future today.
Where I have carried burdens of fear or regret,
Fill me with peace.
Where I have held expectations,
Fill me with trust in Your divine timing.

Let me embrace the future with an open heart,
Ready to receive whatever comes my way.
Guide me to move forward with ease,
Knowing that every step is leading me toward the highest good.

I trust in the journey ahead,
And I walk with lightness, hope, and faith.

DAY 325:
Finding Joy in the Unknown

Lesson for the Day

The unknown often brings with it a sense of uncertainty and fear, but it also holds great potential for discovery, growth, and joy. Finding joy in the unknown means embracing the mystery of life with a heart full of curiosity and wonder. When we approach the unknown with joy, we see it as an adventure rather than a threat, a chance to expand and evolve rather than something to fear.

The unknown is where life's greatest gifts often lie—new experiences, new relationships, and new possibilities. By releasing the need to control every detail and trusting that everything will unfold as it should, we open ourselves up to the joy of discovery. Life becomes more exciting when we learn to see the unknown as an opportunity to learn, explore, and grow.

Today, take a moment to reflect on an area of your life where the unknown feels daunting. How can you approach it with curiosity, joy, and trust? Let go of any fear and open your heart to the possibilities that await you, knowing that the unknown is filled with gifts meant to expand and enrich your life.

Meditative Prayer

Divine Source of Adventure,
Help me find joy in the unknown today.
Where I have felt fear or uncertainty,
Fill me with excitement and trust.
Where I have resisted the unknown,
Fill me with courage and curiosity.

Let me embrace the mystery of life,
Knowing that everything unfolds perfectly.
Guide me to walk forward with joy,
Ready to receive the gifts that the unknown has to offer.

I trust that the unknown is full of possibility,
And I welcome each new discovery with an open heart.

DAY 326:
The Strength to Begin Again

Lesson for the Day

Starting over can feel daunting, especially after setbacks or difficult experiences. Yet, the strength to begin again is one of the most empowering gifts you can give yourself. Every new beginning is a chance to rise, to learn, and to move forward with greater wisdom. The strength to begin again doesn't come from having all the answers or knowing what's next—it comes from trusting in your ability to move forward, even in the face of uncertainty.

When you embrace the power of starting anew, you recognize that each experience, whether successful or challenging, has prepared you for this moment. The strength to begin again lies in your resilience, your courage to face the unknown, and your belief that no matter what has happened before, you are capable of stepping into a new chapter with confidence and hope.

Today, reflect on any area in your life where you feel called to begin again. Trust that you have everything within you to take that first step. Even if the path ahead is unclear, know that the strength you need is already within you, and each new beginning is a chance to grow and evolve.

Meditative Prayer

Divine Source of Strength,
Help me find the courage to begin again today.
Where I feel uncertain,
Fill me with faith.
Where I feel weary,
Fill me with energy and hope.

Guide me as I step into this new beginning,
Trusting that I have everything I need to move forward.
Let me embrace this fresh start with an open heart,
Knowing that each step is leading me closer to my true purpose.

I trust in my strength and my ability to begin again,
And I move forward with faith, resilience, and love.

ALEX McCANN JOHNSON

Day 327:
Holding Hope for What's to Come

Lesson for the Day

Hope is a powerful force that connects us to the future with optimism and faith. Even when the present feels uncertain or challenging, holding hope for what's to come gives us the strength to keep moving forward. Hope is not wishful thinking—it is the belief that, no matter the circumstances, better days are ahead and that we are capable of creating the future we desire.

Holding hope means trusting in the process of life, even when we cannot see the full picture. It is the quiet assurance that the universe, the Divine, or your inner wisdom is guiding you toward what is meant for you. Hope gives us resilience, a reason to keep striving, and the courage to take one more step, even in the face of uncertainty.

Today, take a moment to reflect on the future with hope. What are you holding hope for in your life? Trust that by holding hope, you are actively creating the energy for positive change and growth, and that the future holds endless possibilities for joy, peace, and fulfillment.

Meditative Prayer

Divine Source of Hope,
Help me hold hope for what's to come today.
Where I have doubted,
Fill me with faith.
Where I have feared the unknown,
Fill me with trust in Your divine plan.

Let me look to the future with optimism,
Knowing that everything is unfolding perfectly.
Guide me to move forward with hope in my heart,
And to embrace the future with courage and grace.

I trust that the best is yet to come,
And I am open to the endless possibilities of what's ahead.

DAY 328:
The Peace That Comes from Acceptance

Lesson for the Day

Acceptance is one of the most powerful ways to create peace within ourselves. It is the ability to embrace life as it is, without resistance or judgment. When we accept things—whether it's a difficult situation, a challenging emotion, or another person—we free ourselves from the inner turmoil that often comes from fighting reality. Acceptance doesn't mean resignation; it means recognizing that life is unfolding exactly as it should, and trusting that there is wisdom in every moment.

The peace that comes from acceptance allows us to release expectations, fears, and attachments to how things *should* be. Instead of pushing against what is, we lean into it, trusting that every experience, no matter how difficult, is helping us grow and evolve. With acceptance, we find a deep sense of calm and clarity, and we can approach life with a heart open to whatever comes next.

Today, take time to reflect on the areas of your life where you may be resisting. What can you accept today in order to bring more peace into your heart? Trust that in accepting, you are creating space for healing, growth, and inner peace.

Meditative Prayer

Divine Source of Peace,
Help me accept what is today.
Where I have resisted,
Fill me with understanding.
Where I have struggled,
Fill me with peace.

Guide me to embrace life as it unfolds,
Trusting that all is in divine order.
Let me release the need to control,
And find peace in the flow of life.

I accept the present moment,
And trust that everything is working for my highest good.
Thank you for the peace that comes with acceptance,
And the freedom to move forward with grace.

DAY 329:
Letting Go and Trusting in Divine Alignment

Lesson for the Day

Letting go can be one of the most freeing yet challenging practices in our spiritual journey. When we let go, we release control over the outcome, trusting that everything is unfolding as it should, even if we cannot yet see the bigger picture. Divine alignment is the understanding that the universe, or the Divine, has a plan for us, and that plan is always working in our favor, even when we don't understand it.

Letting go means releasing the need to control every detail and instead trusting that the Divine is guiding us toward our highest good. It is in letting go that we make space for clarity, peace, and the opportunities that are meant for us. Trusting in divine alignment allows us to surrender to life's flow, knowing that we are always in the right place at the right time.

Today, reflect on what you need to let go of in order to align more deeply with the divine flow of your life. Whether it's an attachment to a specific outcome, a fear of the unknown, or a past experience, trust that in letting go, you create space for something greater and more aligned with your soul's purpose.

Meditative Prayer

Divine Source of Alignment,
Help me release what no longer serves me today.
Where I have held on tightly,
Fill me with peace and trust.
Where I have feared the unknown,
Fill me with faith.

Guide me to trust in the divine plan,
And let go of the need to control.
Help me step into the flow of life,
Knowing that I am always aligned with my highest good.

I trust in Your guidance,
And in the divine timing of my journey.
Thank you for helping me let go,
And for the blessings that are unfolding in perfect alignment.

DAY 330:
Closing One Chapter, Opening Another

Lesson for the Day

Every chapter of our lives holds valuable lessons, whether we see them at the time or not. Some chapters are filled with growth and joy, while others may be filled with challenges or uncertainty. Closing one chapter and opening another is a natural part of life's flow. It's an invitation to honor the past, reflect on the lessons learned, and then move forward with an open heart to embrace what is next.

Closing a chapter does not mean leaving behind everything that came with it—it simply means recognizing when it's time to move on and to welcome a new phase of life. Each new chapter offers fresh possibilities, new growth, and new opportunities. By letting go of what no longer serves you and embracing what lies ahead, you create space for transformation and renewal.

Today, take a moment to reflect on a chapter of your life that is coming to a close. How can you honor it and the lessons it has taught you? And as you prepare to open the next chapter, trust that it holds exactly what you need for your continued growth and evolution.

Meditative Prayer

Divine Source of New Beginnings,
Thank You for the gift of every chapter in my life.
Help me honor the one that is closing today,
And the lessons I have learned along the way.

Where I have felt resistance,
Fill me with peace.
Where I have held on too tightly,
Fill me with trust.

Guide me as I step into the next chapter,
With an open heart and a clear mind.
I trust that this new chapter will bring me the growth,
Healing, and opportunities that I need.

Thank you for the courage to close one chapter,
And the faith to open another with grace.

DAY 331:
Gathering the Blessings of the Year

Lesson for the Day

As the year draws to a close, it's a beautiful time to reflect on the blessings we have received, both big and small. Sometimes, we are so focused on what's ahead that we forget to take a moment to appreciate all that has unfolded in the past year. Gathering the blessings of the year means recognizing the gifts, the lessons, and the experiences that have shaped you. It's a practice of gratitude, where we honor the abundance in our lives, even in the midst of challenges.

When we gather the blessings of the year, we celebrate our growth, our resilience, and the love that has surrounded us. Each blessing, no matter how seemingly insignificant, contributes to our journey. By gathering these blessings, we create a foundation of gratitude and positivity that we can carry into the new year.

Today, take a moment to reflect on the blessings you've received this year. What are you most grateful for? What lessons have you learned, and how have they shaped you? Trust that by gathering these blessings, you are preparing yourself to move into the next chapter of your life with a heart full of gratitude and openness.

Meditative Prayer

Divine Source of Abundance,
Thank You for the blessings of this year.
Help me gather them with gratitude and grace,
And recognize the gifts in every experience.

Where I have struggled,
Help me find the lessons.
Where I have been blessed,
Fill me with joy and appreciation.

Guide me to carry these blessings with me,
And to move into the new year with an open heart,
Ready to receive even more blessings, growth, and love.

Thank you for the abundance of this year,
And for the blessings yet to come.

Day 332:
Replacing the Fruits of Your Spiritual Work

Lesson for the Day

Spiritual growth is a journey that requires patience, commitment, and dedication. The seeds of your spiritual work—whether through meditation, self-reflection, prayer, or healing—are sown in the quiet spaces of your heart and mind. Over time, as you nurture your connection with the Divine, these seeds grow into wisdom, peace, love, and understanding. Reaping the fruits of your spiritual work is the moment when you begin to see the results of your efforts manifesting in your life.

The fruits of your spiritual work can take many forms like clarity, inner peace, a sense of purpose, or deeper compassion for yourself and others. It is the natural outcome of the time and energy you have dedicated to your growth. When you reap these fruits, you acknowledge the progress you've made and the wisdom you've gained along the way. You begin to embody the essence of the work you've done, and the changes within you radiate outward, impacting all areas of your life.

Today, reflect on the spiritual work you've put into your journey. What fruits are beginning to ripen for you? What positive changes have you noticed in your heart, mind, and spirit? Trust that your efforts are not in vain, and celebrate the growth you have already achieved.

Meditative Prayer

Divine Source of Wisdom,
Thank You for the fruits of my spiritual work.
Help me see the blessings that have come from my journey,
And fill me with gratitude for the progress I've made.

Where I have labored in the quiet spaces,
Fill me with the fruits of peace and understanding.
Where I have sown seeds of love and healing,
Let them blossom into compassion and clarity.

Guide me to embrace the fruits of my labor,
And to share them with others in love and light.
Thank you for the growth I've experienced,
And for the ongoing blessings of my spiritual path.

DAY 333:
Reflecting on the Growth Within

Lesson for the Day

Growth is a continual process, often occurring in subtle ways. It is not always marked by visible achievements or big milestones, but rather in the quiet shifts that happen within us. Reflecting on the growth within is about acknowledging how far you've come on your journey, even if you don't have all the answers yet. This inward growth—through wisdom gained, lessons learned, and hearts healed—is just as significant as any external success.

As you take the time to reflect, ask yourself, *What have I learned? How have I evolved spiritually, emotionally, and mentally?* These moments of reflection allow you to see the areas where you have expanded, gained clarity, and become more aligned with your true self. It is a time to honor your inner journey and recognize the beauty and strength in your growth.

Today, reflect on the growth that has taken place within you. What inner transformations have you experienced? Celebrate this growth, knowing that it is leading you toward an even deeper understanding of yourself and the Divine.

Meditative Prayer

Divine Source of Growth,
Thank You for the growth that has taken place within me.
Help me recognize the progress I've made,
And honor the journey I have walked.

Where I have gained wisdom,
Fill me with peace.
Where I have learned,
Fill me with gratitude.

Guide me to continue growing with grace,
And to embrace the beauty of my inner transformation.
Thank you for the strength and wisdom that come from within,
And for the continued growth I am experiencing.

DAY 334:
The Joy of a Full Heart

Lesson for the Day

A full heart is a heart filled with love, gratitude, and peace. It is a heart that feels deeply connected to the present moment, to the people around us, and to the Divine. The joy of a full heart comes from recognizing the beauty and abundance in every experience, and from appreciating the love that surrounds us—whether it comes from within ourselves, from others, or from a higher power. When our hearts are full, we experience a deep sense of contentment and connection, knowing that we are held and supported by the love we give and receive.

The joy of a full heart does not depend on external circumstances. It is found in the simple moments of life—the quiet, peaceful times, the acts of kindness, and the expressions of love. It is the warmth that fills you when you are truly present and grateful for what is.

Today, reflect on the fullness of your heart. What are you grateful for? Where do you feel love and peace in your life? Allow yourself to bask in the joy that comes from a heart that is full, and trust that this joy will radiate outward to everyone and everything you encounter.

Meditative Prayer

Divine Source of Love,
Thank You for the joy of a full heart.
Fill me with love, gratitude, and peace today.
Where I have felt empty or disconnected,
Fill me with Your divine love.

Let me recognize the beauty and abundance in my life,
And embrace the love that surrounds me.
Help me carry the joy of a full heart into every moment,
And share this love with those I encounter.

Thank you for the joy that comes from within,
And for the love that fills me and radiates outward.

DAY 335:
Celebrating How Far You've Come

Lesson for the Day

Life is a journey, and every step along the way—no matter how small—deserves to be acknowledged. Celebrating how far you've come is a way to honor the effort, resilience, and growth that have brought you to this moment. We often focus on where we want to go next, but it is equally important to take a pause and appreciate the distance we've already traveled. Every challenge you've overcome, every lesson you've learned, and every breakthrough you've experienced has shaped you into the person you are today.

Celebration is not about perfection, it's about gratitude for the progress you've made. By celebrating how far you've come, you affirm your strength, your courage, and your ability to continue moving forward. It's a reminder that you are always evolving, always growing, and that every part of your journey is worthy of recognition.

Today, take a moment to reflect on your growth. What milestones, big or small, can you celebrate? Recognize the strength it took to get to where you are, and honor yourself for the progress you've made.

Meditative Prayer

Divine Source of Gratitude,
Thank You for guiding me on my journey.
Help me recognize how far I've come,
And celebrate the growth and resilience I have shown.

Where I have felt doubt,
Fill me with appreciation for my strength.
Where I have faced challenges,
Fill me with pride for how I've overcome them.

Let me honor the progress I've made,
And move forward with the same strength and courage.
Thank you for the path I've walked,
And for the journey still ahead.

DAY 336:
Finding Gratitude in Every Season

Lesson for the Day

Life is made up of many seasons—some are bright and full of growth, while others may be challenging or quiet. Each season, however, carries its own gifts and lessons. Finding gratitude in every season means embracing the full spectrum of experiences, knowing that each one has something valuable to offer. Whether you are in a season of expansion, rest, change, or uncertainty, there is always something to be grateful for.

In the difficult seasons, gratitude helps us see the lessons and strength gained through adversity. In seasons of joy and abundance, gratitude allows us to fully appreciate the beauty and blessings of the present moment. By cultivating gratitude in every season, we deepen our connection to the flow of life and the wisdom that each season brings.

Today, reflect on the season you are currently in. What can you be grateful for, even in the midst of challenges or uncertainty? Trust that every season has its purpose, and allow gratitude to guide you through it with peace, clarity, and acceptance.

Meditative Prayer

Divine Source of All Seasons,
Thank You for the seasons of my life.
Help me find gratitude in every season,
Whether in moments of joy, rest, or challenge.

Where I have struggled,
Help me find strength and lessons to be grateful for.
Where I have experienced abundance,
Help me embrace it with full appreciation.

Guide me to move through each season with grace,
And to trust that each one has its purpose.
Thank you for the richness of my journey,
And for the gratitude that helps me honor every season.

DAY 337:
Living in Harmony with Yourself

Lesson for the Day

Living in harmony with yourself means aligning your thoughts, actions, and emotions with your true essence. It is about finding balance within, where your mind, heart, and spirit work together in unity. When you are in harmony with yourself, you are able to listen to your inner voice with clarity, make decisions that reflect your values, and honor your needs and boundaries. Harmony within allows you to live authentically, free from inner conflict or dissonance.

Finding harmony is not about perfection, it's about embracing the ebb and flow of life and accepting all parts of yourself—both light and shadow. It's about being kind to yourself, forgiving your mistakes, and growing from your experiences. When you live in harmony with yourself, you radiate peace, balance, and authenticity, and your external world often mirrors that inner peace.

Today, take a moment to reflect on how you can cultivate more harmony within. Are there any areas where you are out of alignment with your true self? Trust that by embracing your wholeness and aligning your inner world, you create a life of peace, balance, and authenticity.

Meditative Prayer

Divine Source of Inner Peace,
Help me live in harmony with myself today.
Where I am in conflict within,
Fill me with peace.
Where I am out of balance,
Fill me with clarity and understanding.

Guide me to align my thoughts, actions, and emotions
With the truth of who I am.
Let me embrace all parts of myself,
My strengths, my challenges, and my growth.

Thank you for the peace that comes from living authentically,
And for the harmony that flows from within.

DAY 338:
Recognizing the Divine's Blessings in Your Life

Lesson for the Day

The Divine's blessings are all around us, often woven into the fabric of our daily lives. However, in the rush of life, it can be easy to overlook them. Recognizing the blessings of the Divine requires mindfulness and a heart open to gratitude. Whether through moments of peace, acts of kindness, or unexpected opportunities, the Divine is always offering gifts, guiding us with love and care. These blessings come in many forms, sometimes subtle, sometimes grand, but always meant to help us grow, heal, and evolve.

When we take the time to reflect on our lives with awareness, we begin to notice how the Divine is at work in the smallest and largest aspects of our journey. It could be in the support of loved ones, a sense of inner peace, or the clarity that emerges when we ask for guidance. The more we recognize these blessings, the more we cultivate a heart full of gratitude and openness.

Today, take a moment to reflect on the Divine blessings in your life. What gifts have you received that you may not have fully recognized? Trust that as you acknowledge these blessings, you will invite more peace, joy, and abundance into your life.

Meditative Prayer

Divine Source of Blessings,
Thank You for the gifts You have bestowed upon me.
Help me recognize Your blessings today,
In the small moments and in the grand gestures.

Where I have overlooked Your gifts,
Fill me with awareness.
Where I have taken Your blessings for granted,
Fill me with gratitude.

Guide me to see Your presence in my life,
And to walk forward with a heart full of appreciation.
Thank You for the abundant blessings You continuously offer.

DAY 339:
The Power of a Thankful Heart

Lesson for the Day

Gratitude is one of the most powerful energies we can cultivate. A thankful heart is a heart that radiates positivity, love, and peace. When we choose to focus on what we are grateful for, we shift our perspective from lack to abundance. A thankful heart opens us to receive more blessings, more love, and more joy. It transforms ordinary moments into extraordinary ones, helping us see the beauty in the simplest of things.

The power of a thankful heart lies in its ability to create an energy of receptivity. When we are thankful, we align ourselves with the flow of abundance in the universe. Gratitude magnifies our blessings, making them feel more vivid, tangible, and meaningful. A thankful heart doesn't just appreciate the good—it finds peace and growth even in the challenges, knowing that every experience has something valuable to offer.

Today, take a moment to focus on gratitude. What can you be thankful for in this moment? Acknowledge the blessings, big or small, that fill your life. Let your heart overflow with thankfulness, knowing that this energy of gratitude will continue to attract more goodness into your life.

Meditative Prayer

Divine Source of Gratitude,
Thank You for the abundance in my life.
Fill my heart with thankfulness today,
For the blessings I have received,
And for those still to come.

Where I have focused on lack,
Help me see abundance.
Where I have felt discontent,
Fill me with peace and appreciation.

Guide me to cultivate a thankful heart,
And let my gratitude flow outward,
Bringing more love, peace, and joy into my life.

Thank You for the power of a thankful heart,
And for the blessings it brings.

DAY 340:
Embracing the Sacred Rest After the Harvest

Lesson for the Day

Rest is sacred. After seasons of hard work, growth, and striving, the time to rest and recharge is not only necessary but divine. Just as nature has cycles of planting, growing, and harvesting, there is also the season of rest that allows us to honor the fruits of our labor. Embracing the sacred rest after the harvest is about acknowledging that taking time to rest is not a luxury, but a vital part of the process. It is in these moments of stillness and restoration that we gather the energy we need for the next cycle of growth.

In the quiet of rest, we allow ourselves to reflect on what we've achieved, to appreciate the journey, and to prepare ourselves for what is to come. Sacred rest is about nurturing the body, mind, and spirit so that we can continue to grow and evolve with strength and clarity. It is a reminder that life is not just about productivity, but also about honoring the rhythms of pause and rejuvenation.

Today, take time to rest. Whether it's through quiet reflection, meditation, or simply sitting in stillness, honor the sacredness of rest. Trust that in taking this time, you are replenishing your energy and making space for the next chapter of your journey.

Meditative Prayer

Divine Source of Renewal,
Help me embrace the sacred rest after the harvest today.
Where I have overextended myself,
Fill me with peace and stillness.
Where I have neglected self-care,
Fill me with love and restoration.

Guide me to honor the rhythm of rest,
And to reflect on the blessings of the journey so far.
Let me find comfort in stillness,
Knowing that rest is an essential part of my growth and healing.

Thank You for the gift of rest,
And for the strength that comes from taking time to replenish.

DAY 341:

The Gift of Contentment

Lesson for the Day

Contentment is a gift that brings peace to the heart and calm to the mind. It is not dependent on external circumstances or achievements but comes from an inner sense of acceptance and peace with where you are. Contentment allows you to be fully present, finding joy in the now, without constantly striving for something more. It's about appreciating what you have and trusting that you are exactly where you need to be.

When we cultivate contentment, we shift from a mindset of scarcity to one of abundance. We recognize that life is not about constantly chasing after the next thing, but about finding fulfillment in the simple moments, the relationships, and the experiences that already surround us. Contentment does not mean complacency, but rather the ability to be at peace with your current circumstances while remaining open to growth and possibility.

Today, reflect on the areas of your life where you feel content. What aspects of your life bring you peace and joy right now? Take a moment to honor the gift of contentment and trust that it will guide you to a life of deeper fulfillment and connection.

Meditative Prayer

Divine Source of Peace,
Thank You for the gift of contentment.
Help me find peace and joy in the present moment,
And to appreciate all that I have right now.

Where I have sought more,
Fill me with gratitude for what I already possess.
Where I have felt restless,
Fill me with calm and acceptance.

Guide me to live with contentment in my heart,
And to trust that I am always exactly where I need to be.
Thank you for the peace that comes from within,
And for the joy of being fully present in this moment.

DAY 342:
Finding Completion in the Present Moment

Lesson for the Day

True completion is not something we find in the future or by achieving a specific goal. It is found in the present moment. We often seek a sense of completion through external accomplishments, thinking that once we reach a certain point, we will feel whole. However, the fullness of life is experienced when we are present with what is happening right now. The present moment holds all the peace, joy, and satisfaction we need.

When we embrace the present moment fully, we realize that everything we need for a sense of completion is already within us. It is through the small, seemingly ordinary moments that we find fulfillment and a deep sense of peace. In each breath, each step, each interaction, we have the opportunity to feel complete. The present moment offers us everything we need to feel whole, if we only pause and open ourselves to it.

Today, reflect on how you can find completion in the present. What moment can you fully embrace right now, without looking ahead or wishing for something more? Trust that in fully experiencing the present, you will find the peace and completeness you seek.

Meditative Prayer

Divine Source of Wholeness,
Thank You for the gift of the present moment.
Help me find completion in the here and now,
And to recognize the fullness of life in every experience.

Where I have been focused on the future,
Help me return to the present with peace.
Where I have felt incomplete,
Fill me with the understanding that I am whole as I am.

Guide me to fully experience each moment,
And to find fulfillment in the present,
Knowing that everything I need is already here.

DAY 343:
Trusting That All is as It Should Be

Lesson for the Day

Life has a way of unfolding in ways that may not always align with our expectations, yet every moment, experience, and challenge is part of a greater design. Trusting that all is as it should be is an act of surrender and faith. It is the understanding that, even when things don't appear to make sense or when the journey seems uncertain, there is a larger plan at work, guiding us toward our highest good.

This trust doesn't mean that we understand everything or that we are free from challenges, rather, it means we are willing to let go of control and allow life to unfold as it should. When we trust that all is as it should be, we find peace in the midst of uncertainty, knowing that each moment is a stepping stone toward our growth and purpose.

Today, reflect on the areas of your life where you may be doubting the process. What can you trust in today? Allow yourself to let go of the need to control the outcome and trust that everything, even the most challenging moments, is unfolding exactly as it should.

Meditative Prayer

Divine Source of Wisdom,
Help me trust that all is as it should be today.
Where I have questioned the path,
Fill me with peace.
Where I have resisted change,
Fill me with faith.

Guide me to surrender to the flow of life,
Knowing that everything is unfolding in divine timing.
Help me release the need to control,
And trust that every experience is leading me toward my highest
good.

Thank You for the peace that comes from trust,
And for the assurance that all is as it should be.

DAY 344:
A Soul Anchored in Peace

Lesson for the Day

Peace is not a destination but a state of being. A soul anchored in peace is one that remains grounded, calm, and centered, regardless of external circumstances. When our soul is anchored in peace, we are able to move through life's challenges with grace and clarity, knowing that no matter what happens outside of us, we have a deep well of peace within. This peace comes from connecting with our true essence, our inner wisdom, and the Divine.

To anchor the soul in peace, we must first create space for stillness. Through practices like meditation, mindfulness, and self-reflection, we learn to connect with the inner peace that is always available to us. As we cultivate this peace within, it becomes our foundation, allowing us to navigate life with a sense of calm, purpose, and trust.

Today, take time to reflect on the ways you can anchor your soul in peace. What practices or habits help you find your center? Trust that by nurturing your inner peace, you will be able to face any challenge with a calm heart and a grounded spirit.

Meditative Prayer

Divine Source of Inner Peace,
Help me anchor my soul in peace today.
Where I have felt unsettled,
Fill me with calm.
Where I have felt anxious,
Fill me with trust.

Guide me to connect with the stillness within,
And to carry this peace into every moment.
Let me find my center,
And walk through life grounded in the knowledge that peace is
always available to me.

Thank you for the peace that dwells within me,
And for the strength that comes from being anchored in Your love.

DAY 345:
The Stillness That Heals

Lesson for the Day

Stillness is a powerful healer. In the hustle and bustle of everyday life, we often overlook the profound healing that can occur when we simply pause and allow ourselves to be still. The stillness within offers a refuge from the noise of the outside world, allowing us to reconnect with our true essence. In this space of quiet, we can access clarity, release tension, and heal emotional wounds that may have been left unattended.

Healing doesn't always require action; sometimes, it's found in the moments of stillness, where we allow ourselves to simply be. It is in these moments that we create space for deep reflection, inner peace, and renewal. The stillness that heals is a reminder that our bodies, minds, and spirits need rest and quiet to restore balance.

Today, take time to embrace stillness. Whether through meditation, deep breathing, or just sitting quietly, allow yourself to experience the healing power of being present with yourself. Trust that in the stillness, your soul is being nourished and renewed.

Meditative Prayer

Divine Source of Healing,
Help me embrace the stillness today.
Where I have been overwhelmed,
Fill me with calm.
Where I have been restless,
Fill me with peace.

Guide me into the quiet of my soul,
And let me find healing in the moments of stillness.
Let my body, mind, and spirit be restored in Your presence,
And may I carry the peace of this stillness with me throughout my
day.

Thank you for the healing that comes in the quiet,
And for the stillness that renews my heart and soul.

DAY 346:
Resting in the Love of the Divine

Lesson for the Day

Resting in the love of the Divine is a practice of surrender and trust. It is the ability to let go of our worries, fears, and burdens, and to simply rest in the unconditional love that is always available to us. The love of the Divine is constant, unwavering, and all-encompassing. When we allow ourselves to rest in this love, we create space for healing, peace, and renewal. It is in the arms of this Divine love that we find true comfort and strength.

Resting in Divine love does not require us to do anything, it simply requires us to be. When we rest in this love, we acknowledge that we are supported, held, and cared for. We do not need to strive or struggle to earn this love—it is freely given. In resting in this love, we are reminded of our worth and our connection to all that is divine.

Today, take a moment to rest in the love of the Divine. Whether through prayer, meditation, or simply sitting in stillness, allow yourself to feel enveloped in this unconditional love. Trust that in this moment of rest, your spirit is being renewed and your heart is being filled with peace.

Meditative Prayer

Divine Source of Love,
Help me rest in Your love today.
Where I have felt weary,
Fill me with Your peace.
Where I have felt alone,
Fill me with the warmth of Your embrace.

Let me surrender my worries to You,
And rest in the knowledge that I am always loved and supported.
Guide me to feel Your love in every moment,
And to trust that Your love is enough to sustain me.

Thank you for the comfort of Your Divine love,
And for the strength that comes from resting in Your care.

DAY 347:
The Peace That Cannot Be Shaken

Lesson for the Day

There is a peace that exists deep within us, a peace that is unshakable and constant, regardless of the circumstances around us. This peace is not dependent on external conditions or achievements, but rather on our connection with the Divine and our ability to stay centered within ourselves. It is the peace that comes when we trust that we are always held, always supported, and always in the right place at the right time.

The peace that cannot be shaken is a peace that resides in the soul. It is the quiet knowing that, no matter what challenges arise, we have the inner strength to navigate them. This peace comes from a deep sense of trust in the Divine, in ourselves, and in the unfolding of life. When we anchor ourselves in this unshakable peace, we are able to move through the storms of life with grace, clarity, and calm.

Today, reflect on the peace that resides within you. Can you connect with that unshakable peace, even in the midst of uncertainty? Trust that this peace is always available to you, and that it will guide you through whatever life presents.

Meditative Prayer

Divine Source of Unshakable Peace,
Help me connect with the peace that resides within me today.
Where I have felt turmoil,
Fill me with calm.
Where I have felt uncertain,
Fill me with trust.

Let me anchor myself in the peace of Your love,
Knowing that no external circumstance can take away the peace I
hold within.
Guide me to move through every situation with clarity, grace, and
inner calm.

Thank you for the peace that cannot be shaken,
And for the strength that comes from trusting in Your Divine
guidance.

DAY 348:
Walking in Alignment with Your Spirit

Lesson for the Day

Walking in alignment with your spirit is the path of true fulfillment. When you align your actions, thoughts, and emotions with your inner truth, you move through life with a sense of purpose and clarity. Alignment with your spirit means being true to yourself, listening to your intuition, and honoring the guidance that comes from within. It is the practice of following your heart's desires while trusting in the wisdom of your soul.

When you walk in alignment with your spirit, you find peace, as you are no longer torn between what you think you *should* do and what you truly *want* to do. You become more connected with your authentic self, and this connection leads you to make choices that feel right, even if they go against the expectations of others. Alignment is not about perfection, it's about being honest with yourself and allowing your spirit to guide your journey.

Today, take a moment to reflect on how you can walk in alignment with your spirit. What areas of your life may need realignment to be more in harmony with your true self? Trust that by aligning with your spirit, you are moving in the direction of your highest good.

Meditative Prayer

Divine Source of Truth,
Help me walk in alignment with my spirit today.
Where I have been out of alignment,
Fill me with clarity.
Where I have struggled to follow my true path,
Fill me with courage and trust.

Guide me to listen to the wisdom of my soul,
And to make choices that honor my authentic self.
Let me walk with peace and confidence,
Knowing that I am always in the right place at the right time.

Thank you for the alignment that brings peace,
And for the clarity that comes from listening to my spirit.

DAY 349:
Releasing the Need for Control

Lesson for the Day

The need for control often stems from a desire for security and certainty. While it is natural to want to shape our lives, the truth is that we cannot control everything. Releasing the need for control is an act of trust—trusting that life is unfolding in perfect timing, even when we can't predict or control the outcomes. When we release control, we allow ourselves to be guided by the flow of life, which often leads us to experiences, people, and opportunities that we could never have planned for.

Letting go of control doesn't mean abandoning responsibility or giving up on our dreams, it means trusting that the universe, the Divine, or our inner wisdom will lead us in the direction that is most aligned with our highest good. Releasing control allows us to experience peace, freedom, and an openness to life's surprises. It helps us move with ease, instead of resistance, through the ever-changing flow of life.

Today, reflect on the areas in your life where you may be holding onto control. What would it feel like to release that grip and trust the process? Trust that by letting go, you create space for new possibilities to emerge.

Meditative Prayer

Divine Source of Freedom,
Help me release the need for control today.
Where I have tried to shape every outcome,
Fill me with trust and peace.
Where I have feared the unknown,
Fill me with courage to surrender.

Guide me to let go of the need to control,
And to move forward with faith in Your divine plan.
Let me trust in the flow of life,
And in the wisdom of the timing that unfolds before me.

Thank you for the freedom that comes from releasing control,
And for the peace that is found in trusting life's journey.

DAY 350:
A Life Rooted in Gratitude

Lesson for the Day

Gratitude is more than just an occasional feeling of thanks, it is the foundation upon which we can build a peaceful, fulfilled, and abundant life. A life rooted in gratitude is one that constantly seeks the good, even in the midst of challenges. When gratitude is deeply woven into our daily lives, it shifts our perspective, allowing us to see blessings even in difficult moments. It helps us focus on what we have rather than what we lack, creating a sense of abundance and contentment.

Living a life rooted in gratitude doesn't mean ignoring difficulties, but it means choosing to focus on the positives, finding something to be thankful for even when things are tough. This mindset brings clarity, joy, and peace, creating a sense of balance and harmony. It allows us to feel more connected to ourselves, others, and the Divine.

Today, reflect on the areas of your life where gratitude can be nurtured. What are you truly thankful for? How can you deepen your gratitude practice to create more peace, joy, and abundance in your life? Trust that a life rooted in gratitude will bring you the fulfillment and contentment you seek.

Meditative Prayer

Divine Source of All Blessings,
Help me live a life rooted in gratitude today.
Where I have focused on what I lack,
Fill me with appreciation for what I have.
Where I have felt dissatisfied,
Fill me with joy and contentment.

Guide me to see the blessings in every moment,
And to recognize the beauty in the ordinary.
Let gratitude flow through my heart,
Bringing peace, joy, and abundance into my life.

Thank you for the gift of gratitude,
And for the life it creates within me.

DAY 351:
Being Present to the Beauty Around You

Lesson for the Day

In the hustle of daily life, it's easy to miss the beauty that surrounds us. We often find ourselves lost in thoughts about the past or future, forgetting to pause and notice the present moment. Being present to the beauty around you means taking the time to engage with the world as it is, without distraction. It's about appreciating the small moments—the warmth of the sun, the sound of birds, the laughter of a loved one, or the quiet peace of nature.

When we slow down and open ourselves to the beauty around us, we reconnect with the present moment, and we begin to see the richness and wonder in everyday life. Beauty is not just something to be admired from a distance, it is something to be experienced and felt deeply. Being present to it cultivates gratitude, joy, and a deeper sense of connection to the world.

Today, take time to pause and notice the beauty around you. Whether it's in nature, in a person, or in a moment of quiet, allow yourself to fully experience it. Trust that in being present, you are creating space for more beauty, peace, and connection in your life.

Meditative Prayer

Divine Source of Beauty,
Help me be present to the beauty around me today.
Where I have rushed through life,
Fill me with the ability to slow down and see.
Where I have overlooked the simple blessings,
Fill me with appreciation and awe.

Guide me to see the wonder in the world,
And to be fully engaged with the present moment.
Let my heart open to the beauty that surrounds me,
And may it bring peace, joy, and gratitude into my life.

Thank you for the beauty in every moment,
And for the peace that comes from being present.

DAY 352:
Living with an Open Heart

Lesson for the Day

Living with an open heart is about embracing life with vulnerability, compassion, and authenticity. It means being willing to experience the full range of emotions—joy, love, sorrow, and everything in between—without shutting ourselves off from the world. When we live with an open heart, we allow ourselves to connect deeply with others, to give and receive love freely, and to approach life with openness and trust.

An open heart allows us to embrace change, to forgive, and to release any walls we've built around ourselves. It's about letting go of past hurts and choosing to move forward with love and kindness. By living with an open heart, we cultivate a deeper connection with ourselves, others, and the Divine. We open ourselves to the beauty of the present moment and the endless possibilities that life has to offer.

Today, reflect on how you can live with a more open heart. Are there areas where you have closed yourself off or held onto past hurts? What can you do today to approach life with greater openness, love, and compassion? Trust that by living with an open heart, you will invite more love and peace into your life.

Meditative Prayer

Divine Source of Love,
Help me live with an open heart today.
Where I have closed myself off,
Fill me with the courage to open again.
Where I have held onto pain,
Fill me with the healing power of forgiveness.

Guide me to live with love,
To give freely and receive openly,
And to approach each moment with compassion.
Let my heart be open to all the beauty and love around me,
And may I walk through life with an open heart,
Embracing everything it has to offer.

Thank you for the gift of an open heart,
And for the peace it brings into my life.

Day 353:
Trusting That You Are Exactly Where You Need to Be

Lesson for the Day

It's easy to become anxious when we don't know what comes next or feel like we're not where we thought we would be. Yet, trusting that you are exactly where you need to be is a practice of faith. It's the belief that, even when things don't seem to be going according to plan, the present moment is exactly where you are meant to be for your growth and evolution. Every experience, no matter how challenging, is leading you toward a greater understanding of yourself and the world around you.

When you trust that you are exactly where you need to be, you release the pressure of striving or chasing after the future. You allow yourself to be fully present, knowing that the journey itself is just as important as the destination. This trust gives you peace and clarity, helping you move forward with confidence and openness.

Today, reflect on the idea that you are exactly where you need to be. What can you learn from your current situation? How can you trust that each step of your journey is part of your divine plan? Trust that the path you are on is unfolding in perfect timing, and that you are exactly where you need to be.

Meditative Prayer

Divine Source of Guidance,
Help me trust that I am exactly where I need to be today.
Where I have felt uncertain,
Fill me with peace and confidence.
Where I have felt lost,
Fill me with trust in Your divine plan.

Guide me to see the lessons in each moment,
And to embrace the path I am on with faith.
Let me trust that every step, even the ones that seem unclear,
Is leading me toward my highest good.

Thank you for the peace that comes from trusting in Your timing,
And for the understanding that I am always exactly where I need to
be.

DAY 354:
Seeing Every Experience as a Gift

Lesson for the Day

Every experience, whether joyous or challenging, carries a lesson or a gift. Life's circumstances often push us out of our comfort zones and into spaces where growth and transformation occur. When we learn to see every experience as a gift, we shift our perspective from one of resistance to one of acceptance and gratitude. Even the most difficult situations can offer us valuable insights, strength, and resilience that we would not have gained otherwise.

Seeing every experience as a gift does not mean we ignore or diminish the struggles we face, it means recognizing that there is purpose in all things. Every moment is an opportunity for learning, healing, and growth. By embracing each experience as a gift, we open ourselves to the fullness of life, trusting that every part of our journey is helping to shape us into who we are meant to be.

Today, reflect on your current experiences and see them as gifts. What are the lessons or blessings in the challenges you are facing? How can you shift your perspective to see the gift in every situation? Trust that each experience, no matter how it appears, holds the potential for growth and transformation.

Meditative Prayer

Divine Source of Wisdom,
Help me see every experience as a gift today.
Where I have felt frustration or resistance,
Fill me with gratitude and understanding.
Where I have faced challenges,
Fill me with the strength to see the lessons they offer.

Guide me to embrace every moment,
And to recognize the blessings in even the smallest of experiences.
Let me walk through life with the heart of a learner,
Finding growth and peace in every situation.

Thank you for the gifts hidden within every experience,
And for the wisdom they bring to my journey.

DAY 355:
Letting Love Lead the Way

Lesson for the Day

Love is one of the most powerful forces in the universe. It has the ability to heal, transform, and guide us in ways that nothing else can. When we let love lead the way, we are choosing to approach life with compassion, understanding, and an open heart. Love becomes the lens through which we see the world, making our decisions, interactions, and responses more aligned with our true selves and our highest good.

Letting love lead is not always easy, especially when we encounter challenges, disagreements, or fears. However, when we choose love over fear or judgment, we create a space for peace, healing, and connection. Love invites us to be patient with ourselves and others, to forgive, and to move forward with grace. Letting love lead means trusting that love will guide us through every circumstance, no matter how difficult.

Today, reflect on the ways you can let love lead in your life. How can you choose love in your decisions, your actions, and your thoughts? Trust that when love is your guide, you are always moving in the right direction.

Meditative Prayer

Divine Source of Love,
Help me let love lead the way today.
Where I have felt fear or doubt,
Fill me with love and confidence.
Where I have felt separation,
Fill me with compassion and connection.

Guide me to make decisions rooted in love,
And to see the world through the lens of kindness and
understanding.
Let love be the force that drives my actions,
And the peace that calms my heart.

Thank you for the power of love,
And for the peace it brings when it leads the way.

DAY 356:
The Joy of Simply Being

Lesson for the Day

In the busyness of life, it's easy to overlook the simple joy that comes from simply being. We often get caught up in doing—achieving, accomplishing, and moving forward—thinking that our worth is tied to our productivity. However, true joy is found when we allow ourselves to simply be, without the pressure of having to prove anything or meet any expectations. When we stop striving and just allow ourselves to exist in the present moment, we connect with a deeper sense of peace and fulfillment.

The joy of simply being is about embracing life as it is, without needing to change anything. It is in the quiet moments of rest, reflection, and presence that we can truly connect with our essence. By letting go of the need to constantly do, we open ourselves to the beauty and peace that come from simply existing in the world. In these moments, we are reminded that our worth is inherent—not based on what we do, but on who we are.

Today, take time to just be. Let go of the need to do, and allow yourself to fully experience the joy of simply existing. Trust that in these moments of stillness, you are connected to your true self and to the peace that resides within.

Meditative Prayer

Divine Source of Presence,
Help me embrace the joy of simply being today.
Where I have focused on doing,
Fill me with the peace of simply existing.
Where I have sought to prove my worth,
Fill me with the understanding that I am enough, just as I am.

Guide me to rest in the present moment,
And to find joy in the stillness.
Let me embrace the beauty of being,
And trust that in simply being, I am fulfilling my purpose.

Thank you for the peace that comes from simply being,
And for the joy that fills my heart when I release the need to do.

DAY 357:
Finding Sacredness in the Everyday

Lesson for the Day

The sacredness of life is not found only in special moments or extraordinary experiences—it is present in the everyday. Every task, conversation, and moment holds the potential to be a sacred experience if we approach it with mindfulness, gratitude, and reverence. The sacred is not limited to spiritual practices or places, but is woven into the fabric of our daily lives, waiting to be noticed and appreciated.

When we see the sacred in the everyday, we shift our perspective. We recognize the divine in simple moments: a warm cup of tea, the laughter of a friend, the beauty of nature, or the act of cleaning and caring for our space. These seemingly mundane activities are infused with meaning when we choose to engage with them fully and with presence. By finding sacredness in the everyday, we bring more peace, joy, and connection into our lives.

Today, reflect on the everyday moments in your life. What can you recognize as sacred today? Take time to slow down and appreciate the beauty in the ordinary, knowing that every moment is an opportunity to connect with the divine.

Meditative Prayer

Divine Source of All Life,
Help me find sacredness in the everyday today.
Where I have rushed through moments,
Fill me with presence and gratitude.
Where I have overlooked the simple blessings,
Fill me with reverence and awe.

Guide me to see the divine in the ordinary,
And to approach each task and moment with mindfulness.
Let me find beauty and meaning in all things,
And connect with Your presence in every experience.

Thank you for the sacredness in the everyday,
And for the peace that comes from recognizing Your presence in
all.

DAY 358:
Allowing Yourself to Rest in Spirit

Lesson for the Day

In the busyness of life, it's easy to forget that rest is not only physical, but spiritual. Allowing yourself to rest in spirit is an invitation to surrender to the divine flow, to trust that you are held and supported, and to give yourself permission to simply be. It is in this space of rest that we reconnect with our inner wisdom and receive clarity, healing, and peace. Just as the body needs rest to replenish, the soul requires moments of stillness and surrender to renew its energy and deepen its connection with the Divine.

Resting in spirit doesn't require doing anything—it's about releasing the need to control or strive and allowing the divine presence to guide and restore you. When we rest in spirit, we acknowledge that we are not alone in our journey, and that we can trust the process of life. It is in this state of surrender that we find peace, renewal, and inspiration for the next step of our journey.

Today, take time to rest in spirit. Whether through meditation, prayer, or simply sitting quietly, allow yourself to surrender to the divine flow and trust that you are always supported. Trust that this rest will nourish your soul and bring you the peace and clarity you need.

Meditative Prayer

Divine Source of Peace,
Help me rest in spirit today.
Where I have felt restless or anxious,
Fill me with calm.
Where I have tried to control,
Fill me with trust in Your divine plan.

Guide me to surrender to Your love,
And to allow my soul the rest it needs to replenish.
Let me be still and open to Your guidance,
Trusting that You are always with me, supporting me.

Thank you for the rest that comes from resting in You,
And for the peace that fills my soul when I surrender.

DAY 359:
A Heart Overflowing with Love and Peace

Lesson for the Day

A heart overflowing with love and peace is a heart that is fully connected to the divine flow of life. Love and peace are not just fleeting emotions, they are states of being that we can cultivate and embody in every moment. When our hearts are full of love, we naturally share that love with others, creating a ripple effect that spreads warmth and compassion. Similarly, when we are at peace, we radiate that tranquility into the world, offering calm to those around us and to ourselves.

Overflowing love and peace come from recognizing the abundance within us. It is the understanding that love and peace are limitless resources that we can tap into, no matter the circumstances. As we open our hearts to give and receive love, and as we cultivate inner peace, we create a space for healing, connection, and transformation in our lives.

Today, reflect on how you can allow your heart to overflow with love and peace. How can you share love with others, and how can you nurture your own peace? Trust that when you cultivate these qualities, you not only transform your own life, but you also contribute to the collective peace and love of the world.

Meditative Prayer

Divine Source of Love and Peace,
Fill my heart to overflowing with love and peace today.
Where I have felt closed off or disconnected,
Open my heart to give and receive freely.
Where I have felt unsettled,
Fill me with Your calming peace.

Guide me to share love in every interaction,
And to be a source of peace for those I encounter.
Let my heart be a vessel of compassion,
And may my peace ripple out into the world,
Bringing healing, love, and tranquility.

Thank you for the abundance of love and peace in my life,
And for the strength to share it freely.

DAY 360:
Embracing the Divine Plan for Your Life

Lesson for the Day

Trusting in the divine plan for your life is an act of surrender and faith. Life's journey is often unpredictable, and we may face obstacles, detours, and moments of uncertainty along the way. However, when we embrace the divine plan, we acknowledge that there is a greater purpose guiding us. Every experience, both joyful and challenging, is part of the larger story unfolding in our lives. The divine plan is always working in our favor, even when we can't see the bigger picture.

Embracing the divine plan means letting go of the need to control every outcome and trusting that we are being guided to exactly where we need to be. It involves releasing fears and doubts and allowing ourselves to move forward with faith that we are always on the path we are meant to be on. The divine plan is one of love, growth, and transformation, and when we open ourselves to it, we find peace, purpose, and a deeper connection with our true selves.

Today, reflect on the ways you can embrace the divine plan for your life. Are there areas where you are holding onto control or resisting change? How can you trust that every step of your journey is part of your divine unfolding? Trust that by embracing the divine plan, you are aligning yourself with your highest good.

Meditative Prayer

Divine Source of Guidance,
Help me embrace the divine plan for my life today.
Where I have resisted change,
Fill me with trust and faith.
Where I have feared the unknown,
Fill me with courage and peace.

Guide me to trust that every step is leading me toward my highest good,
Even when I cannot see the full picture.
Let me surrender to Your plan with an open heart,
And walk forward in faith, knowing that I am always exactly where I need to be.

Thank you for the divine plan that is unfolding in my life,
And for the peace that comes from trusting in Your loving guidance.

DAY 361:

Trusting in the Journey Ahead

Lesson for the Day

The future is often filled with uncertainty, and it's easy to feel anxious or unsure about what lies ahead. However, trusting in the journey ahead is an invitation to surrender the need for control and to embrace the unknown with confidence and faith. The journey ahead may not always be clear, but every step you take brings you closer to your highest good. Trusting in the journey means believing that, even when you cannot see the road ahead, you are being guided and supported every step of the way.

The journey is not about rushing to a destination—it's about embracing each moment and trusting that every experience is an essential part of your growth. The twists and turns, the challenges and successes, all contribute to the person you are becoming. When you trust in the journey, you open yourself to the lessons, blessings, and opportunities that are waiting for you, knowing that everything is unfolding exactly as it should.

Today, reflect on how you can trust in the journey ahead. Are there areas where you are feeling uncertain or worried about the future? How can you release the need for control and allow yourself to embrace what's coming with openness and faith? Trust that the journey ahead holds exactly what you need for your growth, healing, and fulfillment.

Meditative Prayer

Divine Source of Guidance,
Help me trust in the journey ahead today.
Where I have felt uncertain,
Fill me with peace and confidence.
Where I have been anxious about the future,
Fill me with faith in Your divine plan.

Guide me to take each step with trust,
Knowing that I am always supported and guided.
Let me embrace the unknown with openness,
And trust that everything is unfolding for my highest good.

Thank you for the journey ahead,
And for the peace that comes from trusting in Your loving
guidance.

DAY 362:
Honoring the Path You Have Walked

Lesson for the Day

The path you have walked is a testament to your strength, resilience, and growth. Every step, whether easy or difficult, has shaped who you are today. It's easy to focus on where you are going, but it's equally important to honor the journey that has brought you here. Each experience, challenge, and lesson has contributed to your wisdom and understanding. By honoring the path you have walked, you acknowledge the courage it took to move through the highs and lows, the patience you've developed, and the inner strength you've cultivated along the way.

Honoring the path you have walked is not about perfection—it's about recognizing your efforts, your growth, and your transformation. It's about celebrating the lessons you've learned and the person you've become through all that you've experienced. Every step you've taken has led you to this moment, and that in itself is worth celebrating.

Today, take a moment to reflect on your journey. What steps can you honor today? How can you recognize the growth and strength that have come from your experiences? Trust that by honoring the path you've walked, you are empowering yourself to continue moving forward with confidence and gratitude.

Meditative Prayer

Divine Source of Reflection,
Help me honor the path I have walked today.
Where I have doubted my journey,
Fill me with appreciation for how far I've come.
Where I have struggled,
Fill me with compassion for myself.

Guide me to see the growth and strength in every step,
And to celebrate the lessons I have learned.
Thank you for the path I have walked,
And for the wisdom it has brought into my life.

DAY 363:
The Completion of One Cycle, The Beginning of Another

Lesson for the Day

Life is a series of cycles—each one leading to the next, with moments of completion and new beginnings. Every cycle we go through—whether it's a season, a chapter, or a phase in life—offers us valuable lessons and experiences. The completion of one cycle is an opportunity to reflect on what we've learned, what we've gained, and what we've released. It's a moment to honor the growth and transformation that has taken place.

The beginning of another cycle is a fresh opportunity for growth, healing, and new experiences. Just as we honor the completion of the old, we welcome the new with an open heart and mind. Embracing this flow of life allows us to move forward with purpose and confidence, knowing that each new cycle is a chance to continue evolving.

Today, reflect on a cycle in your life that is coming to a close. What lessons have you learned, and what are you ready to release? As you look ahead to the new cycle, trust that it holds the potential for new beginnings, growth, and transformation. Embrace both the completion and the beginning with gratitude and openness.

Meditative Prayer

Divine Source of Renewal,
Thank you for the completion of this cycle in my life.
Help me honor all that I have learned and experienced,
And release what no longer serves me.

As I step into the new cycle,
Fill me with anticipation and trust.
Guide me to embrace the new with an open heart,
And to move forward with faith in Your divine plan.

Thank you for the gift of new beginnings,
And for the strength to embrace each new cycle with grace.

DAY 364:
Living Each Day with Divine Purpose

Lesson for the Day

Every day is an opportunity to live with intention, alignment, and purpose. Living each day with divine purpose means recognizing that your life has meaning in every moment, and that you are part of a larger, interconnected plan. Every action, thought, and feeling contributes to your spiritual growth and the greater good. Divine purpose is not just about grand achievements or milestones, but about the small, everyday moments where you show up authentically, act with love, and align with your values.

When we live with divine purpose, we move through the day with clarity and focus, trusting that even the most ordinary tasks have significance. Purpose is not always something we can see immediately, but when we trust that our actions are part of a bigger picture, we find fulfillment in even the smallest acts. By living with divine purpose, we are reminded that our lives are meaningful and that we are always contributing to something greater than ourselves.

Today, reflect on how you can live with divine purpose today. What small actions can you take that align with your higher self? How can you embrace your unique purpose in every moment, knowing that each step is part of your divine path? Trust that living with intention will lead you to greater fulfillment and alignment with your true self.

Meditative Prayer

Divine Source of Purpose,
Help me live each day with divine purpose today.
Where I have felt uncertain,
Fill me with clarity and intention.
Where I have felt disconnected,
Fill me with the understanding that I am part of Your greater plan.

Guide me to move through my day with purpose,
Aligning my actions, thoughts, and emotions with my higher self.
Let me trust that every moment is meaningful,
And that I am always contributing to the divine flow of life.

Thank you for the gift of purpose,
And for the guidance to live each day with intention and grace.

DAY 365:

A New Beginning

Lesson for the Day

A new beginning is a powerful invitation to step forward with fresh hope, renewed energy, and an open heart. It represents a chance to release the past, embrace the present, and trust in the infinite possibilities that lie ahead. Each day, each moment, is an opportunity to begin again, to realign with your soul's purpose, and to move forward with a sense of clarity and purpose. A new beginning is not just about starting over—it's about integrating all that you've learned, all the wisdom you've gained, and all the strength you've cultivated along your journey.

This new beginning doesn't require you to be perfect or have everything figured out. It simply asks you to trust in the process, to surrender to the flow of life, and to take that first step with faith. The beauty of new beginnings is that they are full of potential. They are full of hope, and they are full of opportunities to create the life that you desire.

Today, reflect on what new beginnings are calling you forward. What are you ready to step into with confidence? What dreams or goals are waiting for you to embrace them? Trust that each new beginning is an opportunity to grow, evolve, and continue your beautiful journey.

Meditative Prayer

Divine Source of New Beginnings,
Thank you for the gift of a fresh start today.
Where I have been held back by the past,
Fill me with the courage to release what no longer serves me.
Where I have felt uncertain,
Fill me with faith in the journey ahead.

Guide me to step forward with an open heart,
And to embrace the possibilities that lie ahead.
Let me trust in the divine timing of my path,
And in the power of new beginnings to lead me toward my highest
good.

Thank you for the opportunity to begin anew,
And for the peace that comes with trusting in the unfolding of my
journey.

Continue to Sit with Meditation

As you reach the end of this journey through *Meditative Pathways*, I hope you've found moments of peace, clarity, and connection to your higher self. The path of meditation is not one that has a finish line—rather, it is an ongoing process, a continual unfolding of understanding and awareness. Each day, each moment, offers new opportunities to deepen your practice, to listen more closely to your inner voice, and to connect more deeply with the divine.

I encourage you to continue your meditation practice beyond the pages of this book. Let the lessons and meditative prayers you've experienced here become a part of your daily life. You may not always have the time for a long session, but even a few minutes of focused breathing or quiet reflection can center and nourish your spirit. Meditation is a practice that only grows stronger the more you give yourself to it, and it will support you in countless ways as you continue your journey.

Remember that meditation is a sacred space you can always return to. Whether you need clarity, peace, or simply a moment of stillness, meditation is there to guide you. It will always meet you where you are and provide what you need, even when you don't know exactly what that is. Trust the process, and trust yourself.

You have already taken the first step toward growth, mindfulness, and spiritual connection. Let that momentum carry you forward, knowing that the path of meditation will always offer you new insights, new peace, and new possibilities. May you continue to walk with a heart full of gratitude, a mind rooted in clarity, and a spirit open to the wisdom of the universe.

Thank you for allowing *Meditative Pathways* to be a part of your journey. May your practice continue to evolve, and may you find joy, peace, and guidance in every moment of meditation. Keep going—your spirit is ready for the next chapter, and the universe is always there to guide you.

www.ingramcontent.com/pod-product-compliance
Lightning Source LLC
Chambersburg PA
CBHW060400130626
46555CB00005B/1954